# ASSAULT ON THE GUNS OF MERVILLE

# ASSAULT ON THE GUNS OF MERVILLE

*D-DAY AND AFTER*

ALAN JEFFERSON

John Murray

© Alan Jefferson 1987

First published 1987
by John Murray (Publishers) Ltd
50 Albemarle Street, London W1X 4BD

All rights reserved
Unauthorised duplication
contravenes applicable laws

Typeset by Inforum Ltd, Portsmouth
Printed and bound in Great Britain
at The Bath Press, Avon

British Library Cataloguing in Publication Data
Jefferson, Alan, 1921–
Assault on the guns of Merville.
1. Great Britain. *Army. Parachute Regiment
Battalion, 9th* 2. World War, 1939–1945
— Campaigns — France — Normandy
I. Title
940.54'21   D756.5.N6
ISBN 0-7195-4423-8

For Jacques
and in memory of those
of all ranks and nations
who died at Merville in
the summer of 1944

# CONTENTS

Foreword: Lt-General Sir Michael Gray KCB, OBE    13
Introduction                                     15
Acknowledgements                                 18

1  WOODHAY  · Preparation & Training for D-Day   21
2  WOODHAY  · The Finishing Touches              39
3  ROMMEL   · Strengthening the Atlantic Wall    59
4  BUSKOTTE · Building the Battery               67
5  MARS     · Silencing the Battery              94
6  POOLEY   · Another Attack on the Battery    129
7  STEINER  · Defending the Battery            140
8  PADDLE   · Expulsion of the Wehrmacht from
              Normandy                          164
9  MERVILLE TODAY                               172

Notes                                           180

Appendix
1  British Commanders                           192
   Unit Composition
2  Instructions to Commander 3 Para Bde         194
   Officers in action at Merville
   9th Parachute Battalion Strengths

3  Royal Air Force Intelligence Reports          198
   The Drop: Stanley Lee ASC, DFM
   The Drop: Official Reports
   The 00.26 Glider landing at Merville

4  German Commanders                             212
   Unit Composition
   Officers of 716 Artillery Regiment

5  The Skoda 10cm Howitzer 14/19                 215
   The Tasks of the Merville Battery
   Blowing the Merville Guns

6  'At the Orne Estuary': article from *Das Reich*  220
   'Parachutists take a Battery': article from
   *The Times*

Bibliography                                     230

Index                                            234

# ILLUSTRATIONS

*(between pages 112 and 113)*

1. Back of No 1 Casemate, Merville, May 1944
2. 2/Lt Raimund Steiner, acting CO of Merville Battery
3. The 10cm 14/19 Czech howitzer in action
4. Maj-Gen. Richard Gale, Gen. Sir Bernard Montgomery and Brig. the Hon. Hugh Kindersley inspecting Airborne Troops
5. King George VI, Queen Elizabeth and Princess Elizabeth inspecting Airborne Troops at Bulford Fields, May 1944
6. Lt-Colonel Terence Otway
7. Major Allen Parry
8. Captain the Hon. Paul Greenway
9. The Revd John Gwinnett
10. Mass parachute drop from Dakotas, March 1944
11. Dakotas of 512 Squadron at Broadwell shortly before D-Day
12. Lieutenant Michael Dowling
13. Major John Pooley MC, RA
14. Casemate being constructed at Colleville
15. Vertical aerial photograph of the Merville Battery, 20 March 1944
16. Merville Battery area after raids on it up to 6 June 1944
17. Sgt-Major Hans Buskotte
18. Artillerymen of the Merville Battery
19. Sgt-Major Buskotte on his favourite mount
20. Sgt-Major Buskotte, Major Karl-Werner Hof and Captain Schimpf

21 FM Erwin Rommel at Merville, 6 May 1944
22 The 2cm Flak 38 dual-purpose AA gun, nicknamed 'Erika'
23 Front of a 10cm 14/19 Czech howitzer
24 Lt-Gen. Erich Marcks's inspection of Merville, 23 May 1944
25 *Withdrawing from the Battery after the Battery's guns had been destroyed. The MO sets up his RAP in a bomb crater*: a watercolour by Capt. Albert Richards, War Artist
26 Col-Gen. Friedrich Dollmann's visit to Merville, 25 May 1944
27 Rommel's urgent inspection at Merville, 27 May 1944
28 Top of Buskotte's Command Bunker as it is today
29 No 1 Casemate at Merville in 1984

ILLUSTRATION SOURCES

1, 2, 24, 26: Prof. Raimund Steiner; 3: Bundesarchiv, Koblenz; 4, 5, 10, 11, 14, 23: Trustees of Imperial War Museum, London; 6, 12: Mary Ross; 7: Allen Parry; 8: Cordelia, Lady Greenway; 9: Michael Hensman; 13: Brig. Peter Young; 15, 16: Airborne Forces Museum, Aldershot; 17, 18, 19, 20, 21, 22: Hans Buskotte; 25: Trustees of the Tate Gallery, London; 27: Peter Timpf; 29: *Basingstoke Gazette*

# FIGURES

1. Enemy coastal battery — 25
2. General Mongomery's personal message to all men in his 21 Army Group, early June 1944 — 57
3. General Eisenhower's message to the French immediately after the Invasion had begun — 96/7
4. Northern part of 6 Airborne Division's battle area, 6 June–16 August 1944 — 103
5. Merville Battery area: attack by 9th Battalion The Parachute Regiment — 109
6. Second British Army's approach and 6 Airborne Division's position on left flank of the Invasion — 128
7. Range Card taken from No 1 Casemate, Merville Battery — 150
8. Buildings in central battery position still identifiable — 175
9. DZ 'V' and approximate positions of sticks of 9th Battalion The Parachute Regiment — 204

# FOREWORD

## Lieutenant-General Sir Michael Gray KCB, OBE
*Deputy Colonel Commandant The Parachute Regiment*

This is a human story about young men reflecting on their part in a battle which took place in Normandy some forty-three years ago. These narratives relate how they saw events at the time and how they remember them now. Alan Jefferson was a Platoon Commander in the 9th Parachute Battalion, which was given what seemed to be the almost impossible task of raiding and destroying the guns of Merville. His research reveals the equally seemingly impossible task, which befell a young Austrian Second Lieutenant and his German Sergeant-Major who, together with others, tell their personal story of what it was like defending the Battery. This is the first time, to my knowledge, that the German side of those events has ever been told. There are some who may doubt the accuracy of what is said but, even if the descriptions have blurred or become exaggerated by the passage of time, you can piece together the heroism and determination of those who stayed put and fought, no matter what the odds – this characteristic is well known of the German soldier who was a formidable opponent.

So dramatic is the story of the attack on the Merville Battery that it has been re-enacted on several Regimental Days since the Second World War: indeed it has become a legend in our time. The thought that went into meticulous planning and training, allied to the courage of the men who commanded and took part in the operation, has also fascinated generations of students at the Army Staff College. For twenty-seven years they have toured the Normandy battlefields to see for themselves what happened to the best-laid plans in war, once battle is joined. I was one of the students who listened to the officers and men who took part, telling their story of the attack on the Merville Casemates. It is a narrative that was always controversial and we found it easy, with knowledge of hindsight, to stand back and to ask critical questions. After all, this is why we were at the Staff College; but there, of course, we were not fearful for our lives, nor beset by the fog of war. The men who fought did what was asked of them and more, with great fortitude, and showed us what the tenacity of the human spirit can overcome. In his talk to the officers, just before D-Day, Brigadier James Hill, Commander of the 3rd Parachute Brigade, told them: 'Do not be daunted if chaos reigns – it undoubtedly will!' It did, but thanks to the preparation and training, which are well described in Alan Jefferson's book, and to the sheer guts of the attackers, they achieved their objectives and eventually won the day.

What is new to all of us, and is very startling, is the convincing German account that none of the guns was destroyed and that all fired again, were re-supplied and continued in sporadic action until they were withdrawn from Normandy on 16 August. You must judge the truth of what you read and, like me, perhaps speculate on whether a check that the guns had been knocked out would have been possible. You may even muse on an even more important lesson, that too much dependence had been placed on the safe arrival of the gliders bringing in the Royal Engineers with special explosives to destroy the guns. Perhaps every infantryman could, or should, have been taught how to immobilise them effectively.

As you read, remember that each sees these events through his eyes many years afterwards, when memory can play tricks. You will also note that Alan Jefferson has chosen not to make a judgement, he leaves this for you to do. I caution the reader, do not come too hastily to a conclusion or be too critical of detail. Just be thankful that these brave young men made sacrifices so that we, in our time, have been spared the horror of a Nazi tyranny.

MICHAEL GRAY
Lieutenant-General

November 1986

# INTRODUCTION

The guns of the Merville Battery in Normandy, well sited a mile inland and equidistant from the Orne estuary and the channel coast at Franceville, were in enormously thick concrete casemates and were believed to be pointing directly at the beach codenamed 'Sword'. This was where British and Canadian troops were due to land from the sea early on the morning of 6 June 1944, and it seemed to the British High Command that the Merville guns posed a direct threat to the left flank of the beach-landings. The guns were also important to the Germans who had installed them there to command a vital segment of the Atlantic Wall.

The silencing of the guns of Merville by 9th Battalion The Parachute Regiment, before the seaborne invasion, has remained the most widely acclaimed of the Battalion's battle honours. The glory and pride of this particular battle has been rightly shared by all members of the Battalion, and their families, whether or not they themselves were involved in the action.

I had joined the Battalion as a subaltern and reserve 3-in. Mortar Officer (with two years' commissioned service) towards the end of 1943, and I am proud to have taken part in the long preparation, with its rigorous training and rehearsals, for the eventual assault on the Merville Battery. I shared the fears and the zest of parachuting with all ranks in the Battalion whom I came to respect and admire far more than those in my previous units. The deep friendships forged at that time, and during succeeding campaigns with the Battalion in North-West Europe and Palestine, have remained. They demonstrate the depth of feeling brought out in all ranks by wartime service which transcends personality conflicts, personal ambitions and worldly acclaim. They have remained important and durable in the subsequent careers of many of us.

My early view of the battle was that of a junior officer in a recently formed Battalion of a volunteer force, and it was my first action, as it was for practically every member of the Battalion. But circumstances dictated that I was later to acquire a knowledge and understanding of that battle far wider than the startling, cinematograph-like flashes which impressed themselves upon my mind at the time. Seven years as a 'guest artist' with the Staff College Battlefield Tours in Normandy each summer in the 1960s, when I met some of today's generals, raised questions, doubts and a need for revaluation.

In 1984, during the fortieth anniversary of the Invasion, a chance encounter at a Norman auberge opened another door and stimulated extensive research into the involvement of other units directly concerned with efforts to destroy or to defend the Merville Battery and its guns: the Royal Navy, the RAF, the 6 Airborne Division, the Commandos – and the Germans.

The results are here in this book, where I am an observer, impartially relating what I remember coupled with the memories of others. My attempt has been to recapture the ways in which we thought and behaved at the time. In some respects they differ from today's perspectives; but I have taken great pains to ensure the accuracy of the facts revealed.

The main emphasis of the story is on the four howitzers while they were in Normandy, and up to their final destruction or disappearance in the autumn of 1944. Those guns account for the presence of the soldiers of the units herein described, and the various Air Force Squadrons, being sent to Merville at different times to engage in bloody battle.

It has been suggested that facts about all of us should have been gathered far sooner than in 1984–6; and although much has already appeared in print about the action of 9th Battalion The Parachute Regiment, only incomplete accounts of No 3

Commando, and nothing about the Germans has been revealed. The Germans say that they 'would not have been ready to talk' any sooner. NATO, the EEC, President Reagan's humanitarian involvement at the German national cemetery at Bitburg and an increased understanding of our former enemies have all helped create a more stable atmosphere. We are approaching the time when old scores can be forgotten and new friendships can develop over comrades' graves.

# ACKNOWLEDGEMENTS

There are many people for me to thank, and it is not practical to itemise the different kinds of assistance they have all so willingly given. In enlarging upon the help given by a few, I ask the rest to read into my appreciation an extension to each and all of them:

Jacques Blaat, to whom this book is primarily dedicated, was responsible for urging me to think seriously about writing it. Without his multilingual abilities, his strategic situation in West Germany (where he lives and works although he is a Luxembourger) and his determination – quite apart from his interest in warfare – I would have been unable to overcome so many hurdles nearly as quickly as he has enabled me to do. His generosity in driving me about West Germany in 1985, and in coming to Merville in 1986 is also gratefully acknowledged.

General Gray has shown his wholehearted support by agreeing to write the Foreword, which would be enough in itself; but he has also effected several introductions for me, and has been enthusiastic about progress since Jacques Blaat and I visited him in Mönchen-Gladbach in July 1985, and told him what we had found out so far.

Stan Lee has been unstinting in supplying me with information about the RAF when he was 512 Squadron's Chief Wireless Operator, and dispatcher on the leading aircraft. He has also been several times to the Public Record Office on my behalf and has answered numerous questions from his own extensive war-library of books and video tapes.

Bobby Marquis, one-time Regimental Medical Officer of

## Acknowledgements

9th Battalion The Parachute Regiment is a natural editor of English, as well as being accomplished in French and German. He read my text in a formative stage, making invaluable suggestions and improvements, sometimes sending me back with 'do better next time!' It was worth it. I am especially grateful to him for all he has done by subscribing to the whole idea of the book, and in upholding its purpose.

Lieutenant-Colonel Allen Parry MC has provided me with much illuminating information from his keen memory concerning the 9th Battalion's attack, and has remained patient and unprejudiced whenever I have put forward contradictory reports from elsewhere, and we discussed them.

Major Mike Strong REME, a French and German linguist, has assisted considerably with technical German translations, and has himself translated the article from *Das Reich* (at Appendix 5). He has also done a great deal of research into German weapons of the time, and joined the meeting at Merville in March 1986, parts of which he filmed. His zeal has been most stimulating.

Brigadier Peter Young DSO MC was kind enough to entertain me at his house for our first discussion and then to keep in close touch by telephone and correspondence while I wrote the Commando Chapter. He arranged for me to meet one of his former officers and enabled me to find and to write to other ex-members of No 3 Commando. Brigadier Young finally read and re-read Chapter 6, making valuable corrections, before he approved it.

Professor Raimund Steiner, Johannes Buskotte and Friedrich Waldmann have together provided a considerable amount of information about Merville candidly, sincerely and willingly. They were kind enough to see me first at their homes and then to join the meeting at Merville in 1986 so that we could walk the ground together and talk about the battles on the spot. I am also exceedingly grateful to Wilhelm Bleckmann whom I met at Herr Buskotte's house in July 1985, and whose voluminous correspondence has provided much of importance and interest, as well as being generally confirmatory of others'.

## Acknowledgements

I feel much in debt to the following, who have answered questions, either verbally or in correspondence, enabling me to fill in gaps or, sometimes even, to open up new avenues of research: Karl Althoff, the late Harold Bestley, Frau Busekow, Sid Capon, Leslie Cartwright, Lieutenant-Colonel M.J.P. Chilcott RAOC, Robert W. Christopher, Dr Heinfried Collin, Brigadier W.A.C. Collingwood, Lieutenant-General Sir Napier Crookenden, Rémy Desquesnes, Colonel John Drummond, Ian Dyer, Cordelia Lady Greenway, Lord Greenway, George Hawkins, Michael Hensman, Karl Heyde, Sir Havelock Hudson, Percy Hull, Daniel Jamard, W.E. Jones, Stepan Kazmierciak, Werner Kortenhaus, Brigadier F.H. Lowman, Colonel R.I.C. Macpherson REME, Dr Hans Malsch, G.D. Miller, W.R. Mills, Fred Milward, Odwig Mitlehner, Alan Mower, Mme Nazart, Major G.G. Norton, Lieutenant-Colonel T.B.H. Otway, Steve Patterson, Dr Alan Pollock, Hugh Pond, Bob Rees, Mary Ross, Rudi Schaaf, Brigadier R.F. Semple, John Speechley, Charles Strafford, Stroma Sutherland, Frank Tavener, Colonel John Tillett, Peter Timpf, Commander St Clair Tisdal RNVR, Karl-Heinz Tubbesing, V.C. Whibley, H. Williams, Michael Willis.

My grateful thanks are extended to these organisations for the help they have given me during the writing of this book: Air Historical Branch RAF, London; Airborne Forces Museum, Aldershot; *Basingstoke Gazette*; Belgian Embassy, London; Bundesarchiv-Militärarchiv, Freiburg; Commando Association, London; Commonwealth Graves Commission, Maidenhead; Deutsche Dienststelle (WAST), W. Berlin; Imperial War Museum, London; Plymouth City Public Library; Polish Institute & Sikorski Museum, London; Royal Marines: Office of the Commandant General, London & RM Museum, Southsea; Mosslands School, Wallasey; Tate Gallery, London; Victoria & Albert Museum, London; Williamson Art Gallery, Birkenhead.

Deviock, Cornwall                                          A.J.

# 1
# Woodhay

## Preparation & Training for D-Day

'What do you think, sir?'

'What do I think?' Alastair Pearson, the tough, Scottish lieutenant-colonel had been in many battles already. Not quite thirty, he had two DSOs, had been parachuting since 1941 and was known for the simplicity of his planning and determination in action.

He and the Brigade Major were standing together on the rim of a natural amphitheatre among the Berkshire Downs, watching an exercise-battle below them with what looked like toy soldiers. These soldiers were attacking four, square constructions of canvas and scaffolding with great determination.

As the two spectators continued to watch carefully, the Scot shook his head slowly. He had been appointed by James Hill, the Brigade Commander, to prepare himself as shadow commander of the battalion hard at work down there, in case anything happened to Lieutenant-Colonel Terence Otway, the commander who had devised the plan and was practising it so industriously on that hot afternoon in May 1944.

'Look after that man, Bill,' said Pearson to the Brigade Major, 'see him safely over the other side, for God's sake. It's all far too complicated for me.'

They turned away together in silence and climbed into the staff car which was waiting behind them, out of sight of the battle.

'Awa' wi' ye, driver!'

It was a baking hot Thursday in that dust-bath near West Woodhay where we were rehearsing the destruction of 'four big coastal guns', ready for our assault – where? We had not been told, but it was surely France, and it must be soon.

My job was the assault of No 1 Casemate, represented here by the right-hand canvas construction containing the imaginary gun. I commanded No 12 Platoon of 'C' Company in 9th Battalion The Parachute Regiment, a lieutenant's command. There were no second-lieutenants in the Battalion.

'Don't bunch as you come through the wire, Jeff,' Ian Dyer, my company commander, was saying; 'and you, "Jock" ', to No 14 Platoon Commander, 'maintain direction and don't be put off by the craters you'll find in your way.'

I nudged 'Jock', who looked as if he was trying not to go to sleep. 'Dizzie' Parfitt (13 Platoon Commander) was in the same somnolent condition. We were listening, but not listening. Dammit, we'd been doing this since October 1943 in one way or another, and now it was 18 May. The whole Battalion was keyed up to fever pitch: the barometer of morale was absenteeism, and that registered O. Each man had been made to feel indispensable and consequently he felt important; but the CO (Commanding Officer) was the one who bore all the responsibility, and we trusted him completely.

The village of West Woodhay, where we were camped, is in the flat countryside south-east of Inkpen, below and between Newbury and Hungerford in Berkshire. The troops were bivouacked in parkland but the officers were installed in the delightful West Woodhay House. It was built by Benjamin Rudyard, a friend of King Charles I, in 1635, and may have been designed by Inigo Jones. The Henderson family owned the house and Johnny Henderson, who was General Montgomery's ADC at the time, was to inherit it after the war.

Because of the high level of security that surrounded us, we were surprised to be allowed out of camp for one evening, on a rotational basis of companies. 'Dizzie' and I, alone in Hungerford, were more interested in finding food than in anything else. Our normal, Army rations were said to be on a higher scale than the ordinary infantry's allocation, but the rate at which we burned up energy was never quelled by the food we had in barracks or, least of all, on exercises.

So 'Dizzie' and I made straight for Hungerford's famous old hostelry, the Bear, sat down and tucked in. Hungerford – how well named. That was not nearly enough. In those days all restaurants, even the Savoy Grill, were limited to a charge of five shillings per person per meal. There might be a 'cover charge' of a few pence, and a 'service charge' but everybody concerned was rationed and controlled. Our three slender courses had not sufficed. We looked at one another, nodded, paid the bill and walked straight over to the Three Swans where we went through their (all-too-similar) meal immediately. That then felt a little better.

Our soldiers, some of them, were engaged in different pursuits. Our Divisional Intelligence had recruited a number of outstandingly pretty WAAFs, dressed them in 'civvies', and had planted them round the villages and towns near West Woodhay in an effort to test our security by endeavouring to extract information from us. Who were we? What were we doing there? How long were we staying? Where were we going next? Were we going to be in the 'Second Front' (as the Invasion was commonly called)? Knowing the ways and the wiles of parachutists, I don't mind betting that those lads got a fair way with the girls before they were stopped, because absolutely no information was forthcoming.

Then we were allowed to go on a long weekend's leave, from Friday to Sunday night immediately following our day in the sun. The authorities were taking a risk of a sort, but they felt that morale would benefit and who knew better than they when our next leave was to be? On our return there was to be a divisional exercise, the climax of all our training.

By now our families knew better than to ask questions. 'Be like Dad, keep Mum' the posters said. It was a matter of honour, of pride. And we were proud – oh so proud!

Thinking back on how I got into the Battalion and especially into 'C' Company that was going to be at the sharp end of the attack, several events came to mind. Marches gave one plenty of opportunities for reflection and consideration.

In the previous winter at Bulford on Salisbury Plain[1] – it must have been towards the end of November – all officers were called into the mess billiards room one evening after dinner. At the far end of the room was a blackboard covered by a cloth, and Joe Worth, the Intelligence Officer, was beside it, looking important. When we were all assembled, the CO came in and joined Joe. We sat down again and waited. There was an air of expectancy about it all: this was not merely an announcement of some Brigade exercise.

The Colonel was brief. He had been given our 'Second Front' objective in some detail, although he did not know the place nor the date of the operation. Yet with what he knew, he was going to be able to begin our training in earnest. A parachute operation, certainly, and this was our objective – or something very much like it. He signalled to Joe Worth. The cloth was whisked away from the blackboard disclosing a drawing (see Fig. 1). There was dead silence.

I glanced round to see the reaction, because I was still only a reserve officer of the Battalion, and did not truly 'belong'. The others were all craning forward, mouths slightly open, eyes gleaming, nostrils slightly distended as though scenting the prey. This gave way to some licking of lips, relaxation and settling back. All this in no more than four or five seconds.

The Colonel was speaking: 'If it is not clear to you what this diagram represents, I'll go over it, a stage at a time.'

Joe handed him a billiard cue.

'Here, (a), is a cattle fence of wire all round the position. And here, (c), is an anti-tank ditch. Between them, (b), a minefield. We don't know what kind of mines, but if there is an anti-tank ditch there are certain to be anti-tank mines as well as anti-personnel. They take various shapes, as you know, and the "S", or *Sprung-mine* is the most unpleasant. (d) is a heavy concentration of wire, probably some five feet high and deeper than that. The cattle wire (a) won't cause us any trouble, but (d) will have to be blown up so as not to hold us up.'

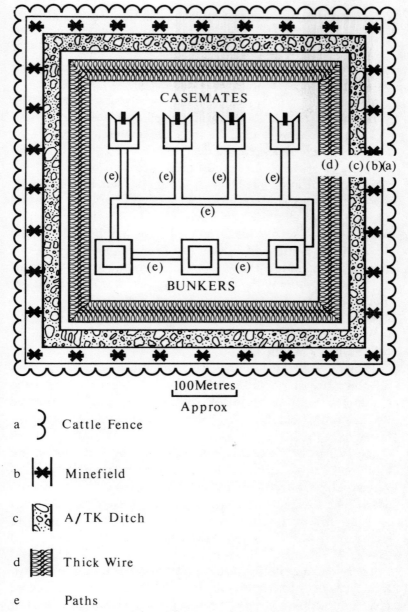

Fig. 1 Enemy coastal battery

I was noting the definite tense, as though it were already happening.

'You see these paths, (e)? They are used by the defending troops and will be clear of mines, of course. Elsewhere in the position we must assume to be dangerous.

'Now we've got through all that, we have arrived at the important part.' He looked up, paused and smiled grimly.

'Here – 1, 2, 3 and 4 – are large concrete bunkers or casemates.' He repeated the description: '1, 2, 3 and 4. The concrete is probably about six feet thick and impervious to aerial bombardment. That's why we are needed. Inside each of these casemates is a large coastal gun, probably 105mm or 150mm. They are the objective. Our task will be to drop reasonably close to this Battery – reasonably close – get through the cattle wire, cross the first minefield, cross the anti-tank ditch, blow the wire, cross the main minefield, storm the bunkers, destroy the guns and their crews. Then we'll get out.'

He stopped, looked all round and lowered the billiard cue.

'Well?'

Everybody laughed.

The CO understood perfectly. Given out pat, like that, it seemed more than a tall order, but we were certain that if the Colonel thought we could do it, well so we could. The laughter was a kind of safety valve, because it all sounded perfectly horrible.

Joe Worth proceeded to relate details about the guns, the kind of German troops who would be manning them, his views on booby-traps and mines, and then asked for questions. There were a few silly ones. The CO stressed the need for absolute security, security of the most stringent kind, and told us that from now on we would all be involved in what he called 'Battery Training'. Our course had been set.

There was a rush for the bar and a good deal of excitement. Ian Dyer got going on the piano, and the usual singing began. It seemed almost a normal evening in the mess. In the course of it, the 'S'-mine joke between Mike Dowling and me was born.

## Preparation & Training for D-Day

Mike was my chum. We had got to know each other at the Airborne Battle School[2] in September 1943. He was already commanding a platoon in 'B' Company of the Battalion and had been transferred to us from 1st Battalion The Royal Ulster Rifles in the Airlanding Brigade, having decided that he preferred the idea of parachuting into battle rather than coming down in a glider.

There was something else about Mike as well, and it did not take me long to find out what it was. His left arm was very weak, due to an accident when learning to jump and completely useless when it came to trying to support himself with it alone. One of the nastier tests given us during the Battle Course was a water crossing. We had to go along a rope, upside down, hands and head first, across a fast-flowing stream of about 30 ft in width. When one reached the middle of the rope it was sagging below water, and the upward climb from a complete ducking was the hardest part. A blazing bonfire beckoning from the opposite bank was the only consolation, apart from a small boat downstream, carrying vigilant members of the demonstration platoon, some rowing furiously to keep themselves in place, others armed with hooks on poles, ready to save those who had been unable to hang on to the rope.

Mike was ahead of me. It was cold and raining and we were wearing only denim overalls and boots.

'You'll never manage it,' I said to him, 'not with that arm.'

'And if they find out, I'll not be able to stay in the Battalion, will I?' he replied, with his smile that alone must have got him straight into an Irish regiment, and now silenced further argument.

So off he ran without a moment's hesitation, plunged in, hung on for a few thrusts, lost his grip, splashed, fell in and was promptly hooked out of the water as he floated, half-submerged, past the boat.

Afterwards, as we stood with the others who had come across, all stark naked round the fire, roasting ourselves dry and then putting on fresh clothing, Mike winked at me.

'Bad luck, losing your hold like that,' I said.

We returned to the Battalion after the Course had finished, as best of friends. We both enjoyed a sense of the ridiculous and a joint desire to deflate the pompous. Our joke about the 'S'-mine was really a desperate bet: whichever one of us first trod on one inside the Battery had lost. Nobody else was party to this jest, so nobody was particularly interested. They probably thought we were both rather silly.

While Mike and I had come from different regiments, and the majority of the subalterns had done the same, bringing with us many different experiences and skills, there was a nucleus of senior officers in the Battalion who had come from a single unit. This was 10th (TA) Battalion The Essex Regiment, which had been turned over to parachuting in late 1942 and became 9th (Home Counties) Battalion The Parachute Regiment in the new 3rd Parachute Brigade.

Although some officers, warrant officers, NCOs (non-commissioned officers) and men were not able to parachute for varying reasons of age, health or desire, the strength of the new unit lay in its officers and highly trained NCOs who remained, already comrades and friends of some four years' standing.

A year after formation, all company commanders in the Battalion were ex-10th Essex, and so were two captains and several others who had gone to Brigade or Division as staff officers. Our Quartermaster, Albert Chilton (senior quartermaster in the Army Air Corps) was an Essex man. Our Commanding Officer and second-in-command were regular serving officers from other regiments and so was one subaltern, Hugh Smyth MC. He had been prepared to come down from captain to join the Battalion, and was posted to 'A' Company led by Major Allen Parry. Smyth was the only decorated officer in the Battalion at this stage.

Our Adjutant, Hal Hudson, had done his jumps at the same time as I did mine. I discovered that he and I shared the luxurious habit of smoking a pipe in the bath. He had first been a medical student but had then gone into his father's marine insurance business at Lloyd's.

## Preparation & Training for D-Day

On 23 December 1943, 6 Airborne Division was mobilised, that is to say it was ordered to put itself on a war footing and be prepared for action fairly soon. This meant a great deal of extra administrative work all round, especially for our Adjutant and Quartermaster who burned the midnight oil for weeks on end while the rest of us caroused as usual.

I was still on the reserve of the Battalion and had still not been given a command of my own, and this irked me considerably.

Before mobilisation there was a captain's appointment for the future officer who would command the Reserves when the Battalion went to war. Long before mobilisation this third pip had been given to Frank Tavener, the senior subaltern at the time, ex-10th Essex and 3-in. Mortar Platoon Commander, which, strictly speaking, was a lieutenant's command. It was an awkward situation because Frank was a much-liked member of the Battalion and it was unthinkable that he should be left behind.

On 7 January 1944, owing to a gradual change in officers' appointments, mainly the consequence of ill-health or injuries, I was suddenly appointed OC (Officer Commanding) 'R' (Reserve) Company and had hardly taken over my new responsibilities when, two days later, on 9 January I was given 12 Platoon in 'C' Company. Nine is my birth number, nine has always shown up to advantage throughout my life, and here I was on 9 January with a longed-for rifle platoon in 9 Parachute Battalion.

But my joy had another side to it. For two or three weeks, Frank Tavener's fate had hung in the balance, but finally bureaucracy had triumphed to his disadvantage. On 8 January he was formally ordered to hand over his Mortar Platoon and to take over 'R' Company, vacated that day by me.

Frank went to see the CO and declared this to be nonsense. He had been the 3-in. Mortar Officer for a long time and would, of course, gladly throw in his third pip to keep command of his platoon and to go into action with the Battalion. The answer shattered him.

'No, Frank. You've had it too long. You've been paid for

your third pip. Sorry. You're OC "R" Company and that's an end to the matter.'

So Lieutenant Peters, an ex-guardsman and only recently commissioned, who had been Frank's assistant, took over the 3-in. Mortar Platoon, and Frank Tavener, still a captain – but a most unwilling one – retired to command 'R' Company. We were all very sad at this outcome.

With a stabilisation of officers, with mobilisation and a general feeling of 'nearness' to battle, our training took on a different tone. Between 7 February and 24 May 1944 there were five large-scale exercises involving the Battalion. Their code-names are still remembered, though most of the details concerning them, and their individual purposes are probably forgotten: *Co-operation* (though there was little of it, according to my diary); *Thrust; Bizz II* (for the whole Division); *Mush; Banger II* – these last two within ten days. One or two events stand out, however.

On *Co-operation* we were given the '24-hour pack' for the first time. This was a ration pack for one man for the time stated and contained dehydrated meat cubes (rather nasty) and a slab of concentrated oatmeal to be eaten raw or made into porridge. It was rather good. There was also some very concentrated plain chocolate, no doubt full of energy-giving vitamins, a few cigarettes, some boiled sweets and several sheets of 'Army Form Blank'. (A very old quartermaster in a train during the war once told me that the regulation number of sheets per man per day was three: one up, one down, one polishing. I think there were more in our 24-hour pack.) Every man carried a water-bottle containing 1¼ pints and some of this was considered necessary to reconstitute the meat and the oatmeal, but far more importantly it was used for making tea. The pack had several 'tea, milk and sugar' cubes which, when boiling water was poured over them, produced a faint imitation of the real thing. Cooking was an individual matter, done in a mess-tin over a tiny portable stove with solid-fuel tablets (such as campers use). The only article which the soldier had to provide for himself to get going with his meal was a light for the solid fuel. Generally speaking, the 24-hour pack was a great success, and we carried it on all subsequent exercises, and later into action.

There was special excitement attached to Exercise *Bizz II* in March. We took off at 17.10 hrs and flew south, across the coast and over the Channel towards France. It was still broad daylight and sunny, and certainly gave me an odd feeling. As soon as it was calculated that we had shown up forcibly on the enemy radar screens, we turned about and returned to England to jump at 19.00 and begin the exercise proper. We had fighter cover, but nothing of the Luftwaffe was seen.

During the first few months of 1944 we worked very much harder than before because the incentive was increased. We knew that we were coming nearer and nearer to the real thing. We put in many solid hours, not only in daytime but also at night until we were well accustomed to forming up, moving about and operating efficiently in complete darkness. Endurance tests continued, too. Every so often – and it seemed too often – every man had to cover 10 miles on foot in two hours, in battle order with rifle. This weighed 60 lb. No matter what the weather was like, this was the most arduous of our tests demanding a steady double (run) on the flat and downhill, and a brisk march uphill in order to cover the distance in the set time. It was far worse than the 50 miles in 24 hours that we all had to do once: 36 miles in the daytime, a pause for dinner ('don't take your boots off, or you'll never get them on again') and the remaining 14 miles at night.

All this received the reward that every soldier enjoyed most, even more than money: leave. Between Exercise *Co-operation* and 22 May, which was the watershed of our training, my diary reminds me that I had a total of 20 days' leave in short periods of weekends, or even one day at a time. Looking back, it seems amazingly generous and magnanimous of trust. Admittedly, several of the days were 'fudged', when we had no parades, but were forbidden to travel by train. My fiancée then took the train from London to Andover, where I journeyed by bus. There were no private cars.

At the beginning of May we were ordered to get ready to leave barracks and move to a special exercise area, and on the night of 8 May (still a strong emphasis on night operations) we marched from Bulford Camp to West Woodhay, north-east across Salisbury Plain, a distance of about 30 miles, mainly on minor roads.

There our mock battery was built, and the area round it sealed off rigorously. In spite of the high degree of security, General Gale[3] was confident in our ability to keep our mouths shut, so was Brigadier Hill[4] and so was Colonel Otway[5]. And because our CO – even more than his superiors – was prepared to vouch for our corporate loyalty, we went on leave *twice* from West Woodhay.

In our absence, the 'Battery' had to be camouflaged because it represented such a close likeness to the real thing. In the doubtful event of a German aeroplane passing over, it might blow the gaffe. We had to be super-cautious.

Leave between 19–21 May was, as many of us feared, the last one. Waterloo station, where we debouched from the train in a human – some considered it an in-human – avalanche, was the scene of a demonstration never before seen there. The soldiers were so determined that no porter nor ticket inspector dared resist. Some of the troops were whooping and shouting as though they were charging those scaffolding and hessian objects on the Berkshire Downs. Others pretended to have fixed bayonets, others lobbed imaginary grenades in front of the grand assault as they cascaded through the barricades, winning another battle of Waterloo. Observed from above it must have looked solid red: the berets were bunched so closely together – 9th Battalion The Parachute Regiment was unstoppable.

The obverse of this action on the Sunday night was similar. There were three trains to take us back to camp. The first train was empty. The second contained a mere handful. The third and last train was standing with steam up and the platform gates still shut. 9th Battalion The Parachute Regiment arrived almost together from all over London and the Home Counties,

600 determined men with wives, sweethearts – and just one or two looking round the dark corners of Waterloo station for a tart, and not in vain.

The situation looked hopeless to me: I was most unlikely to be able to get on that train. Yet there was one way. I climbed over the railings between the roadway through the station and the nearest platform, crossed the line and experienced an electric shock. Climbing, rather shaken, into the nearest 1st class compartment from the wrong side, I was glad to see one of the Brigade doctors there. I told him what had happened.

'That won't do you any harm at all,' he said. 'It'll tone you up. Jump in.'

At that moment, the terrified inspector opened the gates of two adjacent platforms and stood well back. The red-headed mass passed through the gap as though it had been blown, and commandeered the train. There was no time for fond farewells (which was probably a good thing) and the wives and sweethearts, who had come to see their loved ones on to the train, merely gasped at the force and energy of the stamping boots and sea of khaki that had swept the loved ones away from them.

While on leave, I had seen a toy metal horn-shaped instrument in a junk shop. Not a horn at all, it had one note, and I bought it for 1s 9d. It gave me an idea and it was going to be useful.

When we paraded the next morning for the exercise, I told my platoon – 12 Platoon of 'C' Company – 'Obey the last command, the last sound you hear, though it may not be a word.'

'Plat-oon, *parp*.'

'Stand at *parp*.' They got it straight away, and from then on that was how I gave them my commands, apart from a few blasts here and there when the occasion demanded it.

Our ultimate exercise – and I've lost its name – took place between 22–24 May 1944. It was a complicated exercise involving several marches, attacks and ending up at West Woodhay. On the first day we had to outwit a strong enemy of the 1st Airborne Division[6] and a Polish unit.

At some time on the first day it leaked out among the Battalion — not surprisingly — that 50 men of 'A' Company were being given a special task of landing inside the Battery in three gliders. Although I was not personally involved, I was astonished at this unconventional method of employing trained parachutists. The unique force was going to be commanded by Captain Robert Gordon-Brown (known familiarly as 'GB') a curious character, older than most of us and bald-headed. He had already passed his Staff College examination, was a celebrated architect in civilian life and possessed a good brain. He was the second-in-command of 'A' Company.

Major Allen Parry, his Company Commander, was very cut up at not being selected to lead this *coup de main* force, already called the 'GB Party' or 'GB Force'.

A subaltern in 9th Battalion The Parachute Regiment did not necessarily grasp the complete plan at once, in every detail, as it was envisaged by Colonel Otway, though gradually it was taking shape in my mind. Now I found it added up for me at last, in all its complexity and elaborate preparation for which, we were told, nothing had been refused nor spared us. All the meticulous planning and rehearsal was obviously going to pay dividends in the real assault, the success of which was ingrained into us all. As CSMI[7] 'Dusty' Miller put it: 'We ate, drank, slept and thought bloody Battery!'

This was the plan. The two main elements were the body of the Battalion on the ground, and the *coup de main* 'GB Force' in three gliders arriving simultaneously by air. There were also a number of subsidiary groups with different, though vital tasks.

Two advance parties were to precede the Battalion by half an hour in a single aircraft, dropping by parachute on the DZ (dropping zone). This lay about 1¼ miles from the Battery, involving an approach march. One was called the RV (Rendezvous) Organisation Party under Major Parry; the other, the 'Trowbridge Party' under the command of Major Smith.

Major Parry's party consisted of himself and one representative from each company. He was to do his best to encourage the main body, after they had landed on the DZ, towards the RV by flashing an Aldis lamp and blowing an artificial bird whistle. (This, in Quartermaster's terminology, was known as 'Ducks, bakelite'.) Once the Battalion had assembled at the RV in woods and well-concealed ditches, and the CO had given the order to advance, Major Parry was then responsible for leading us all to a prearranged spot near the Battery.

Here he would be met by Major Smith. George Smith, an entirely unflappable man, and a fearless one, commanded HQ Company which, composed of separate, specialist platoons, needed a Company Commander only for administration. Oddly enough, George had a loud, snuff-taker's sniff, although his job demanded complete silence. Together with two of the toughest men in the Battalion – the two physical-training sergeant-majors, 'Dusty' Miller and Bill Harrold – he was to do as Admiral Trowbridge had done before Trafalgar: go ahead and search out the enemy dispositions. Our 'Trowbridge Party' was required to do 'anything useful' such as spotting the distribution of sentries, cutting any wire they found and leading the next party up to the edge of the minefield.

This was euphemistically named the 'Taping Party' and was led by Captain the Hon. Paul Greenway[8]. He was something of an eccentric, he loved life and was not only endowed with a crazy brand of humour, but also with great courage. His task was to lead eight men of 'B' Company, of which he was the second-in-command, to the outside wire of the Battery defences. Having been shown where the minefield began, Greenway and his men, equipped with 'Polish' mine detectors (in reality metal detectors) were to locate, lift and neutralise enemy mines until they had cleared three lanes, which were to be marked with white tape. All this had to be done in complete silence and, presumably, under the noses of German sentries.

Captain Greenway and his eight men were scheduled to

travel in the CO's aircraft, the leading one, so that they might have a good start. By the time they had cleared their paths, Major Smith would return to the prearranged spot, meet Major Parry and the Battalion and bring them up to the edge of the minefield.

We had been allocated some heavy stores which were to be delivered by gliders. They included three jeeps and trailers loaded with 'Bangalore' torpedoes for blowing the thick concentration of wire across our path, and some lightweight bridging material for crossing the anti-tank ditch. There were also two six-pounder anti-tank guns, and the main body of Royal Engineers with their special explosives for destroying the large guns in the casemates. In addition there was spare ammunition, particularly the heavy 3-in. mortar bombs and medium machine-gun belts. Altogether we had five gliders of supplies.

The mortars and machine-guns were being dropped in containers among their respective sticks of parachutists – containers being cigar-shaped metal boxes released from below the aircraft in the middle of each stick and coming down by parachute to land among those responsible for them.

Of the three rifle companies dropping with the main body of the Battalion, 'C' Company which included my 12 Platoon, was the assaulting company. The three platoon commanders and our kindly second-in-command 'Robbie' Robinson (who hated putting any soldier on a charge or being tough with him) each had one of the four casemates to clear of the enemy and to eliminate all opposition so that the Engineers could do their job of destroying the guns undisturbed.

'B' Company were to breach the wire obstacle with their 'Bangalore' torpedoes, then follow 'C' Company into the assault as a second wave. In case there might be a delay in getting 'Bangalores' from the gliders, a few lengths were dropped in 'B' Company containers. They were metal tubes filled with explosive which, when ignited, sprayed the air round them with small pieces of the tube which had been fractured into particles of the right size to destroy wire entanglements.

Then there was the other half of 'A' Company, the land-based, not the glider-borne half. They were to be the Battalion's reserve at the Firm Base outside the Battery position under command of Major Eddie Charlton, a regular officer from the King's Own Shropshire Light Infantry, the Battalion's second-in-command. Close beside him, one of the 3-in. mortars was detailed to fire flares into the air so as to light up the whole Battery position for the Glider Pilots of the 'GB Force'. These gliders were, respectively, commanded by 'GB' himself, by Lieutenant Hugh Smyth MC, and by Lieutenant Hugh Pond. A Royal Engineers officer and seven sappers were also on board, and with the 47 men of 'A' Company made a complement of 58 to crash-land inside the Battery at 04.30 hrs.

At that precise moment, I would be running towards the glider which had finished up between Casemates 1 & 2, possibly with its wings shorn off, because the taking of No 1 Casemate was my responsibility. So that we might know friend from foe, we had a call-sign: 'PO' answered by 'Olly, Olly' since neither can be pronounced properly by a German speaker.

Finally there were four different bugle calls, each for a specific purpose, to add a touch of brass to Colonel Otway's score.

The timings for each event from the moment the Battalion's first man touched down on the DZ, to the actual assault, with its many component parts, were calculated to the last minute – in one case to 30 seconds – and were all dovetailed together to make a monumental plan centring on 04.30. We had also to be clear of the position by 05.10 in case our success signal had not been received by HMS *Arethusa*, transmitted to her by the naval officer who was jumping with us. *Arethusa* was offshore in the English Channel, ready to begin bombarding the Battery if nothing was heard from 9th Battalion.

Over the months preceding the last exercise at West Woodhay, each sub-unit had been briefed, rehearsed, tested and tried until its job – its theoretical job on a yet undisclosed target – was known and had become second nature by day and by night, in rain and fine, in cold weather and now, in baking hot summer sunshine. It had then been performed with all the other sub-units until every creak had been eliminated and the whole machine that was 9th Battalion The Parachute Regiment ran smoothly, silently, efficiently and menacingly.

So now we were about to do it all over again, but with a new and thrilling addition: live ammunition. We arrived at the supposed DZ and were strung out as though we had been dropped from the air. On the sound of a whistle we moved.

# 2
# Woodhay

## The Finishing Touches

So here we were, ready to do it all over again: the drop, the rendezvous, the approach march, the forming-up, the gliders landing, the big bang and the charge through the wire into the Battery, yelling blue murder. This time, however, there was the new and thrilling addition: live ammunition.

We arrived at the supposed DZ and were strung out as though we had been dropped there. That's what all the umpires were for. On the blast of a whistle, we moved.

There was hardly any moon and I was relieved to see that most of my platoon were coming in steadily after me. Now for direction. Yes, there it was, Major Parry's 'Ducks, bakelite' quacking away to my left. I gathered up as many of my platoon as I could find in the darkness and we got to the RV fairly quickly. Our Company Sergeant-Major 'Barney' Ross was there to lead them in to 'C' Company's waiting position while I reported to the CO.

He was standing almost alone looking somewhat tense, with the Adjutant a little way behind him, and told me, 'Remind your Company Commander that I require to know his strength every fifteen minutes.'

I saluted and went to the Company area where there was a very good turnout.

'Come on, Jeff,' said Ian Dyer, 'how many of your platoon arrived?' I counted them and produced almost a full strength, but I did not pass on the CO's message. Our training had been too meticulous for Ian to be unaware of his CO's orders.

Shortly afterwards the remainder of my platoon reported to the RV. They included Private Dunk, a stolid Hampshire lad, popular because his father drove the 'Bulford Special' – the train which took us away on leave from Bulford sidings to the main line at Andover, often with young Dunk travelling on his father's footplate because neither of them was catching the express to London.

It seemed a long time before we received the order to get ready to move off. The approach march went without a hitch, with us all silently moving along paths and over obstacles similar to those we would soon be encountering 'over there'. Major Smith and Major Parry made their scheduled Stanley-and-Livingstone meeting, and even more silently we made our way to the edge of the 'minefield'. There was Paul Greenway, there were the unmistakable white tapes, leading us through the safe lanes and up to the edge of the wire: the Start Line.

We crouched there, waiting. This was the moment when I hoped that nobody was going to sneeze, or fall over, or become trigger-happy and loose off an unintentional round into the night. But the training was too good. Right fingers, though not relaxed, produced no spasms, nasal passages remained clear, every man took care where he put his feet.

Our live ammunition included smoke grenades (though not the fragmenting 36s) and we knew our 3-in. mortars were behind us with one ready to fire star shells to illuminate the whole area of our home-made Battery which we were about to destroy. The 'Bangalore' torpedoes were ready beneath the thick coils of wire that barred our path, and Mike Dowling was standing nearby with several of his men, ready to explode them.

I looked round at my platoon. Sergeant 'Tich' Harper was there all right, bouncing about; Sergeant Rose looked more morose than he usually did – had he some premonition? Keen, dependable Sergeant Eric Bedford was holding himself fully in check, breathing hard and slowly and clearly taken up by the excitement of it all. Morgan, my batman, was immediately behind me flashing a look of enjoyment; Privates Capon,

Delsignore, Walker, Smith, Cartwright and others were fidgeting and fretting to go.

'Hold it,' I urged them, 'not long now. Don't spoil it. Then we'll smash the place to smithereens.'

Suddenly – and partly as if in a dream because the whole scene had become so real – the horribly coarse, animal rasp of a bugle sounded Reveille. This was the signal to ATTACK. 'Charlie, Charlie, get out of bed!' are its words.

All right, Charlie, and so we shall. And as if from a catapult, 12 Platoon shot forward through the smoking gap where the wire had been. I, for one, hadn't taken account of the explosion. Mike Dowling egged me on lugubriously and I stuck my tongue out at him as I passed by. All I thought about was the 'casemate', the 'gun'.

Telling my platoon not to bunch and blowing my toy 'horn', alternately yelling with the rest, I led them on towards the 'casemate' that soon seemed to be towering above us.

In went the live bursts of Sten fire and rifle shots, in went the phosphorous grenades. The Sappers came up, but by now some of the hessian had caught fire. Nevertheless, two of them laid their hollow 'beehive' charges, withdrew quickly and there was an enormous bang. Flames took complete control of the 'casemate' but that did not prevent several soldiers from continuing to pour rifle fire into it. War can bring out the primitive in most of us, as we discovered; and although we withdrew in orderly fashion as we had frequently practised, it was in the belief that we had performed something like a rape. I did not want to look into anybody's eyes.

There was plenty of time to reflect upon it – and upon the whole business during the 26 miles' march back to Bulford – and to cool off. Mentally we were refreshed, pleased with ourselves and almost ready to do it again. Physically nothing was quite the same. I also pondered on the danger of over-rehearsal: it had gone so well. There is a saying in the theatre that a bad dress rehearsal makes a good first night. This had been the dress rehearsal . . .

There was only one day's respite in Bulford, but it was a

memorable day. The CO brought all officers together and confided in us. It was the first step in releasing pent-up feelings.

Yes, it was to be a coastal battery of four large guns (not surprisingly) but at present he could not tell us precisely where it was. He would do so as soon as possible, and asked us to be patient. The task, he went on, was a very important one indeed for 9th Battalion had been given one of the two prime tasks in the Division. He knew we realised that things were hotting-up – this was obvious – and we could tell our troops this, to keep the pressure down.

He then added, 'After this operation, we shall go on to destroy an important German radar station nearby, on the coast.'

My platoon were busy cleaning themselves and their rifles after our battle. The atmosphere was one of close companionship among all ranks that I, for one, had never before experienced. I went back to them and took them on to the football field behind their barrack room where what I said could not be heard by anybody else without our first seeing their approach. I told them what the CO had just told me. Among the last intake to 12 Platoon had been a Corporal Dowling – no relative of Mike's. I had not got to know him particularly well, but he was efficient and very quiet – something of a loner.

On the following day, 25 May, we all got into trucks with our full kit and moved to a tented camp on the edge of RAF Station, Broadwell. Broadwell is in Oxfordshire, very close to Stow-on-the-Wold, which is in Gloucestershire.

Albert Chilton, our Quartermaster, and Frank Tavener had made the camp as comfortable as they could, considering the equipment available. Everybody was to sleep in tents – a luxury after the last few exercises – and I shared one with 'Dizzie'. The Officers' lines, with the mess tents behind them, were separated from the other ranks by a large expanse of grass, which was our parade ground. The only two solid buildings served as the men's mess hall, and the Briefing Room that was always heavily guarded, day and night.

The weather was fine and very hot. Next door to us on the

airfield were our old neighbours from Bulford, 1st Royal Ulster Rifles, the regiment from which Lieutenant-Colonel Otway, Captain Gordon-Brown and Mike Dowling had all come. Huw Wheldon was a captain in the RUR and his voice could generally be heard above everybody else's. He and their Battalion doctor were both Welshmen and used to converse together in their own tongue. What they were doing in the Ulster Rifles was never satisfactorily explained.

By the morning of 26 May, a Friday, we had all settled in and were thoroughly enjoying the relaxed atmosphere and the glorious sunshine that enabled us to strip to the waist as we did final kit-checks and cleaned weapons.

The Company Commanders suddenly disappeared *en masse* inside the Briefing Room, and there was a moment of general silence as the Battalion watched. The Briefing Room could be seen by all companies and this was a dramatic moment. Each man felt that the CO was, perhaps, a little further than at arm's length; but his Company Commander was close enough to be more of a father figure. Consequently each man felt himself being drawn closer and closer to learning the big secret of his life.

The atmosphere was tense and all eyes were on the door of the Briefing Room. After about an hour it opened.

The Company Commanders and a few others officers emerged with looks of immense satisfaction and excitement on their faces. Now it would not be long before we were all 'in the picture'.

For the rest of the day the Company Commanders were among us, talking to us perfectly normally, but nobody was fool enough to attempt to extract any advance information. Our turn would come. Patience . . .

It came, sure enough for 'Dizzie', 'Jock' and me on the Saturday, 27 May. Yet we had to wait until the other platoon commanders had been briefed. After watching their comings and goings the summons arrived at about midday. Our gentle Company second-in-command 'Robbie' Robinson accompanied the three of us. Ian Dyer was excited. He briefed us carefully on the most wonderful model I had ever seen[1]. It was about 1.5 m square with each building beautifully constructed out of plaster of Paris. The four casemates and the blockhouses were there in correct colours, the anti-tank ditch, the wire entanglements, trees and bushes, grass and chewed-up earth, the houses in the village and every bomb crater. It had been painstakingly made from an ever-increasing series of aerial photographs, of which there were many in the briefing room for us to consult. But there was still no indication of where.

Ian Dyer clearly explained his plan and said that we would each have several opportunities of briefing our own platoons on this model, though in no more than 15-minute sessions, for it was obviously going to be in great demand throughout the Battalion.

I gazed at the work of art in front of me, full of admiration. It was like looking at the real thing from high in the air through a cloudless sky.

When it came to my turn, 12 Platoon were as ecstatic as I had been when I gave them their first briefing that afternoon. Fifteen minutes went by in no time, and then 'Dizzie' was there with his platoon, banging at the door. Never before had soldiers wanted to prolong the parade as they did with the model. They were fascinated.

We went away and talked about it together. Every man had to draw a picture of his own part in the action, so that I knew he had grasped exactly what he had to do, and there was no mistake. Although some of my soldiers were not very adept at translating their thoughts graphically, I was convinced that they all understood it. There was such keenness and total commitment to the job in hand by every one of them that it was a pleasure to . . .

'CO wants to see you, sir.'

It was the orderly room runner.

'Carry on, Sergeant Harper.'

Funny, what now? I marched in and saluted.

'What's the matter with you, Jefferson? Have you no sense

of security at all? Have you lost your wits altogether?'
I was flabbergasted.
'You have passed on information of great sensitivity and of importance to the enemy. A coastal battery next to a radar station doesn't exist all along the coast of Europe, you know. Two or three at the most. What have you got to say?'
'You told us in Bulford that we could pass on the information to our troops, sir.'
'I told you no such thing. The information about the radar station was for officers only.'
'I did not understand it like that, sir.'
'Then you're a fool. A bloody fool. Hal,' turning to the Adjutant, 'has any other officer passed this on?'
'Not that I've heard, sir.'
Colonel Otway eased himself in his chair and looked at me hard, fingering his pipe which was on the table in front of him.
'You really have been a BF, you know, Alan. I know you're keen, but this is immature . . . immature. For *God's sake*,' he banged his hand on the table, 'don't let your enthusiasm run away with you. There isn't time for me to . . . I don't want to do anything about it now, but you could have been in the most enormous trouble. Solitary until the Battalion had left.'
I shuddered, and my knees felt weak.
'Any questions?'
'First of all, thank you, sir.' I was feeling sick now. 'But might I ask how you knew?'
The CO paused and then turned to the Adjutant, Hal Hudson.
'Tell him.'
Hal looked at me in his kindly way. 'It's sometimes necessary to look after our own security from within. Your Corporal Dowling is SIB. Now you're to keep *that* to yourself.'
SIB – no wonder then, if I'd made such a boob.
'I see. Yes. I understand it all now. And thank you again . . .'
I was going to extend my gratitude but decided not to pile it on. But I felt it, all the same, felt it to the point of bursting into tears.

SIB: Special Investigation Branch, top security chaps who often wear a false rank. Dowling might even be commissioned and masquerading as a corporal. I'd heard that SIB were drafted into units to check on senior officers sometimes.

When I got back to my Platoon lines, I had the impression that they already knew what had happened. They all stared at me.

'Listen. I've told you too much and I've just had a bollocking from the CO. It was a misunderstanding on my part and I've apologised to him. So I'm not going to be court-martialled or anything like that.'

A few men laughed quietly. They all went on staring at me.

'I want to let you know that it was Corporal Dowling who sensed the need to keep me in check. He is wiser than I am and has a far better feeling for security.'

Dowling remained impassive while they all stared at him.

'Now you all know far more than any other platoon, more than the CO thinks is good for you. Don't let him hear I disagree because I know you'll keep it to yourselves. You have a privileged secret. Back me up, won't you?'

They looked rather pleased and murmured assent. I dismissed them, but Corporal Dowling remained.

'Permission to speak, sir?'

'Yes, Corporal Dowling, of course.'

'Thank you for what you said, sir. I'm glad it's . . . I . . .'

'All right, Dowling, I understand, thank you again.'

'It's just, well, sir – I've not been with you for long but the Platoon's a grand platoon, sir, and they're all behind you. I'm very glad I've got you as my officer.'

And as if that wasn't enough trouble for a parachuting subaltern of 23 summers, entering on his 24th, I was immediately plunged into more. I had absent-mindedly scratched away at a tree-stump while waiting for the assault on our last exercise and had trapped a splinter of bark under the fingernail which had gone septic. Now it was hurting like hell and I went to see Harold Watts, our MO (Medical Officer).

'You chump,' he said. 'I can't do anything about that, it needs surgery.'

'Surgery?' I yelled. 'What do you mean, Harold?'

'Don't you see? The whole nail is infected because of that splinter under it. What on earth have you been picking at?'

I told him.

'You'd better go and see Johnny and ask him what's best to do.'

'Can't you bandage it up or something?' I asked Harold.

'Yes, of course I can, but that's not going to remove the poison. Run along and see Johnny Johnston.' He shook his head and gave me a pitying look. My finger was already feeling worse after that diagnosis.

Johnny Johnston commanded the 224 Parachute Field Ambulance section that would be jumping with us. The skilled section would augment Harold Watts's small unit by treating casualties on the spot, especially early on when the Battalion was isolated. If Johnny couldn't deal with my finger now, he had to send me back to the Field Dressing Station at Brigade; then to the Casualty Clearing Station at Division, then . . . No, none of this bore a single thought.

'Let's have a look, Alan.' The good-looking, humorous, rugby-playing doctor took my hand.

'Not so good. What did Harold say?'

I told him.

'It's poisoned all right and it's my duty to send you back. The nail will have to come off, and that's something I'm not allowed to do here. In the field, perhaps, but not here. I *can* do it, though,' he added slowly. 'I know what's needed, though I'm not meant to use a scalpel under the present circs.'

I looked at him appealingly. We must have presented a curious sight: the tall doctor bending over me, sitting on a chair, one of my hands in his. I might almost be expecting him to propose to me.

'I'm not supposed to do it, Alan,' Johnny said slowly, and then very quickly 'but I will. It won't be very pleasant but I'm certain you'll grin and bear it.'

Afterwards he bought me a whisky, which I needed, and gave me a brand-new leather finger-stall with which to protect my nail-less digit when I jumped into action.

That evening we had our Platoon Party in a tent. I had invited Brian Browne of the Anti-Tank Platoon, and Mike Dowling as my guests. Johnny Johnston said he'd be glad to come along later – I wanted to thank him for services rendered, and 12 Platoon had already heard that he had done me a great favour by disobeying the medical rules.

The Platoon had all contributed towards the £7 for a pin of ale, and we drank it without difficulty. A pin is 4½ gallons (or half a firkin – which went down equally well as a joke) so we had just about a pint each. There were various parachuting songs and 'turns', ranging from the vulgar to the obscene. CSM (Company Sgt-Major) Ross, who looked in, was prevailed upon – without much difficulty – to give his famous rendering of 'The Old Girl Sat by the Fire'. Then I was called upon and recited 'The Village Farting Competition'. As my soldiers considered me puritanical because I was never heard to utter oaths, my turn dispelled all future notions and had made me 'one of the boys' as Morgan told me afterwards.

Johnny Johnston appeared at last. I made some sort of fatuous introduction and he gave 'The Old Girl Sat by the Fire' to our surprise, because it was considered 'Barney' Ross's copyright. I very much hoped that he wasn't going to be squashed with cries of 'Stale! We've heard it already!' but no. They all sat listening quietly and politely until Johnny reached the lines:

> The neighbours called a doctor;
> The neighbours called a doctor;
> When he got there
> I do declare
> The dirty old sod, he blocked her.

when there was loud applause. I was much heartened by their good manners. It hadn't always been like that.

Sunday 28 May was Whit Sunday, and our much-loved padre, John Gwinnett[2], held a special Church Parade. He always gave an apt sermon, so intimate that it didn't sound at all stuffy or sermon-like, but was more like a friendly chat.

## The Finishing Touches

John was completely attuned to his audience, and used to include the occasional remark or suggestion which the attentive listener might pick up and digest for himself. His text was

> Fear knocked on the door.
> Faith opened it.
> And there was no one there.

It was most impressive. Afterwards 'Fight the good fight' from 700 lusty throats and strong hearts sounded as it has never sounded since, to me. There was no accompaniment, so far as a musical instrument was concerned, but we were all absolutely together.

Our faithful Women's Voluntary Service ladies, who came with us everywhere with their canteen, had made a flag for the 9th Battalion, and John dedicated it. It had Pegasus emblazoned on a maroon ground, and the figure 9: it was ours and ours alone. As far as we knew, we were the only Battalion to possess one.

That afternoon we were all given lighthearted lessons in Dinghy Drill by the RAF — how to inflate and operate the rubber dinghies which were in all aircraft in the event of ditching in the Channel. The cry 'Dinghy! Dinghy!' was thereafter to ring round the camp in slight mockery of the useless articles. Why should we think of ditching? We were all going to make pansy-landings[3] on firm ground.

Then came the palaver of fitting 'chutes.

The parachute which we used was stored in a canvas covering like a bag, with a wide white piece of webbing, and a D-ring on the end, projecting from the top of the bag, or 'pack' as we called it. This webbing was properly called the static line but was known as the 'strop'. Before jumping we fitted four other webbing straps to the contours of our bodies, one over each shoulder and two between the legs, three of them fitting with a click into a metal box secured to the fourth one. One had only to twist the top of the box, give it a bang with the fist, and the straps dropped away, releasing the body from the harness.

The single piece of webbing from the top of the parachute pack had a D-ring that was attached to a snap-clip, like the end of a dog's lead. This clip slid along a stout wire running the whole length of the aircraft on the port (door) side, temporarily attaching the parachutist to the aircraft but allowing him free movement up and down inside. This wire was called the strong-point and it was common practice for several soldiers to pull on it with all their strength, so as to test it. Were it to break in flight, our parachutes would not be opened by their static lines.

When a man jumps from the aircraft, the strop unravels from the canvas bag containing the parachute, until it is at its fullest extent of 12½ ft. At that moment it is taut and straining against two pieces of thread (or 'ties') that hold the canvas 'pack' together. Immediately the man's falling weight is added to the tension of the strop against the 'ties', they break, the 'pack' falls apart and the man and his parachute part company with the aircraft. The upward rush of air helps the parachute canopy to develop, and with a satisfactory and heart-warming crack it opens fully.

The empty canvas bag on the end of the strop is left hanging out of the aircraft's door (or aperture), flapping about in the slipstream and winding itself round the others which belonged to the rest of the recent stick, now on their way to earth.

The parachute has to be packed in a very special way (in the war this was done by WAAFs) so as to avoid any possibility of its becoming tangled or knotted and prevented from developing. The canopy of khaki nylon for parachutists (various individual colours for containers or panniers for supply drops) is divided into 28 equal panels. The 28 shrouds (unfortunate words) or ¾-in. woven nylon lines are then found to be attached to the harness worn by the parachutist via 'lift-webs' or more webbing within arm's reach and used for pulling down to assist in changing direction or in landing.

In the unfortunate event of the canopy failing to develop or being collapsed by a 'thrown line' across it rather than below it, the man comes down without the benefit of his parachute's

## The Finishing Touches

arresting powers. This is known as a 'Roman Candle':

'Glory, glory what a helluva way to die . . .' as it goes in the old parachuting song.

The RAF found us, on the whole, to be very touchy about our parachutes. A man is entitled to refuse the 'chute offered him if: (a) he does not like the serial number on either the 'chute itself, or the static line – they are always different; (b) the 'pack' looks dirty or worn; (c) the static line looks worn – a bad sign; (d) it doesn't feel comfortable or 'right' when handled.

An aircrew member has been known to tell a parachutist (in fun) that the 'chute he has just drawn contains a blanket. The soldier, remembering the line of the same old song:

> I'd like to find the WAAF who put
> A blanket in my pack
> 'Cos I ain't goin' to jump no more.

didn't think it in the least amusing. He took back the 'chute and drew a different one.

No serial number, on 'chute or on static line, was ever acceptable if it ended in OO. That was considered too final. Some soldiers objected to a single O at the end, or in the middle of the number. Usually the old hands took the 'chute they were given without bothering to look at all.

Then there were the ju-jus. Most parachutists carried one: a small gift from a girlfriend, wife or mother, or something he felt was going to bring him luck. I used to jump with a tuning fork (A=440) and a paperback edition of *Hamlet* – but they weren't quite of the same order.

So going back to the particular fitting of 'chutes on Whit Sunday 1944 at Broadwell, we all went through the process, were satisfied with what we had, adjusted the webbing harness to suit each man's body as tightly as possible, took it all off again and placed each 'chute carefully on the seat of the aircraft which we would be occupying for the trip abroad that was not going to need a passport.

There were 20 men in each stick. I had two sections of

12 Platoon with me and Sergeant Harper took the others in the aircraft immediately following us. We chatted to our crew and I arranged with the pilot to give us the red warning light one minute before the green for GO! instead of *five* minutes before, which was the regulation. We'd had that once on an exercise and it was agony. The pilot agreed to this after some discussion, provided we stood up – ready to move down the aircraft – one minute before that. To indicate this one minute before the last one minute, he would flash the red light. We shook hands on it.

Whit Monday was windy, and we didn't much care for that. Now that we had all been through our platoon tasks, the CO briefed the whole Battalion to bring together the individual strands. We all gathered in the mess hall, waiting for the Where and the When.

He began by outlining the Divisional plan, and showed us how we fitted into it, emphasising that the destruction of our Battery was 3 Brigade's prime task. Our former CO, James Hill, had, in his wisdom, given it to his old Battalion. Of course! But it was Lieutenant-Colonel Otway, our present CO, who went on: 'There is a different aspect to this attack, as you will already have realised. Most of "A" Company will be above us in three gliders, in a force commanded by Captain Gordon-Brown, preparing to land right inside the position.' After a pause, in which there was complete silence, he went on: 'Mr Worth will now show you the Brigade dispositions.' He gestured towards a blackboard where a number of maps were displayed to view, and at last we all saw the name: MERVILLE.

Joe Worth had what the troops called a 'lah-di-dah' voice, and as he explained the positions of various units in the Battalion, one repeated word got on the nerves of his audience. When he finally described ' "B" Company – heah; "C" Company – heah; the CO's Order Group –' the soldiers all broke in: '*Heah*!'

On the morning of 2 June we had another massive kit inspection with Company Commanders also taking part, and live ammunition on display, so there was need for special care

## The Finishing Touches

We heard an explosion in the Ulsters' lines: a grenade had gone off accidentally, killing an officer and wounding several soldiers. We didn't want that sort of mad Irish trick, as I carefully pointed out to Mike Dowling.

While this kind of remark would normally be considered in poor taste, many of our 'jokes' were even further beyond the pale. We were given to scoffing at death, treating it with ridicule in an attempt to stave it off. Mike and I and the 'S'-mine was an example. That nasty booby-trap, when trodden on, released a packet of steel balls into the air, usually between the legs of the man who set it off. Silly, for he and I would go a very long way in reality to protect one another; it was only a nonsense cliché in the heady atmosphere of those days.

The Divisional Commander came and spoke to us. Richard Gale, known affectionately as 'Windy', was an impressive man who spoke words that every soldier understood. We all admired him. General Gale was full of pride and confidence in us, and in his Division as a whole.

'Finest command I've ever had. And I tell you something else. Know the seventeen-pounder anti-tank gun? The big bugger? You do? Think the enemy likes it – those Panzer crews? Course they don't. But *I'll* tell you what: I'm putting some of 'em in gliders, taking 'em over with us. What about that, eh?'

Cheers and applause.

'And as for the op itself, only a bloody fool would think of going where we're going, so that's why I'm going there!'

We cheered him to the skies.

I came in for a good deal of chivvying and teasing at breakfast on Saturday 3 June. My engagement to be married was announced in the *Daily Telegraph*. Even the CO joined in, and I felt, with a good deal of relief, that my grave misdemeanour had been forgotten.

The following day was expected to be D-1 and there was to be no drinking after midday. However, there was still a strong wind and after the sergeants' mess tent had become uprooted and blown away, it seemed that General Eisenhower concurred, and called off the whole operation for another 24 hours.[4]

This reprieve deserved something special, and the RAF officers sprung a surprise by inviting all the 9th Battalion officers to their mess that evening.

512 Squadron, which was flying us, had a most interesting history. It was born out of 24 Squadron whose crews were mainly ex-Bomber Command and ex-Coastal Command. They were brought back from supplying Chindits in Burma, from campaigns in North Africa and Italy and from Fighter Command in Europe. Many wore campaign stars and some had been decorated.

24 Squadron of 44 Group in Transport Command was responsible, among other things, for the transportation of VIPs, including members of the Royal Family and foreign heads of state in exile. The Squadron's CO was Winston Churchill's pilot, and they operated several different types of aircraft, including the Flamingos of the King's Flight, on a variety of different jobs, many of which were top secret. The crews were of many nationalities but they had one thing in common: almost without exception they were very experienced and highly qualified. 24 Squadron was an élite squadron and those who served in it were very proud to do so.

One unit of 24 Squadron, 'C' Flight, operated the Malta 'shuttle'. Using Lockheed Hudsons with turrets removed, and stripped of all armour and armour plate to reduce weight, they operated a service from London via Gibraltar to Malta and return, throughout the very long months of the siege. Outbound loads consisted of a hundred and one different bits and pieces of equipment as well as replacement air crews and other service personnel necessary to maintain the island. Return flights were usually utilised for the repatriation of service personnel wounded on the island.

In May 1943 the Flight was re-equipped with Dakotas, among the first to reach the RAF. With the lifting of Malta's siege some of the Flight were attached to the American Army

## The Finishing Touches

Air Force for the invasion of Sicily. In the event they did not take part because they were untrained in paratrooping or glider-towing; instead they operated in the supply areas of Algeria and Tunisia.

On return to base at Hendon in August 1943, they learned that 'C' Flight of 24 Squadron had been formed into a completely new Squadron – 512. They continued to be based at Hendon and to operate exactly as they had been doing.

On 17 January 1944, 46 Group came into being. Before that date there was only one Group involved with Air Support Work and that was 38 Group. It had been responsible all along for development-work relating to airborne operations. 38 Group's aircraft were military types such as Stirlings, Halifaxes, Albermarles (and, for training purposes, the old Whitley with its aperture in the floor, commemorated by the song 'Jumping through the hole').

The new 46 Group had five squadrons of which 512 was the parent squadron and, in the beginning, the only one equipped with Dakotas. They moved to Broadwell in February 1944 and were told, when briefed in May, that they were to carry 9th Battalion The Parachute Regiment of 6 Airborne Division. The Battalion was to be dropped on the most easterly DZ, also the most difficult because of its size and close proximity to the coast: only 75 seconds inland.

They were also told that although they had been selected for this particular and important job on account of its difficulty and the Squadron's experience, they would not be doing their own pathfinding as they had done many times already on exercises. Pathfinding would be undertaken by 38 Group. The crews of 512 were not pleased.

We learned a few random pieces of information from the Squadron's history in their mess that night, but not very much. We were far more interested in getting to know the individuals and in drinking their beer. A Wing Commander, also called Jefferson, entered into amiable conversation and in no time we were calling each other 'Jeff', much to the surprise of my brother subalterns. Eternal loyalties and confidences were sworn, and we felt happy about being flown out by such splendid 'light-blue jobs'.

On Sunday 4 June, John Gwinnett held a Drumhead Service – implying a summary affair under urgent conditions. Once more he inspired us and gave us confidence in the Almighty: 'God helps those who help themselves', he told us, but the old lags of the Battalion, now obliged to behave with decorum, read it the other way.

James Hill, the Brigadier, had taken part in this service, and addressed us afterwards, uttering those famous words frequently attributed to him since: 'Gentlemen, in spite of your excellent training and good orders, do not be daunted if chaos reigns – it undoubtedly will!' It is doubtful whether anybody in the 9th Battalion considered that chaos on a grand scale was ever likely to interfere with the well-laid plans we had now absorbed and digested.

From then on and into the next day we had 'enforced rest'. I spent some of it with my platoon, chatting, exchanging ideas and making myself as one with them. That night I was awoken again by 'Dizzie' moaning and restlessly moving about in his sleeping bag. I asked him whether I could do anything for him, but he didn't answer. If he had a fever there were no signs of it in the morning, and this had happened before. He was extremely disturbed while asleep, to the point of hysteria.

Nobody felt especially hungry on 5 June, when we had late Reveille and mainly fatless meals were on offer. The day passed slowly, but at 19.00 hrs we got ourselves together, sealed up the last envelope to be posted only after we had gone, like the pile already kept back since briefing. We assembled, by habit, in our advance battle order, though without the glider boys of 'A' Company who, after much ribbing and suggestions tat they should dispense with their parachute wings, had disappeared to another airfield at Tarrant Rushton, Dorset, taking with them the Battalion flag.[5] It was considered to be safest in GB's glider.

Then we left our camp on Broadwell airfield, through the gate and past a knot of people who were remaining: Albert Chilton, the Essex Quartermaster (an old man by our stan-

# 21 ARMY GROUP

# PERSONAL MESSAGE FROM THE C-in-C

### To be read out to all Troops

1  The time has come to deal the enemy a terrific blow in Western Europe.

The blow will be struck by the combined sea, land, and air forces of the Allies – together constituting one great Allied team, under the supreme command of General Eisenhower.

2  On the eve of this great adventure I send my best wishes to every soldier in the Allied team.

To us is given the honour of striking a blow for freedom which will live in history; and in the better days that lie ahead men will speak with pride of our doings. We have a great and a righteous cause.

Let us pray that 'The Lord Mighty in Battle' will go forth with our armies, and that His special providence will aid us in the struggle.

3  I want every soldier to know that I have complete confidence in the successful outcome of the operations that we are now about to begin.

With stout hearts, and with enthusiasm for the contest, let us go forward to victory.

4  And, as we enter the battle, let us recall the words of a famous soldier spoken many years ago:

> *'He either fears his fate too much,*
> *Or his deserts are small,*
> *Who dare not put it to the touch,*
> *To win or lose it all.'*

5  Good luck to each one of you. And good hunting on the mainland of Europe.

*B. L. Montgomery*
*General*
*C.-in-C. 21 Army Group*

1944

Fig. 2  General Montgomery's personal message to all men in his 21 Army Group, early June 1944

dards); Frank Tavener, a real fighting man obliged to stay behind; some of the cooks and orderlies; Lance-Corporal Flitton and his sanitary squad; the post corporal. They stood to attention, saluting, and there was scarcely a dry eye among them. As the Royal Ulster Rifles were not joining us in Normandy until the following afternoon, they sent a contingent to bid us farewell, which was decent of them. There were also the Broadwell NAAFI canteen-girls and a cluster of elegant and beautiful WAAF security girls who all had tears rolling down their cheeks.

Everybody there knew without doubt that 9th Battalion The Parachute Regiment, the original 9th Battalion on its way to battle, was marching together for the last time.

# 3
# Rommel

## Strengthening the Atlantic Wall

The British and Canadian raid on Dieppe in August 1942 provided the Nazi Minister for Propaganda, Dr Joseph Goebbels, with a great story about the invincibility of the Atlantic Wall, part of 'Fortress Europe'. The Wall was supposed to be a line of fortifications stretching from Denmark to the Pyrenees. The raiders at Dieppe had been decisively beaten on the beaches (though there had been some penetration inland by Commandos) and therefore – according to Goebbels – the whole French coastline was equally as impregnable as Dieppe had been. Certainly ports such as Dieppe, Boulogne, Le Havre, Cherbourg (and the Channel Islands) were veritable fortresses but, in between, many of the defences were lamentably understrength or, in some sectors, altogether neglected.

As the tide of war turned against the Nazis in 1943, it became evident that the Allies were planning a determined assault from southern England upon the Atlantic Wall. Hitler boasted of his 'reprisal weapons', the V1 and V2 (somewhat behind schedule); and also his 'miracle weapon', the atomic bomb (whose progress had been severely hampered by Allied raids on heavy-water plants). These, proclaimed Hitler, were going to bring Germany through to victory on both the Eastern and the Western Fronts.

At the end of 1943 (with North Africa lost and most of Italy in Allied hands) Hitler appointed Field Marshal Erwin Rommel of Afrika Korps fame to command the new Army Group 'B'. Rommel was ordered to take this formation to Normandy and to report to Field Marshal Gerd von Rundstedt, C-in-C West who, in spite of equivalent rank, was his superior officer.

von Rundstedt was an old man of sixty-eight years in December 1943. He was a Prussian of the old school and an aristocrat. He had been retired in 1940, sacked twice by Hitler for failing to complete impossible tasks, such as the holding of the Southern Front in Russia during the winter of 1941/2; yet was brought back twice to active service because he was one of the ablest generals Hitler had. von Rundstedt realised that he had been given yet another impossible job to make the Atlantic Walls impregnable and did not unduly tax himself in preparing the defences, whose unified strength lay only in Hitler's mind and Goebbels's words.

von Rundstedt did not care at all for the Nazi lot, least of all for the 'corporal' who led them, but his only alternative was to obey commands and to behave like a Junker. Nor did he seem to have much in common with Rommel, when he first arrived in France. To von Rundstedt, Rommel was an upstart, had never attended Staff College, had never fought on the Eastern Front and had attracted the sort of hero-worship which he considered vulgar, and smacked of a 'personality cult'.

Rommel was aware of the gaps in his service and character that von Rundstedt would very likely find objectionable, and it was probably a shared sense of humour that brought the two Field Marshals into a reasonable relationship. In any case, Rommel was the man who had fought against the British in France in 1940, and later in the Western Desert. Then he had encountered the British and the Americans in Sicily and Italy. He had a good deal to tell von Rundstedt about their methods. Rommel could tell, could advise, could even prompt, but he could not command. He knew, beyond doubt, that Allied air superiority was going to play the biggest part in the forthcoming war in the West, and pointed this out forcibly.

Since the Battle of Britain, the Luftwaffe had never commanded the skies over the English Channel. It was now, in 1943, quite impossible for any German aircraft to get half-way across the Kanal, as they called it, before being intercepted and probably shot down. There could be no photo-reconnaissance of the Channel ports and marshalling areas in the south of England, and this severely hampered German intelligence. By contrast, Allied aircraft entered, photographed, bombed and strafed at will in German-occupied air-space.

In early December 1943, Rommel began a tour of the Atlantic Wall, starting in Denmark. That took ten days. He then moved his headquarters to Fontainebleau and began an intensive study of the French coast. Shortly before Christmas he started to make a number of lightning – though long – visits by car, accompanied by a few staff officers, and always without warning. He was not given to shouting nor to insulting his subordinates, but his obvious distaste for what he saw, coupled with an immediate grasp of the remedy, instilled the required respect and alacrity into a lot of old 'dug-outs' who were expecting to see out the rest of the war in comfort and trouble-free seclusion. Rommel changed all that after a single visit.

From mid-January 1944, Rommel obtained an independent command. Nobody seems certain how it came about. Naturally, Rommel wanted it, von Rundstedt was delighted to have a heavy load of responsibility removed from him, and Hitler would have liked the idea of the two Field Marshals disagreeing over details. Rommel was appalled by what he saw in the West. On 17 May, Rommel went to the Carentan area to inspect the 91st Airlanding Regiment, and spoke to its officers. In the course of his address he uttered the prophetic words about the Allied Invasion: 'They will come with cloud and storm, and after midnight.' The situation there had deteriorated almost beyond belief since he had commanded the 7th Panzer Division in the push to Dunkirk in 1940. The much-vaunted Atlantic Wall was a sham. Furthermore his powers to authorise actual, physical work by – in particular – the Organisation Todt were non-existent. It was a world away from the Western Desert where he had been supremo.

Fritz Todt[1] was a civil engineer who had been responsible

for building the Siegfried Line and the autobahns. He was consequently accustomed to dealing in massive supplies of concrete. Over the years he had so ingratiated himself with Hitler that he was now responsible to no one else, and could not be ordered about by anyone else. While his influence extended to the Western Defences, he often contracted out to local building firms, because he was interested only in the prestige jobs. Todt was killed in an air crash in 1942, but the Organisation remained under Hitler's personal control for the rest of the war.

In 1943–4 most of the 'important' work lay in rebuilding – or endeavouring to put a brave face on – the bombed cities of the Reich. A few bunkers and emplacements in Normandy were not the concern of the Organisation Todt's head office, though the very name was very powerful in civil engineering throughout occupied countries.

The degree to which Rommel found himself hampered is best expressed by General Dr Hans Speidel, his Chief of Staff[2]:

> The chain of command in Western Europe conformed neither to the timeless laws of warfare nor to the demands of the hour nor even to common sense. Hitler thought that he could apply his revolutionary principle of divided responsibilities to the conduct of the war and play off one commander against another to his own advantage. Under the Commander-in-Chief for the West (Field Marshal von Rundstedt) there were Army Group 'B' (Rommel) in the Netherlands/Loire Sector and Army Group 'G' (Blaskowitz) in the Loire/Spanish frontier/Mediterranean coast/Alps Sector. The western naval command (Admiral Krancke) received orders direct from the German Naval Staff, while the Third Air Fleet (Field Marshal Sperle) received orders from Göring. Thus operations at sea and in the air could neither be directed nor co-ordinated by C-in-C West nor by commander of Army Group 'B'. The military commanders were only partially informed ... by ... the other two services, and usually too late.

Thus the 'Wall' which Rommel saw was perched on the cliffs and along the coast. Its sea and coastal artillery was the prerogative of the Navy. Above was the sky, which a rather chary Luftwaffe was supposed to command. But even if it did so, Rommel was unable to command or order *it*. Yet as soon as an enemy soldier set foot on a beach or came down by parachute or glider inland, it was Rommel's responsibility to deal with him.

Between the coastal strongpoints, and generally further inland, there were Army field batteries linked – to a certain extent – with naval batteries so as to cover the whole coastline. Because of the shortage of steel, revolving turrets could no longer be supplied to the Wehrmacht, so that the Army gunners, who also needed a wider arc and elevation of fire than that obtainable from within concrete emplacements, preferred to serve their guns in the open where possible.

On the other hand, the heavy naval guns were in steel turrets which revolved and secured for the gunners the arcs of fire they wanted. This sharp division between arms of the German services presented many other, similar examples to illustrate the total lack of co-ordination.

It was not long before Rommel noticed that there were inadequate concrete shelters round the naval gun positions for protection of their crews during air raids. There were neither minefields round the strongpoints, nor effective beach and shallow-water obstacles against seaborne landings. The German High Command had failed to supervise the Engineer-in Charge (a General) who, in turn, lacked altogether the vision and keenness to create a comprehensive defence system.

Hitler's directive to von Rundstedt had always been to fight the decisive Invasion battle on the Wall itself, to break up all Allied opposition at the time of landing, and to refuse a foothold. As at Stalingrad there was to be *no retreat*, even for regrouping, and thus the generals – and sub-unit commanders – were denied the ability to manœuvre to obtain strategic advantage.

Rommel had different ideas. Always the Panzer General, he was certain that his armoured divisions, brought well forward towards the coast, would be vital so as to wipe out the initial 'soft' troops before enemy tanks and anti-tank guns could be delivered. He was reckoning on a battle of opportunity where his Panzers might pounce, rather than relying on a thin grey line. There were other considerations as well.

Rommel had initially insisted on the need to 'stop the enemy in the water and destroy his equipment while it is still afloat'[3]. But the Navy had not co-operated fully by agreeing to mine the sea lanes, and Hitler would not allow the Luftwaffe to drop 'pressure-mines' around the Isle of Wight as Rommel had requested. Hitler's reason was that there was no known way of sweeping them, but it is very doubtful whether they could have been sown there in the first place. Hitler was still loyal to Göring.

The defences of Le Havre on the eastern edge of the Bay of the Seine, and Cherbourg at the western side, were very adequate as strongpoints and were no more likely to be taken from the sea than Dieppe had been two years earlier. As these were the only substantial ports in the Bay, Rommel did not believe that a major landing in this area was feasible. He believed, rather, that there might be several Allied landings either together, or in close succession, with one or more feints to keep German troops tied down in wrong places. Paris, he considered, was to be a fairly rapid objective ('for operational, political and psychological reasons')[4] while the isolation of Brittany with Cherbourg as its prize was a certainty. But how?

Hitler thought he had the answer to this, and to almost every other problem that teased his generals. On 6 May 1944, Rommel received a surprising signal from the Führer's headquarters[5]:

> The Führer is of the opinion that an invasion along a 500-km-wide strip is unlikely; that attacks will occur primarily at Normandy and to a lesser extent at Brittany. The most recent information once more points in this direction.

The signal went on to deal with 243 Infantry Division's supply of horses.

Hitler's generals disagreed entirely with the Normandy and Brittany landings theory, which had probably come about as a result of Hitler's 'intuition'. Such a theory went against all conventional strategy. The Allies would be entirely unable to secure a port for themselves in the early days of the landings when a massive and rapid rate of supplies was vital. If they landed elsewhere, without a port, the distance across that wider part of the Channel would make adequate supply impossible. The generals were convinced that the attack, when it came would be – must be – in the Pas de Calais.

Hitler was determined to improve his somewhat dented image as generalissimo of the Third Reich throughout his armed forces and civilian population by masterminding the forthcoming repulse of the Allies; yet he managed only to effect contradictory measures by pointing one hand at Normandy and then transferring vital reinforcements away from there with the other.

Vice-Admiral Friedrich Ruge, Rommel's Chief of Staff, has also highlighted the Führer's indecisiveness, and has stated that thought and planning at Hitler's HQ was based far more on tactical than on strategic principles. On 10 May, Rommel received another signal which read[6]:

> The Führer expects the enemy attack to begin in the middle of May. Especially 18 May – a potentially favourable day. Irrefutable documentary proof is, of course, not available. Point of concentration first and foremost: Normandy; secondly: Brittany.

It has been suggested that superior British counter-espionage activities were partly responsible for making the enemy think the Allies' main assault was going to be elsewhere[7]. As long ago as 1941, Dieppe was chosen as the site for an experimental landing because it was never going to be in the main Invasion area when the offensive against 'Fortress Europe' began.

Rommel was constantly on the move, inspecting, checking and impressing everybody who saw him by his grasp of what was needed. 'Unlike many of the General Staff he was very much interested in technical things. . . . He had a strong mechanical bent and his suggestions were always sound.'[8] He was often able to end rivalries between 'experts' in former disassociated arms under his command, where all ranks were now inspired by his simple explanations, the logic of his ideas and the manner in which he associated himself with all ranks. Quite often he used to eat with the soldiers, one of his attributes as a great commander.

Rommel's old adversary and victor in the Western Desert, General Montgomery, had sized up what to expect when his troops reached the other side. In May 1944 he said of Rommel[9]:

> It is now clear that his intention is to defeat us on the beaches... He is an energetic and determined commander; he has made a world of difference since he took over.... He will do his level best to 'Dunkirk' us – not to fight the armoured battle on ground of his choosing but to avoid it altogether and prevent our tanks landing by using his tanks well forward.

Montgomery was a step ahead of Rommel in his appreciation of the man who had brought forward the 12th SS Panzer *Hitler Jugend* Division, and the 21st Panzer Division. The fact remains that while the struggle to get ashore and establish the bridgehead would be a fierce one, the Allies did not have to face such a formidable defence-system along its whole length as many had feared. Some of the installations were easily overcome, others were equipped with smaller weapons than Allied intelligence had anticipated. Others were dummies. Had Rommel been sent to the French coast sooner and had he begun his programme there instead of in Denmark in December 1943, the opposition which he was creating might have been tougher and the delicate balance of those first few days in June 1944 could have tilted in his favour. But that is not what happened.

We now need to look more closely at a small unit under Rommel's command that he knew and inspected twice. It was called 1/1716 by the Germans, and the Merville (or Sallenelles) Battery by the British Staff.

# 4
# Buskotte
## Building the Battery

The end of 1942 was the turning point in Hitler's military might, in spite of all his vainglorious boasts. Belief in an easy conquest of Russia was now fading and the Führer rounded on his generals, blaming them for the results of his own bad orders. He saw the tide turning against him in North Africa, which he partly blamed on the unreliability of his Italian allies. He also recognised the need to repair his Atlantic Wall, the northern bastion of 'Fortress Europe', even though the Allied failure of the Dieppe Raid in the previous August had greatly enhanced the propaganda value of the Wall.

Among all these diminishing returns, the Stalingrad Front in Russia was proving to be the most critical. Many more divisions were needed there, and Hitler did not wish to count those that had been massacred in the snowy wastes. Pitiful remains of once-brave soldiers were returning to the Fatherland, many to die on the way. Those who survived were cripples, invalids and nervous wrecks all requiring rehabilitation. As many as could still bear arms were sent to North-West Europe.

Partly to conceal the immense losses, formations were regrouped and renumbered. One of these was Infantry Division 656. It had gone over from Finland into Russia in June 1941 and now, more than two years later, its remnants had been redesignated Infantry Division 716 and ordered to take over a sector of the Atlantic Wall in Normandy by Christmas 1942.

Each infantry division contained its own artillery regiment and this was subdivided into three sections, with three batteries in each. Every battery had four guns. (See Appendix 4, p. 21.1.)

The first battery of the first section of the 716 Artillery Regiment (belonging to 716 Infantry Division), known as the Merville Battery, is the unit which concerns us and which bears investigation. Among its men was a Sergeant called Buskotte. Although he had not served on the Russian Front – considered to be the hallmark of proper Wehrmacht soldiery – he was clearly marked for promotion.

Johannes Buskotte was born into a family butchery business in Osnabrück. They were all ardent Catholics. On 2 November 1937, aged twenty-one, he joined the *Arbeitsdienst* (literally Work-service, a nominally non-combatant pioneer force) at Quakenbruck, near his home town. He was too old for the Hitler Youth, but by volunteering for service he chose the Labour Corps in preference to the fighting forces.

Buskotte and his squad were put through a full training, including arms drill and marching, fieldcraft and observation exercises. It was a way of having a part-trained army in reserve while keeping to the post-First World War restrictions imposed by the League of Nations. Instead of rifles, they carried spades, always scrupulously cleaned and polished, and because the spade weighed about the same as a rifle, it was easy enough, when the time came, for these back-row pioneers to be turned into front-rank fighting soldiers.

In 1939 Buskotte transferred voluntarily to the Wehrmacht at Detmold, partly because it enabled him to continue his service near home at Osnabrück. He was still able to go home often, to help his father in the shop, and to keep his own hand in. He was trained as a gunner, joined the newly formed 716 Artillery Regiment and was posted to No 1 Battery.

The Regiment was equipped with Czech (formerly Austrian) 100mm howitzers dated 1914/19, First World War weapons that were unsuited to the requirements of modern artillery regiments in Russia and therefore retained for European defence. In contrast to later howitzers they had shell and primer in two parts. The shell would not fire without a bag of up to six powder containers inserted into the breech after the shell[1]. The four guns in Buskotte's Battery were independently marked '1916', but no log-books nor record of service came with them. German artillerymen who had been trained on the conventional 105mm howitzer found little difficulty in adapting to the Czech weapon which they usually referred to as '105' – 'What's 5mm, here or there?'[2] (See Appendix 4, p. 211–14.)

During the second week in December 1942, the 1/1716 (as the Battery was officially described – 1st Battery in the 1st Section of the 716 Artillery Regiment) – began its march to new quarters. With six horses – or equally acceptable oxen – to each howitzer and two to a limber, they marched until the animals were exhausted. They were then let loose and fresh ones were taken or requisitioned 'in accordance with the Wehrmacht's mobilisation orders' from the nearest farm or stud along the way.

The journey from Saxony to Normandy took a week and was uneventful. When the Battery reached its destination, the soldiers found themselves in the middle of several fields, about a mile from the Channel coast and a mile east of the River Orne. It was 20 December, and the location did not seem a particularly festive one in which to spend Christmas.

Three Norman families owned the requisitioned fields: Legrix, Duval and Delfargueil were still permitted, however, to graze their cattle outside the perimeter wire, although inside that was out of bounds to all but essential suppliers and workmen.

The Battery was established out-of-doors between the village of Merville (from which it takes its name) and a hamlet called Descanneville, really part of Merville for it includes the Château de Merville.

The entrance to the Battery was (and is) approached from a narrow road off the Descanneville crossroads. On the corner, then as now, stands a shuttered cottage painted green and white; while the largest house on the left side of the road was the Mairie and behind it the little school. Then, further on, and behind that, was the stone wall surounding the Château de Merville.

This pleasant building, probably seventeenth-century, was taken over for the Battery's administrative offices, and for sleeping quarters. A cider-press in one of the outhouses was soon put to good use. The school house was requisitioned as an officers' mess for the artillery and infantry officers in the immediate area.

Grooms and farriers all lived down the road near Gonneville, in a stud farm called Haras de Retz, with their animals. In the event of an emergency, they were ordered to report at once to the Battery position and to leave the horses out of danger.

As the soldiers settled in and looked round for the means to enjoy themselves, some enterprising French people opened a 'Café Merville' in Descanneville, beyond the front gates of the Château. It was neither as large, nor as welcoming, nor as well stocked as another in Franceville, nor yet as the Café Gondrée beside the Bénouville Bridge[3]. Although this café was rather far away, it was on the route to all the other units in the Regiment.

WO Peter Timpf of the Battery remembers it[4]:

> It wasn't much of a place. Located two houses east of the Merville Château, it was staffed by local French civilians. German soldiers were tolerated but not welcomed. I used to go there sometimes for matches and a drink or two, just for a change from the regular canteen drinks. Canteen supplies came up [at the Battery] once monthly and lasted for about two weeks. We used to send someone to Caen to purchase what we needed from the French: Benedictine, Cognac, Calvados, wines and tobacco.

All soldiers had two weeks' leave every six months, with immediate compassionate leave if home or possessions had been bombed. Air raids by the RAF were becoming more prevalent on German towns and cities as the Allies stepped up their round-the-clock raids.

Off-duty time locally was spent either in Cabourg or in Caen. The best way to get to Cabourg was by bicycle, though it was a garrison town, holding many soldiers. Caen was a real

## Building the Battery

city with everything to offer by way of entertainment. The soldiers reached it by travelling on the French buses. But Caen had its disadvantages. It housed the HQ of the regional Gestapo and other intelligence units. Its streets rang with the sound of jackboots and there were far too many military police for comfort because it was the main railway centre. Soldiers going on leave from Merville took the little train from Ouistreham to Caen along the Orne, then changed on to the main line for Paris and Germany.

Some of the soldiers liked to go to Franceville. Timpf recalls[5]:

> Yes, once a week for a change of scenery and a few drinks. On Sundays the bakery there sold good cream cakes, and we were good customers.

Although it was dull at Merville, it was very peaceful. Nobody bothered about pep talks and propaganda: it was all free and easy. Nor was there very strict censorship of mail so that some veiled criticisms of the war's progress often got through from Normandy to the soldiers' families. It was becoming evident, to even the simplest soldier, that Germany was either going to become involved in a much longer war than they had all been told, or in a defeat. Each man who was eating the cream cakes from Franceville, or drinking the Calvados began to feel better. He had plenty of exercise, plenty of work, plenty of fun too. The weakest and most unhealthy of them began to feel better, and if this led to an upgrading in health the next time there was a general check from the MO, the saying went: 'Get well to get killed!' as back to Russia some of them went.

There was one odd-man-out belonging to the Battery. He was a fervent Nazi, a lance-corporal who took Hitler's creed very seriously and was, strangely enough, a Swiss national. He had volunteered for the Wehrmacht, imbued by Goebbels' rhetoric, and entered into soldiering with enormous zest. His name was Lutz[6]. He was always smartly turned out, he relished polishing his badges and singing the Party songs. He was disliked, and was held in some mistrust by his comrades lest he should report any of the careless remarks they uttered after a few drinks. For apart from Lutz, the Battery enjoyed being in this backwater, away from the sickening propaganda, the barking voices, the exaggerated claims.

The Wehrmacht magazines *Signal* and *Das Reich* came round, both well produced but giving highly coloured reports of current (and sometimes not so current) events, showing how splendidly the three German services were doing all over Europe.

The stepping-up of Allied bombing of German towns upset the soldiers in Normandy far more than anything else. 'Bomb-leave' became more frequent, and when the soldiers returned to their Battery it was, more often than not, in mourning and with grief marking their features. In many cases it was the cause of strengthening their purpose and making them want to get their own back on the enemy. On the occasion when a soldier went absent, or contemplated desertion, he very seldom succeeded, for the long and ferocious arm of the Gestapo took him back and inflicted severe punishment – often execution – that British authority would never contemplate.

When the sun came out in early 1943, the howitzers were still sited in the open, although they had been moved about in between, under the cover of trees in orchards. They always needed attention and maintenance against the rain and the sea breezes, laden with salt, awaiting proper shelter. This kept the soldiers busy and so did the occasional exercises as well as practice shoots.

In the spring, the job of constructing concrete bunkers and casemates for the Battery was put out to contract by the Organisation Todt and was secured by a pro-German French engineering company called Entreprises Rittmann of Paris. They had local offices at Rouen and, even nearer, at Houlgate on the coast beyond Cabourg. Rittmann began work on No 1 Casemate in June 1943.[7]

This was the most important of the four casemates to be built because it would protect the right, and ranging gun which the three others would follow in a shoot. Numbers 1 and 2 worked as a pair, so did Nos 3 and 4; Nos 1 and 3 Casemates were therefore more elaborate than the other two, with accommodation for the gunners and underground chambers for ammunition.

When work began on No 1 Casemate there seemed no great urgency. It was constructed in an elaborate fashion with solid concrete walls, fully reinforced, and a large pair of rooms 4m below the ground at floor level, approached only by means of a vertical, iron ladder through a trapdoor. At this depth it needed an efficient pumping system and as there were to be steel doors at the back of the casemate and a thick steel curtain at the front, which could be lowered over the gun port, there was also going to be a good ventilation system installed. It was altogether no mean undertaking and, at the rate of progress with No 1 Casemate and preparations for the other three, to fulfil artillery and safety requirements, would take at least two years to finish. Work was also progressing on the Command Bunker, the Stores Bunker and the Cookhouse (see Fig. 8 on p. 175).

Seven months spent with the howitzers in the open used to cause some concern over their safety. Lieutenant Karl Heyde, Commander of No 6 Battery on the other side of the Orne (until he became the Regimental Adjutant), had his own views about this. His battery had been in a field without any form of camouflage, except that there were cows grazing all round them. On one visit, the CO expressed surprise and apprehension at this state of affairs. He did not think it at all sensible, in view of the frequent appearance of RAF aircraft.

'I do not agree, with respect, Colonel,' replied Heyde. 'The cows afford us the best camouflage!'[8] He was later proved correct because No 6 Battery was not identified from air-reconnaissance photographs.

It was a different matter in the case of Merville. While the members of the Battery carried on with their work of making the place safer for themselves, they were unaware that it and they were now under British Intelligence scrutiny. For the Allied planners, Merville had become a subject of constant analysis, anxiety and apprehension. They felt certain that the casemates, progressing slowly, were of a size that must be intended to protect large, coastal guns; and as the casemates were being built to face north-west towards Riva Bella, across the Orne Estuary, the chosen left flank of the Invasion must be suspected – if not already known.

The four howitzers, said a British Intelligence Report, are

> ?150MM (5.9″) at present mounted in open circular emplacements ... in front of each existing emplacement a concrete casemate is being constructed. Work started in June 1943.[9]

In the previous November, an American Intelligence estimate had put the calibre of the Merville guns at 155mm.

They were, of course, the Czech 10cm howitzers, and Intelligence had been unduly convinced by French Résistance as well as by photographic interpretation that it was a coastal battery, not an Army unit. All coastal batteries, it will be remembered, were under control of the German Navy.

The four casemates were certainly being built to face Riva Bella, but not with the emphasis on the beaches. The howitzers' main task was to guard or to menace the important feature of the Orne Canal: its locks and estuary. German High Command had always been of the opinion that should an invasion take place in this part of Normandy, the enemy would want to capture Caen as quickly as possible. As the most direct route to the city was up the Orne Canal, it seemed likely that assault boats, full of troops, were to be expected. Although the lock gates on the canal were prepared for demolition, an artillery barrage on and round the Canal would be an added deterrent.

A secondary target was the flat, open ground which lay to the east of the Orne estuary, in the event of enemy landings there. All trees and a farmhouse, which had stood between the Battery position and the area known as 'Les Dunes', had been razed to the ground.

A third – a 'target of opportunity' – had also been suggested:

enemy ships in the Channel. Although it might not appeal to the more conventional German artillery officer, it should not be ignored.

While the casemates were being built, a German sergeant, Fritz Waldmann, was responsible for the fire-plan of the howitzers and for their installation inside the casemates as they were built. As one of three close friends in the Battery, he was the brains of the trio, the mathematician concerned with indirect fire and the trigonometry it needed. Aged thirty-seven, he was nine years older than the second member of the trio, Hans Buskotte. Buskotte was the practical gunner and disciplinarian, soon to be promoted to Battery Sergeant Major.

The third was Peter Timpf. He acted as a FOO (Forward Observation Officer) with a platoon of No 3 company of the 736 Infantry Regiment billeted in Descanneville. As their 'advanced ground observer' he went with advancing infantry ahead of static positions, advising the Battery OC at first hand as to how his fire might support them. He was able to direct the howitzers' fire when the OC was unable to do so, but the OC gave direct orders to the Battery position.

Timpf was a particular friend of Buskotte's and they shared a room in the Château above the Battery Office, later sharing a corner in No 1 Casemate. Timpf provided a good and useful liaison with the infantry although he was, first and foremost, a gunner and a member of the Merville Battery.

The Officer Commanding 1/1716 was Captain Karl-Heinrich Wolter who had been brought back from the Russian Front in a sad, nervous condition. As he got better, he became prone to all kinds of excesses. Buskotte, who was regimental, upright and moral to the last degree, did not admire him. Wolter's frequent womanising – not unusual among all ranks in Normandy – was one of the bad habits which Buskotte and all the soldiers observed in their commander's way of life. The worst over-indulgence that Buskotte could think of to express Wolter's gluttony was: 'He drank Calvados – with cream on the top!'[10]

Lieutenant Rudi Schaaf was the Battery Officer, with whom

Buskotte, as senior WO (Warrant Officer), shared the Command Bunker when they were working. This was equipped as an office: clerks and the telephone exchange to OP (Observation Post) and each casemate, against the necessity for a general withdrawal from the Château into the Battery position.

Wolter disliked having to be tied down to the OP, or to sleeping inside No 1 Casemate where there was a corner for him, on the right inside the door. It was more comfortable and secluded at the OP, though two WOs were always there: Kath and Rauch. There was a 'Tobruk Stand'[11] (a machine-gun position with a steel cupola over it) on top of the bunker, and a little way off across the dunes, another bunker manned by Lieutenant Rix of the 736 Infantry, where there was a telephone line to Division.

As every other battery in the Regiment was on the other side of the Orne, No 1 at Merville was isolated. That had its advantages as well as its drawbacks. They seldom saw the Regimental Commander, Lieutenant-Colonel Hans-Joachim Andersen. He had taken over in July 1943 after being severely wounded in Russia. He was still a sick man and, at the age of forty-eight, was one of the oldest officers in the Regiment. He was very popular for his fairness and his mild manner, but he found his command rather a strain.

Sometimes the Section Commander, Major Karl-Werner Hof, visited Merville, but more often Wolter saw his brother officers at conferences when he was called to Regimental HQ in Colleville. On these occasions he left Schaaf in charge, and then the third officer on the Battery's establishment, Lieutenant Hans Malsch, known as 'the maid of all work' was sent to the OP. Malsch had this job from December 1943 until March 1944. This was a happy arrangement for Wolter, who made use of his journey to Colleville for other 'conferences' of a more personal nature.

At the end of 1943 there was a sharpening up of all troops in Normandy because of Field Marshal Rommel's arrival, and

716 Division found themselves under his command when Army Group 'B' was formed.

On 6 March the Field Marshal made an unannounced visit to Merville on his way to Caen. The big black Horch car (Horch = Audi) pulled up at the main gate of the Battery. The Field Marshal briskly jumped out and was met by Captain Wolter. (See Plate 21.) With Rommel were his Adjutant; the Engineer Commander of Army Group 'B', General Meise; Rommel's Chief of Staff, General Dr Hans Speidel; and Vice-Admiral Ruge.

Rommel quickly took in every essential detail and expressed his opinion that the Organisation Todt was taking far too long about their construction. He wanted the pace of building to be stepped up – fast. He came and went. It had taken no more than twenty minutes, but he had left a strong impression on those who were close enough to take in his brief, measured words. From now on, nothing was going to be quite the same as it was before.

Buskotte was promoted to Battery Sergeant Major and was told to be prepared to move out of the Château and to set up his office permanently in the Command Bunker when ordered.

Rommel had seen a great deal of inadequacy in his area of command since he arrived, and gave orders that there was to be a dummy battery constructed near every real one along the Atlantic Wall. As things were, there could be little doubt as to where the real batteries were situated and the Allies were taking a great number of photographs of all positions along the Wall. On 20 March the last picture of the Battery was taken before the first bombing raid on it. There was no dummy battery constructed near Merville, but the old field position, 600m from the casemates, shows up as a white line, and may have been considered sufficient as a means of deluding photo-reconnaissance. (See Plate 15.)

The first air raid, when it came, was an inevitable shock after so many months of peace, but as the raids continued, they constituted a series of great annoyance and frustration to the defenders, quite apart from their effect on the nerves. Rommel's continual pressure to make his units more efficient meant increased activity on the site, which was then detected and dealt with by the Allied aircraft. No sooner had work begun on new buildings, new trenches, new weapon-pits – no sooner had stores been delivered – than the RAF came back to wreck it all. Most of the raids were at night, but when the daylight hit-and-run fighters came over, the only AA defence in the Battery sprang into action.

This was the 20mm Flak 38 Gun (known as 'Erika' in the Wehrmacht, perhaps because of the marching song of that name). It was the conventional weapon for both AA and horizontal roles against soft-skinned vehicles on the ground. This 'Erika' was inclined to be temperamental – 'just like a woman'. (See Plate 22.) There seemed no reason why she should suddenly refuse to fire, and those detailed to operate the weapon found her to possess a truly wayward disposition. She was mounted on top of a triangular building, below which was the cookhouse, until (when the raids became more frequent) the cookhouse was moved away from the centre of the position to the guardroom near the Quartermaster's bunker. Two men handled the AA gun and two others handed up the ammunition. This team of four was relieved throughout the 24 hours because they had always to be on the alert. They had a stuffed dog as a mascot which stood beside 'Erika', often watching silently as the soldiers cursed while they once more stripped down the gun in an effort to discover what was wrong.

On the night of 9/10 May there was a concentrated aerial raid on Merville by 56 Lancasters, but all their bombs fell to the south of the target. A German report which ridiculed the effects of this raid read[12]:

> Out of 1000 bombs only fifty landed near the Battery and of these only two hit a casemate (No 4) though without penetration. But in the farm at Le Mavais a building was destroyed; in the Grande Ferme La Buisson a large bomb fell in the vegetable garden; and in the adjoining Descanneville every window was broken. In the

outlying fields, 27 cows were killed, 11 had to be put down and 40 ran away. A rabbit warren suffered a direct hit.

This was the time when Hitler's advisers had told him to expect an invasion: weather, tides and winds were all suitable. The day prophesied, 18 May, came and went without interruption. Vice-Admiral Ruge wrote[13]: 'Glorious Whit weather. Everyone surprised and delighted that the enemy has not taken advantage of it. We are playing tennis and table-tennis.'

Colonel Andersen was suddenly taken ill and was evacuated to Germany on 15 May for an urgent gall-bladder operation. He was replaced by Major Helmuth Knupe (promoted to Lieutenant-Colonel), a very different type of man: dashing, daring, full of ideas yet no younger than Andersen – only fitter.

A captain in the Regiment called Schimpf was well known as a liar and a braggart. Most people loathed him, but he was somehow able to ingratiate himself with Andersen, who had earlier recommended an Iron Cross, subsequently awarded to Schimpf. Schimpf had gone on 'bomb-leave' the day before Andersen was evacuated, and on his return was not at all happy about a new CO, and one such as Knupe.

Colonel Knupe began to develop new ideas for an improved disposition of officers in his Regiment. He did not want Schimpf hanging about at HQ any longer and posted him to Merville – as far away as he possibly could. Wolter, on the other hand, could do with a bit of supervision, so he was transferred to Colleville.

On his return from leave Schimpf was taken to Merville by his Section Commander, Major Hof, to look round his new command before he took it over. Wolter was not there, so Buskotte met them. (See Plate 20.) Schimpf talked all the time about how he would blow everything out of the water if it attempted to land in *his* area.

Another lieutenant called Tubbesing was to become Battery Officer under Captain Schimpf, while Rudi Schaaf (whose place Tubbesing took) was promoted to take over a new and important appointment: commander of No 3 Battery, called 'Graf Waldersee'[14], self-propelled and with 150mm guns.

On the night of Saturday/Sunday, 19/20 May 1944, the Battery suffered its twentieth air raid[15]. The fact was of critical importance to Wolter, because it was the last air raid he experienced on the last night of his life.

He had arranged to spend the night with a delightful French girl known as Denise 'Bernard' (her real name is unknown[16]) and was prepared to flout all the regulations and to sleep with her in the officers' mess. After all, he was on the point of being transferred to Colleville.

Denise and her sister Jacqueline were fanatical members of the Résistance – unbeknown to the Germans – and had Wolter taken the trouble to have Denise investigated, it might well have emerged. But he was not interested in her background. The Bernard sisters were well known to most of the officers in the Regiment and along the coast, and they had free entrée to all the messes. As a result they were able to send back vital information to London, reports that were augmented by local tradesmen's discoveries during their 'authorised' visits to batteries, strongpoints and most of the headquarters establishments. They were not always accurate, not always correct. (On 20 April the howitzers had been taken out of the Merville Battery for 'war games'. They were always moved at night, during the curfew, so it was difficult for the French to observe them. Yet a report came back to London that they had 'gone'.)

On the evening of 19 May, Denise and Wolter had many drinks and retired to bed and at about 01.30 15 Lancasters and 51 Halifaxes of the Royal Canadian Air Force were over the Battery.

Buskotte, in his Command Bunker, was patiently noting the details of the raid, and reporting them to the OP. But Wolter was not there. Lieutenant Rix of the infantry took the messages and passed them on to Division. When it was apparent that the raid was over, Buskotte went outside to survey the damage, as was his custom. Once more the topography of the place had been altered by the appearance of new craters. When he approached the main gate he saw the guard commander coming towards him in a state of panic and distress. The officers' mess had been completely destroyed and Buskotte found himself staring at the rubble in disbelief.

Taking a party of men with him, Buskotte began calling and searching among the ruins for signs of life. But there was no answer. With the aid of one of Rittmann's mechanical diggers they began to move the stones and to recover bodies. Among the eighteen they found were those of Captain Wolter and Denise 'Bernard'.

In order to protect his Battery Commander's reputation, Buskotte stated in his report that 'the body of an unknown French woman' had been found some distance away from the school building, and he arranged for it to be laid out separately from the others.

Wolter's funeral took place on the following Monday. Lieutenant Tubbesing expressed his grief at 'the tragedy of Wolter's death' for the fun-loving captain was popular among his brother officers on account of his *joie de vivre* and carefree attitude to life.

Colonel Knupe's first action, on hearing the news of Wolter's death, was to consider whom to appoint in his place. Schimpf, true to form, had evaded his responsibilities by claiming additional 'bomb-leave' from Knupe without going via the Adjutant, and had already left for Halle. Knupe had no available captain, nor yet a lieutenant at the moment, only a second lieutenant called Steiner, an Austrian who was recuperating from a rough time on the Russian Front and fighting the partisans in Yugoslavia.

Raimund Steiner came from a respected Innsbruck family who had lived there, in the same house, for 500 years. His father was a town councillor and clung to independent, freedom-loving views. These were contrary to Nazi ideology when they annexed Austria in 1938, and the Steiner family was placed under close scrutiny. The father and two sons were harassed and the father died prematurely from his ill-treatment in a concentration camp.

Raimund Steiner was forced to enlist on his nineteenth birthday in April 1939. He opted first for the Pioneers and in the following October transferred to the mountain artillery. As an ordinary soldier in the 111 Mountain Artillery Regiment he was sent to northern Norway in 1940, at first enjoying the cheerful comradeship and strong discipline, criteria of crack troops the world over. Then the 111 Regiment crossed Finland and into the USSR on the first day of that campaign: 21/22 June 1941.

The division had orders to capture Murmansk, 125 miles north of the Arctic Circle on the Barents Sea and Russia's only ice-free port the whole year round. They failed in their task and suffered severe casualties, in the course of which Steiner was blinded. He had fought bravely and received an Iron Cross 2nd class. Although he thought he had lost his eyesight altogether, a doctor in the field hospital decided to perform a risky operation, which succeeded. It was a miracle, Steiner believed, and after nineteen months on the Eastern Front, he was sent to the Officers' School at Thorn (Torún in Poland, then within the Third Reich). To be an officer would endow Steiner with power to protect his family from persecution.

He was commissioned and rejoined his former regiment as a second lieutenant (see Pl. 2.) They were now engaged in 'fire brigade missions' on the outskirts of Stalingrad in 1942: being sent wherever their guns could do most damage to the Russians. The regiment was nearly wiped out and Steiner was posted to Mountain Artillery Regiment 112 in the Crimea. He had been wounded again several times and another, more serious, injury caused him to be evacuated to the reserve army at Solbad Hall in Austria, only 10 km from Innsbruck.

After recuperating and seeing a great deal of his mother, Steiner was sent to Udine, north of Trieste, where German troops were attempting – unsuccessfully – to prevent the Italian Marshal Badoglio from making peace with the Allies after Mussolini's death. Then Steiner found himself fighting the Jugoslav partisans in particularly bitter encounters and appallingly difficult terrain. Again wounded, he was sent to northern France and on Christmas Day 1943 was marched in to the Commanding General of 716 Division, wearing his mountain artillery breeches and uniform.

'Ha! A gentleman in baby's nappies, I see!' said the General sarcastically. 'Get yourself a correct officer's uniform immediately and report to the second battery at Colleville.'

Steiner marched straight out, feeling that he had made a bad start, and duly reported to No 2 Battery of the 716 Artillery Regiment at Colleville. The tactical headquarters were 'fully bunkered' beside a ring contour 61, but Steiner found the officers' mess in a house in the village. There he was received by a warrant officer called Jüngling, in the absence of the battery commander, Lieutenant Ebenfeld, out celebrating.

Steiner waited in the mess on the first floor of the building above the Battery Office. In the comfortable and well-appointed ante-room, with some fine stained-glass in the windows, stood a large sideboard. On its shelves – incredible for one used to the Russian Front – was a liberally stocked bar: Calvados, Cognac, wines and other luxuries.

He waited for nearly an hour, taking down notes from the orders on a notice-board, and the light was fading when suddenly the door opened, and in came an attractive ash-blonde young woman aged between twenty and twenty-five. She was well dressed in a fur coat (rather differently from wartime clothing in Germany and Austria) and at once said to him in almost perfect German: 'Ah, you must be Lieutenant Steiner, the new battery officer. You are coming to K5 on the beach.'

Steiner was flabbergasted. He had no idea what she meant by 'K5' and was greatly astonished that this Frenchwoman knew not only his name, but that she seemed so knowledgeable about military strongpoints.

'I am Jacqueline Bernard,' she told him, and offered to take him straight away to his future position in 'K5' bunker on the beach, not considering that it was 'Siegfried' (Lieutenant Ebenfeld) to whom he had first to report. Siegfried, she said, with a laugh, was out with his female friend in Riva Bella, and would probably come back quite drunk in the early morning.

Mlle 'Bernard' then gave Steiner a report on the positions: a description of the military posts in the area; accounts of officers and NCOs in each strongpoint and the daily goings-on in the region. It was incomprehensible and most uncomfortable for the security-conscious Steiner to encounter this young woman so soon after his arrival. She seemed to him to pose a very real threat.

Later on, Lieutenant Ebenfeld arrived with his French friend, both intoxicated. Steiner reported himself correctly but Ebenfeld dismissed him abruptly, saying in a slurred voice: 'That can wait until morning. Where's supper?'

Ebenfeld's friend was between thirty and forty and presented a wretched appearance. Her thick makeup was smeared and a false eyelash had stuck to one cheek. Their behaviour seemed commonplace to Jacqueline who began to prepare a meal for them all. Then they sat down together. The three others chatted about various officers and soldiers, as a result of which Steiner learned that Jacqueline's sister Denise was a close friend of Captain Wolter, commander of the Merville Battery on the other side of the Orne.

Steiner could scarcely believe that all this was happening to him on his first evening in Colleville, and it was obvious to him how deeply the French Résistance or the Allies – or both – had penetrated these German military positions. He was glad when the meal was over and he could retire.

A couple of days afterwards, Steiner expressed his fears to Ebenfeld, but nothing was done to stop the free-and-easy comings and goings of several Frenchwomen. Ebenfeld did not appreciate Steiner's interference in what he considered to be his own business, and the other officers soon regarded the Austrian second lieutenant as priggish, especially as he had no liaisons with local women and drank sparingly.

Colonel Knupe had noticed this, and that Steiner preferred to spend his time with either the warrant officers or the Italian labourers working for the Enterprises Rittmann. Not a good idea. Steiner would be far better off elsewhere, and Merville seemed an ideal place. Knupe gave the necessary orders and then warned Buskotte whom he had got to know.

Everybody knew Buskotte. He was one of those warrant

officers who, in a strange way, earned universal respect and affection by his fairness and his own scrupulous behaviour. Young Steiner would be better off under Buskotte's wing.

After dark on 20 May, Steiner gathered his kit together and gratefully left Colleville for Merville. In the vehicle lent him for the purpose, he crossed the well-guarded bridge at Bénouville and then crossed the smaller one over the River Orne. This pair of bridges was the only way across this double water-obstacle until one reached Caen. Steiner turned left, past the hamlet of Ecarde and through the narrow streets of Sallenelles. As he approached the outskirts of Franceville he was flagged down by alert sentries, but was allowed to proceed. 'Up the hill to your right, and right again at the top by the water-tower', was the direction.

Buskotte was waiting for him, with a small guard turned out politely to welcome their new battery commander. Steiner was then shown his accommodation inside No 1 Casemate on the right. This was his daytime office and his occasional night-time lodging, should he be up at the position and not at the OP – for instance, if he got caught there in an air raid.

After stand-to at dawn, and breakfast which followed, Buskotte put him 'in the picture'. He did not need to tell Steiner much about the Regiment, for he had been in it for five months, although he described some of the men in the Battery and took Steiner round to meet them. Because the commander at Merville had been a captain since the Regiment was raised, the soldiers were somewhat surprised to find a second lieutenant now in command of them. Either he must be an exceptional officer, soon to be promoted, or else the Wehrmacht was in a sorry state.

Buskotte explained about the buried cable from the Battery to the OP, and the similarly placed ones (all 1.2m deep in the ground) from the Command Bunker to each casemate. As they went together down to the OP on the beach at Franceville, Buskotte told Steiner about their close relationship with many of the officers and men in the 736 Regiment of Infantry now all dependent upon one another: the infantry could be called upon to protect the Battery from land attack; the infantry could call on the Battery for artillery support.

Steiner was enchanted with the beach outside his bunker and the waves which came close to it at high tide. He was able to see past Cabourg and towards Le Havre to the east; and Ouistreham very clearly to the west, with the close-packed houses of Riva Bella beyond. The OP was, at water-level, not well situated to observe fire on the Orne Canal. Buskotte said that when the howitzers had ranged, observation by Timpf had been from the water tower beside the Battery, and that offered an excellent view all round. It would not be a safe place with an enemy about, for all towers, chimneys and church steeples were far too obvious observation posts and drew an immediate 'stonk'.

Buskotte took Steiner along to the next bunker where he met Lieutenant Rix and discovered that he knew Rix's wife who, like himself, was an inhabitant of Innsbruck.

It seemed to Steiner that much hard work was necessary to put the Battery in good order, especially after the damage caused by the last raid. Many of the mines had been exploded by bombs falling on or near them, and new ones had to be sown. Buskotte explained that there was always much to be done after every raid, and that they had increased of late. He was beginning to realise that in spite of his low rank, Steiner was far from inexperienced and that the two of them were going to be able to work well together.

On 23 May, General Erich Marcks, commanding 84 Corps, arrived unannounced at the Battery, the first of a succession of high-ranking officers of all three arms who would from now on be inspecting this interesting unit. Marcks was from the general staff and had a high reputation as a strategist. He had lost a leg in Russia and walked with a wooden one. He was ascetic, with a thin face, strong, earnest and absolutely correct in his manner. He wore spectacles in plain, metal frames. General Marcks made a thorough inspection of the Battery, adding frequent remarks about its features, then began to climb up the bank of earth beside No 1 Casemate, roughly resisting Steiner's offer of help. Buskotte stood by observing. With the greatest difficulty, and unaided, the general eventually reached the top of the casemate and looked all round. (See Plate 24.) From there he was able to see and to comment on the disposition of defensive weapons; he also observed the craters carefully, especially those made by larger bombs, and close to No 1 Casemate.

When Steiner ventured to ask him how long the Battery was to be armed with the 'temporary' howitzers, General Marcks replied shortly, but not unkindly: 'That is a strategic matter and you will be informed about it in due course.'

The plan had initially been for long-barrelled guns with a flat trajectory like ships' artillery, and with far greater range than the howitzers possessed. Not only were the ports facing north-west in each casemate restrictive in their lateral arc, but impossibly small for a military field-gun's need to fire with its barrel at a high angle. (Buskotte had explained that the first state of the howitzers, in the open, was really ideal for the artilleryman. Installed, as they were now, it was impossible to fire to the rear and very restrictive.)

Because he had been so well briefed by Buskotte, Steiner was able to answer General Marcks's precise questions about the trajectory and efficiency of each howitzer, and also about the small arms. Above all, Marcks wanted to know how effective fire would be on the Orne estuary. His manner was harsh, and he left the position without a formal goodbye.

Two days later there was another senior visitor. At 14.00 hrs a Horch staff-car drew up and two men got out. Fortunately Steiner was there, although completely unprepared to receive anybody. The general officer coming towards him was the very opposite of Marcks: considerate in bearing, not lean and hungry in appearance but rather portly, cheeful and with a pipe in his mouth. He stretched out his hand in welcoming fashion to Steiner, who was doubling to meet him, doing up the top button of his jacket and smoothing his other hand down the front of his uniform to make sure that he was properly dressed.

Steiner was aware that the portly one was a general and that the other one was probably his adjutant. Only when the tall, thin and upright one addressed his senior as 'General Oberst' did Steiner realise that he must be Colonel-General Friedrich Dollmann, commanding 7th Army, and known to be extremely 'upset by Hitler's methods'.

Steiner made his report in a breathless and hesitating manner, caught completely unawares by Dollmann's arrival. He explained that the Battery was suffering from many losses of equipment as a result of frequent aerial bombardments, and that some of this equipment was, in any case, rather poor stuff. The general interrupted him with 'Good! Very good, young man!' His adjutant was a typically correct and unforthcoming staff officer, though he showed Steiner some signs of goodwill.

The many deep bomb craters made a strong impression on the colonel-general, and while he was investigating them, his adjutant asked Steiner a number of questions, taking notes of his answers. Steiner drew attention to his weak armament but the complaint was brushed aside when Dollmann, turning round to listen, assured him that the Invasion would not take place in this area – he could be certain of that. Steiner got the impression that Dollmann was interested only in the destructive effect of the numerous air raids.

Although every German had seen pictures of Allied concentrated bombardments, nothing could describe their effect upon those who had not suffered them. On about 25 May there was another raid on the Battery, this time of a different kind. The remarkable aspect of it was in the size of bomb delivered, that shattered the nerves and blocked the ears of the soldiers as none before had done. It was difficult to stop trembling hours after the raid.

Buskotte was first out of the bunker after it was over, as usual, and was horrified to see where a giant-sized bomb had entered the ground some 5–10m outside the entrance of No 3 Casemate and had left a large, cylindrical shaft obliquely in the ground, pointing downwards and in the direction of the casemate's foundations. It was what the Germans call a *Blind-*

*gänger:* it had not exploded. Buskotte ordered the evacuation of No 3 Casemate and reported the event to Steiner. He, in turn, reported the matter to Division and asked for a pioneer troop to come and defuse it.[17]

Instead, the most senior pioneer general in the Wehrmacht arrived in person very soon afterwards, and made his inspection. The general seemed surprised at the angle of entry to the ground, and from the size of the hole it had made, the evident size of the bomb. The 50° angle of strike and penetration into the soft earth seemed to indicate that it could have been delivered only by a fighter-bomber; had it come from a high-flying Lancaster or Halifax, it would have struck the ground at 90°. Steiner and Buskotte emphasised to the general that the bomb was almost certainly lodged *below* the underground chamber, about 10m deep, but the general seemed far more interested – as General Dollmann had been – in seeing the general effects from previous bombardments. He also remarked on the ability of the casemates and other concrete buildings to withstand them. All the same, he saw clearly that between the 2.2m thickness of the outside walls to No 1 Casemate, and the 0.5m of No 4, necessity had yielded to false economy.

During the night of 26/27 May it had been raining hard and the whole Battery position was muddy and slippery. Buskotte was in charge when several large motor cars drew up round about midday. A black Horch was leading them and out of it stepped a familiar figure: Field Marshal Rommel. Buskotte quickly instructed an NCO to telephone Steiner at the OP, and ran to meet the Field Marshal. Buskotte was performing the duties of a lieutenant, as Battery Officer; Steiner that of a captain as Battery Commander. There was no other officer there.

The large party threaded their way through puddles, taking some time to reach the centre of the Battery position, and when Steiner arrived, out of breath, he saw an unforgettable and imposing picture: the large group of senior officers standing rather pompously round Rommel. The Wehrmacht generals had red stripes down their trousers and so had the staff officers; the Luftwaffe wore trousers with white stripes; the Naval staff officers, mostly admirals, were in dark uniforms with bright blue stripes. Second Lieutenant Steiner felt himself small and unimportant as he stood beside this group of High Command, a mere observer, uninvited to the party.

Suddenly there was a cry of alarm and two Spitfires flew very low over the Battery, cannons and machine-guns blazing. Unhesitatingly the officers fell flat among the sticky mud on the ground. Then the Spitfires came back, firing as before. Nobody was hit, but when the generals and admirals rose to their feet, plastered all over with slimy ooze, they were mortified to see Rommel still standing there 'like a steel tower', perfectly clean and as though nothing had happened.[18] The 'imposing picture' had been turned into a grotesque one. And 'Erika' had not spoken.

Rommel went on talking, ignoring the condition of his audience and the interruption. 'The Invasion, when it comes,' he said, 'will last only a short time.' This was understood to mean that the Allies would quickly be thrown back into the sea; but for some reason Steiner thought otherwise. It seemed to him that Rommel was suggesting the very opposite: that the Wehrmacht was going to be overwhelmed almost at once.

There was another RAF raid that night by 55 Lancasters. Immediately afterwards, Buskotte and a couple of medical orderlies went round to assess the damage and losses. After almost every raid soldiers were suffocated in their collapsed trenches or weapon-pits by tons of earth and stones showered over them as the ground-plan of the Battery took on yet another formation. Sometimes the upheaval had been so great that old positions were no longer distinguishable and the bodies – if they were still in one piece – were never found. It was a miserable and unpleasant task, looking for the remains of eighteen- or nineteen-year-olds who had recently joined the Battery only to have their young lives so suddenly extinguished in a moment with a flash and a rumble that shook the earth as it shook them out of it.

The frequent losses and destruction of weapons was another, though less emotional, consideration for Buskotte. Now three of their four machine-guns had been wrecked and the local defence of the Battery was reduced. There were no mortars, there had never been a searchlight, and that 20mm AA gun was still misbehaving. Admittedly, every soldier carried a rifle and the NCOs had Schmeisser machine-pistols, but this was inadequate firepower in the event of a land attack. They were going to have to rely more upon assistance from 736.

On 2 June, Buskotte reported something unusual and possibly ominous. La Grande Ferme du Buisson (which had recently been bombed) lay to the south-west of the Battery, about half-way across the fields towards Le Plein. Many of the soldiers had seen pigeons circling round the farm, and some flying over the Battery wearing rings and capsules on their legs. So they were not wild birds and the capsules had a sinister implication. Buskotte and Steiner went to look.

As they approached the farm it seemed ominously quiet. They knew that it was normally a busy establishment but now it was unoccupied: no sign of animal life, not a dog nor cat. They looked in at the windows and investigated the empty outhouses. Not a soul. The only living creatures there were the pigeons, soaring and swooping overhead, in and out of the eaves or perching on the roof.

They shot a pigeon or two and returned to the Battery, greatly puzzled but with the order to the troops to shoot all pigeons on sight. The soldiers enjoyed searching houses for shot-guns and confiscating them.

Buskotte and Steiner shared their pigeons with a padre who had come to visit the Battery and who said Mass on the following morning inside No 1 Casemate. Although attendance was purely voluntary, every soldier not on duty took part in the service. They seemed to have the feeling that difficult times were ahead.

Another bombardment shocked them that evening. It was prefaced by a great number of flares over the Battery which at least gave the defenders time to get into the casemates and underground chambers. Yet even so there was more loss of life, more destruction of their work.

On Sunday 4 June everybody turned out to clear up again. Steiner decided to make an entirely new allocation of tasks and a reorganisation of the defence layout: Sergeant So-and-So here; Corporal So-and-So there; disposition of weapons there – and there. One machine-gun was sited in the 'Tobruk Stand' of No 1 Casemate. Another, which had been repaired, was given a roving commission so as to create the impression that there was more than one on the ground.

Later that day a platoon from the 'Death Battalion' of pioneers arrived, about twenty of them including one communist – so Buskotte was told by the single NCO in charge of them. These pioneer units were embodied from among deserters, criminals, political delinquents as well as Polish, Russian or Jugoslav prisoners of war. They had the dirtiest jobs of all, including unearthing and defusing unexploded bombs and mines. Some of them had been tortured and most had had the stuffing knocked out of them so that they required the minimum of supervision and escort. This pioneer unit was made up of men who breathed, but who were 'dead' already. Their lives did not matter a pfennig, and if they blew themselves up in the course of their work, they had at least made themselves useful in sparing the life of a good soldier.

This pioneer platoon got to work as soon as they arrived, though they looked as if they had marched from some distance away. They were told to dig down as far as they could in the general direction of the bomb's shaft, but as they had not got very far by nightfall, Buskotte told them that they might sleep in the casemates, wherever they could find room, but without getting in the way of his gunners or disturbing them.

On the following morning, 5 June, clearing up continued and Steiner's ambition was to have the whole Battery ready for action again by evening. Much of the perimeter wire and that forming the inner defences was repaired, new mines were sown, and the pioneers went on digging.

## Building the Battery

Steiner had discussed the defences of the Battery with some of 736, and had spoken to Lieutenant Bleckmann. His task was the placing of obstacles of all kind, on beaches and in fields, as part of Rommel's anti-Invasion plan. Bleckmann told Steiner that he had lately noticed a curious change in the habits of the French inhabitants of Franceville.[19] Every evening, as it was getting dark, they all moved out of their houses and went inland, either on bicycles, with the minimum of possessions, or on foot. Then each morning they returned. They seemed to have little concern for their houses or possessions, but in any case there was no looting.[20]

Bleckmann was acting strongpoint commander at the big blockhouse opposite Ouistreham, and that evening, as he was cycling back there, he was stopped in Franceville by a young Frenchwoman.[21] She told him that she had a long way to go inland in order to leave the coastal strip by dark, but had no bicycle. Could he lend her his? Bleckmann felt sorry for her and handed over his bike, requesting her to leave it outside her house for him to collect in the morning. She expressed gratitude and promised to do as he had asked. Bleckmann watched her riding away. It was beginning to drizzle with rain and he had more than a mile to walk.

It was raining much harder when Steiner, exhausted by his day's work, cycled downhill through Merville village and over the main road at Franceville a couple of hours later. The sea was more choppy than usual and there was a stiff breeze blowing. The moon showed herself only occasionally through thick and thundry clouds. Not the kind of weather for an invasion.

Steiner climbed wearily into his pyjamas and got into bed at the OP. He fell asleep almost at once. It seemed to him only a few moments later when the telephone bell jangled in his ear.

Buskotte's voice, considerably more agitated than his usual, measured tone, sounded loudly and imperatively: '*Herr Leutnant!* A glider has landed in our Battery and we are in close combat!'

The time was 00.26 hrs on 6 June 1944.

# 5
# Mars

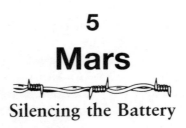

## Silencing the Battery

The first aircraft to fly across the English Channel in the last hour of 5 June 1944 carried Air Vice-Marshal Hollinghurst, and began the air invasion of Normany under the RAF code-name 'Tonga', a part of the major, comprehensive Operation OVERLORD which included the largest invasion force ever assembled.[1] The Air Vice-Marshal's aircraft, an Albermarle of 38 Group, carried officers and men of 22 Independent Parachute Company, the Pathfinders. Their task was to set up illuminations, smoke candles and wireless beacons on the DZs to guide in the main force of parachutists.

9th Battalion The Parachute Regiment was to be dropped by 512 Squadron on DZ 'V' which had been selected from air observation and photographs. From that height it seemed perfectly suitable and was at a convenient distance from the Merville Battery. During briefing the crews of 512 had been told that the country surrounding DZ 'V' had been heavily mined, so it was essential, for the safety of the parachutists, that they were not allowed to overshoot it.[2] Any mines found on the DZ were to be cleared by the Pathfinders.

Shortly before the 9th Battalion were due to arrive over the DZ, the Merville Battery was to be bombed by 100 Lancasters of Bomber Command with 4000–lb bombs.[3]

The enthusiasm in 512 Squadron is well shown by their Operation Officer's record in the hours preceding the operation. Flight Lieutenant Anthony Gough wrote[4]:

D–6 hours. [Day of operations less six hours, i.e. 18.00 on 5 June.]

## Silencing the Battery

Today is the most momentous and exciting in the entire history of 512 Squadron. . . . at 17.00 hrs. Captains and W/Operators were called to the squadron briefing room where the CO informed them that marshalling of aircraft was to take place immediately. Navigators received their final Met briefing and flight plans at 21.00 hrs. and at the same time the troops were emplaned in good time and the squadron, led by W/Cdr Coventry AFC, commenced to take off at 23.15 hrs. . . . 32 aircraft in all, who formed up in vics of 3 aircraft, each vic flying at 30 seconds intervals.

Wing Commander Basil A. ('Champ') Coventry was in aircraft KG392, with the letter V on its nose, carrying part of 9th Battalion's headquarters including the CO, Lieutenant-Colonel Otway. (See Plate 6.) Each Dakota carried a crew of four: Captain, second pilot, navigator and the wireless-operator; the last doubled as dispatcher and nearer the time of the drop he took up his position at the rear of the aircraft opposite the door-opening on the port side. The Dakota had a main door which was, in fact, a double door split in the middle vertically, and opening outwards. The forward half of the door had within it a separate door that could easily be removed, leaving the remainder in position. This inner door-space was the exit for parachutists and it remained open in flight, the door having been left behind on the airfield. The edges of the open door-space were covered all round with tape to prevent the parachutists fouling themselves on any protruberances as they made their exits. The smell of this tape and the dope painted over it was a characteristic of jumping from the Dakota.

The dispatcher stood aft of the open door, facing the 'stick' of parachutists as they ran down the aircraft towards him, and then out. He was attached to the strong-point by a monkey-belt to avoid his becoming swept out with the soldiers.

The dispatcher (or 'jump-master' as the Americans call him) was in contact by intercom with the flight deck at all stages of the run-up to the DZ so as to keep his 'stick' informed as to how long there was to go. At this stage of the flight, each aircraft was independently operated, for there was no radio

## Le général Eisenhower s'adresse aux peuples des Pays Occupés

### PEUPLES DE L'EUROPE OCCIDENTALE :

Les troupes des Forces Expéditionnaires Alliées ont débarqué sur les côtes de France.

Ce débarquement fait partie du plan concerté par les Nations Unies, conjointement avec nos grands alliés Russes, pour la libération de l'Europe.

C'est à vous tous que j'adresse ce message. Même si le premier assaut n'a pas eu lieu sur votre territoire, l'heure de votre libération approche.

Tous les patriotes, hommes ou femmes, jeunes ou vieux, ont un rôle à jouer dans notre marche vers la victoire finale. Aux members des mouvements de Résistance dirigés de l'intérieur ou de l'extérieur, je dis : 'Suivez les instructions que vous avez reçues !' Aux patriotes qui ne sont point membres de groupes de Résistance organisés, je dis : 'Continuez votre résistance auxiliaire, mais n'exposez pas vos vies inutilement ; attendez l'heure où je vous donnerai le signal de vous dresser et de frapper l'ennemi. Le jour viendra où j'aurai besoin de votre force unie.' Jusqu'à ce jour, je compte sur vous pour vous plier à la dure obligation d'une discipline impassible.

### CITOYENS FRANÇAIS :

Je suis fier de commander une fois de plus les vaillants soldats de France. Luttant côté à côté avec leurs Alliées, ils s'apprêtent à prendre leur pleine part dans la libération de leur Patrie natale.

Parce que le premier débarquement a eu lieu sur votre territoire, je répète pour vous, avec une insistance encore plus grande, mon message aux peuples des autres pays occupés de l'Europe Occidentale. Suivez les instructions de vois chefs. Un soulèvement prémature de tous les Français risque de vous empêcher, quand l'heure décisive aura sonné, de mieux servir encore votre pays. Ne vous énervez pas, et restez en alerte !

Comme Commandant Suprême des Forces Expéditionnaires Alliées, j'ai le devoir et la responsabilité de prendre toutes les mesures nécessaires à la conduite de la guerre. Je sais que je puis compter sur vous pour obéir aux ordres que je serai appelé a promulguer.

L'administration civile de la France doit effectivment être assurée par des Français. Chacun doit demeurer à son poste, à moins qu'il ne reçoive des instructions contraires. Ceux qui ont fait cause commune avec l'ennémi, et qui ont ainsi trahi leur patrie, seront révoqués. Quand la France sera libérée de ses oppresseurs, vous choisirez vous-mêmes vos représentants ainsi que le Gouvernement sous l'autorité duquel vous voudrez vivre.

Au cours de cette campagne qui a pour but l'écrasement définitif de l'ennemi, peut-être aurez-vous à subir encore des pertes et des destructions. Mais, si tragiques que soient ces épreuves, elles font partie du prix qu'exige la victoire. Je vous garantis que je ferai tout en mon pouvoir pour atténuer vos épreuves. Je sais que je puis compter sur votre fermeté, qui n'est pas moins grande aujourd'hui que par le passé.

Les héroïques exploits des Français qui ont continué la lutte contre les Nazis et contre leurs satellites de Vichy, en France, en Italie et dans l'Empire français, ont été pour nous tous un modèle et une inspiration.

Ce débarquement ne fait que commencer la campagne d'Europe Occidentale. Nous sommes à la veille de grandes batailles. Je demande à tous les hommes qui aiment la libérté d'être des nôtres. Que rien n'ébranle votre foi – rien non plus n'arrêtera nos coups – ENSEMBLE, NOUS VAINCRONS.

DWIGHT D. EISENHOWER
Commandant Suprême des
Forces Expéditionnaires Alliées

Fig. 3  General Eisenhower's message – especially – to the French immediately after the Invasion had begun, and also distributed in leaflet raids to other Occupied countries in their own languages

contact with the ground or between aircraft.

The so-called 'vics' of three aircraft flew with their leader slightly ahead of and between the two others which were about level with one another. ('Vic' was the phonetic alphabet's way of speaking the letter 'V' for all services during the war, so there was a 'V' on the nose of the leading aircraft in 512 Squadron; 'V' for the shape of each flight of three; 'V' for the DZ – and 'V' for Victory!)

Each 'vic' flew at an interval of 30 seconds from those in front of and behind them, as noted by Flight Lieutenant Gough, and they had low-intensity blue formation lights which could be seen only by the other two aircraft in each 'vic'. All lights were extinguished before approaching enemy territory.

Each aircraft in the squadron was independently navigated so that if any failed to keep visual contact with the other two in his 'vic', as a consequence of their breaking formation for any reason, navigation was unaffected.

The route taken on the night of 5/6 June 1944 was from Broadwell Airfield to Enstone to Fairoaks to Worthing. At Worthing there was a directional beacon. Then over the Channel and across to Cap d'Antifer, north-east of Le Havre, westwards parallel to the coast, and inland through a 'flak gap' known to exist near Cabourg. Then to the DZ.

As they crossed the coast, each aircraft dropped a small cluster of 20-lb bombs, partly to keep the enemy's heads down, partly to conceal the fact that they were troop-carriers and not really bombers. These bombs were carried underneath the fuselage and their release produced a metallic noise inside the aircraft.

Some of this – but far from all – was known to us inside the Dakota on our way to battle. The aircraft's seats, along both sides, were far too narrow to sit on, encumbered as we were with parachute packs on our backs. Most of the soldiers were sitting on the floor with their 'chutes resting on the rim of the seat behind. From experience this was the most comfortable way to travel.

We had no more than a passing word to our RAF crew after emplaning, then they had shut themselves away and the skipper had refused my request to go forward with him. So I sprawled on the floor with my soldiers.

We didn't talk much. Each man withdrew into himself, feeling that he was now at the top of a slide that had only one way out: through that open doorway of the Dakota, smelling strongly of dope and covered by endless bands of tape.

We were part of a great air armada that wound its way in spirals until we were all assembled. Then the engines seemed to take on a different tone and we ceased to turn. We were heading in one direction, presumably due south.

Nobody had moved about very much. There were three containers for circulation among us: a box of sandwiches, bread and jam only; a bucket in which to pee; and the sick-bucket. As it was almost impossible to get one's hand inside one's trousers with the parachute harness clasped tightly between the legs, the first bucket was not in use. But Private Dunk seemed to need the sick-bucket before very long in the air. After he had made frantic signals for it, the bucket was passed down the line only to arrive too late. I looked away.

Each aircraft, which was its own island, contained miniature islands of soldiers, each thinking, wondering, tight inside and fearful of the outcome. Yet once each man was out of that door, the thread of uncertainty would snap as easily as the ties on his parachute pack. The 'chute would develop, the man would develop too and be ready to fight with his feet on the ground. That is where our training led us. But inside the aircraft we were all too introspective, thinking, wondering.

It was impossible from my position on the floor to see outside, or to judge where we were in the stream. We seemed already to have been in the air for hours. Actually it was little more than an hour. The RAF dispatcher had left his wireless set and had taken up his position beside the open door, crouching there like a monkey. He called out: 'We're over the Channel, look!' A gap in the clouds had revealed the white caps of waves far below, reported by those who had the energy to look for themselves. I was too far back, in the middle of the stick. Normally there would have been comedians who asked whether Wigan Pier was in sight, or something of that order, but not tonight.

Remembering my arrangement with the pilot, that he would give us the red light one minute before the green, I had promised him that we would all stand up on the red signal. It came sooner than expected.

'Get up! Get up!' I heard myself shout, as though from a distance. The stick needed no second bidding. We had all had enough of this flight. I called out: 'Mind your arm in the strop!'

Then, when there was no movement I repeated:

'Wake up! Mind your arm in the strop!' I was entirely oblivious of the fact that my own strop was *under* my left arm, extending from the pack that contained the parachute to a snap-hook on the wire 'strongpoint'. The man behind should have corrected me, I think it was my batman, Morgan, but he was probably too immersed in his thoughts to think of me, and I don't blame him.

Then to break the monotony of this intolerably long flight there was a sudden banging under the aircraft as though it was being hit with saucepans.

'What's that?' called one of the soldiers.

'Flak, of course,' I replied, as though I had been flying through it all my life, when it was the first time for me as well. It was not flak at all, but the 20-lb bombs being sent down on the beach below us.[5]

'Will it hit us, sir?' he asked. The question went unanswered. At that moment the pilot made a turn, and although the stick was temporarily unbalanced, nobody fell over.

As we came through the 'flak gap', the aircraft crews were able to see both river estuaries, the Orne to starboard and the Dives to port. There was a little flak, but none close enough to cause interference or to require any form of evasive action.[6]

We now had 75 seconds flying time before reaching the north end of the DZ and this was where the delicate navigational aids came in.[7] Each aircraft possessed two. One, called GEE, was installed inside the aircraft and had the big advantage of being only a radio receiver, hence it could not give away the aircraft's position. Other aids worked on radar principles, emitting radio pulses that could be detected by enemy radars or night fighters.

GEE in the aircraft was relatively small and lightweight and it operated on frequencies which required short aerials. It was a hyperbolic system with chains of transmitters located in various parts of the country covering approaches to Occupied Europe. Each of the chains had a master station and two or three slaves. Display in the aircraft was on a cathode-ray tube with a horizontal time base. The master station transmitted a short pulse of energy which showed on the receiver as a blip on the time base. When the transmitted pulse was received at each slave station, it instantly transmitted an answering pulse and these were also displayed as blips on the time base in the aircraft. By lining markers, the operator could measure the time in micro-seconds between the reception of these three pulses, and by using a specially overprinted chart showing curved lines of equal time difference, an accurate position could be plotted. The system was subject to jamming by the enemy, which could render it useless, although a skilled operator might sometimes get a little information from it, especially when equipped with an anti-jamming device.

On the night in question, one of the slave stations of the chain covering the approaches to Normandy had developed a fault, with the result that it was of little use in giving accurate fixes.

Many of the other types of aircraft operating that night were equipped with H2S, radar sets for ground mapping, by means of which navigators could easily see the coastline and measure their distance from it, and by map reading were able to determine exactly where they were. They also had a bomb-aimer's position giving downward vision that enabled the navigator to see directly below the aircraft as well as ahead, which was a considerable help when trying to find a small field on a dark night. The Dakota had none of this: the only views were to the sides and forward over the nose. Once over the DZ, it was invisible to the crew, and there was no accurate way for the navigator to inform the pilot, or of the pilot being able to see whether they were drifting or on line.

There was another aid, though, which should have made all the difference in the case of the Dakota. This was 'Rebecca', a transmitter/receiver operated on the principle of transmitting a short pulse which triggered a response from a beacon on the ground called 'Eureka'. The aircraft's receiver measured the time difference – the distance between the aircraft and the ground beacon. Two aerials, facing forward, one on each side of the aircraft's nose, presented the operator with an indication of the direction of the beacon: left, right or dead ahead. These 'Eureka' beacons were to be set up by the Pathfinders of

22 Independent Parachute Company on the DZ. The Pathfinders were also to set up DZ markers and 'wind tees' (or smoke candles) to show the speed and direction of the wind, essential information for knowing just where to start the drop. Troops dropped immediately over the DZ would very easily drift outside it in a strong wind, and the higher the altitude from which they were dropped, the further they would be carried away from the right place.

When approaching the DZ, our pilot throttled back and, at the same time, put the petrol-air mixture into 'Fully Rich' and the angle of attack of the airscrews into 'Fully Fine' as he began to make his descent, tail up, to cross the entry point of the DZ at 900 ft for the drop. On his approach, to establish or to maintain the correct direction, he might use the rudder to 'yaw', that is, to make a flat turn. We parachutists were completely unaware of all these niceties, though we recognised changes in engine-sound, in direction and speed, and knew that something different was going on.

Number 1 was standing in the open doorway, hands gripping it on either side, left foot forward, chin up and looking his own height in the textbook attitude. If he allowed his eyes to look down, he must have had a wonderful view. The dispatcher was staring, mesmerised, at the darkened bulb of the green light. Then it glowed and I could see its reflection on the inside of the fuselage – *Green*.

The dispatcher danced about gesticulating, emphasising my previous conviction of his simian attributes; No 1 had gone, No 2 followed.

'Go! Go! Go!' the dispatcher shouted. And I shouted with him. And then we were all shouting and all moving down the aircraft, faster and faster.

Suddenly there was nobody between me and the door. I caught a glimpse of the dispatcher's grinning face (he'd soon be breakfasting on bacon and eggs)[8] and then the slipstream hit my face. The static line tightened and for a moment the whole weight of my falling body was taken by my left arm. It was flung up across my face, a painful wrench. 'Hell!' I

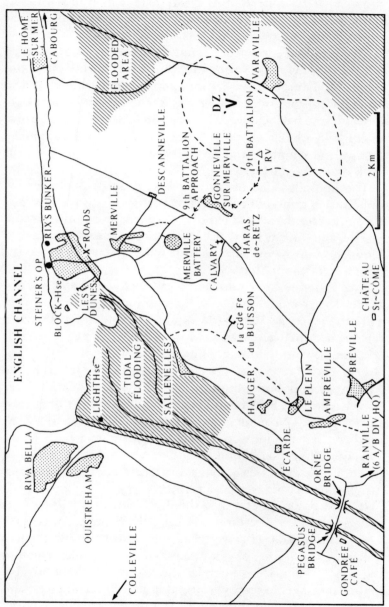

Fig. 4 Northern part of 6 Airborne Division's battle area, 6 June – 16 August 1944

thought, 'I've done it now.' The arm was almost useless though I had to get it up again and secure an even hold on the lift-webs for direction and especially for landing.

One hundred entrechats[9]. That is what I had decided to do while dropping into Normandy. (But I was wasting precious time.) My fiancée was a dancer and I was determined to beat Nijinsky's record of eight – or was it ten? Certainly more than anybody else had achieved. That would show her the calibre of us chaps in 9th Battalion The Parachute Regiment. As I looked below, and counted, and my feet worked away, I could see nothing in the darkness.

The luminous dial of my watch said 00.55 and after the obliterating grind of those aircraft engines it was wonderfully quiet: quieter than I had expected. Twice the moon appeared briefly, and there was a wind. Did I detect some muck and dust blowing about? Not sure. If so it must be coming from the bombing of the Battery.

Two canopies came into view a little below me, so I was not alone. The ground didn't seem far away now. (96, 97 . . . 100, 101, 102 for luck.) Watch it! Coming in right. Pull down more on the left lift-web. Can't. Must. Left weak. Try! Here it co-o-omes. Good landing. Hurrah! This is France!

I smacked the box on my chest to release the straps of the 'chute from my body, bundled up the nylon and left it there (never done that before) and began pulling up tufts of grass – French grass – *Norman* grass! We're here! We are here! Well, I'm here, but I'm blowed if I know exactly where.

Major Parry was standing a little away from the main RV position, in fact he was halfway up a tree, shining his lamp and lustily blowing his Ducks, bakelite.

It guided me in towards the RV and as I followed its aggressive call, I met Jimmy Loring, the Signals Officer. He was carrying a large canvas bag which held the Battalion's T-Panel Code – a set of silk panels, red on one side, white on the other. They were intended for use in daylight to give limited messages to our own aircraft above, by arranging them in certain shapes on the ground. To my amazement, Jimmy suddenly flung the bag down a large bomb crater, and walked on.

'Hey, we'll need that tomorrow – I mean today,' I said and tumbled down to retrieve the bag. Staggering back to the level, I caught up with Jimmy and gave him back the bag, but again he threw it away. Again I saved it. This was becoming tiresome, and me with my game arm. There was no point in my continuing when he cast it aside for the third time, so I gave up and went my own way, leaving him muttering and cursing to himself. I never discovered why he had behaved in that way.

When I reached the RV beside a clump of trees, I saw Lieutenant-Colonel Otway standing there, tense and white. I saluted and reported myself to him. He replied in an expressionless tone: 'You're commanding 'C' Company.'

I stood in astonishment. I, the most junior subaltern of the Company in command? Impossible! Where was Ian Dyer, where was 'Robbie' our second-in-command? Where indeed were 'Jock' and 'Dizzie', the two other platoon commanders? Why, it's ridiculous.

'Well, don't *stand* there, go and take over your Company.'

I went.

And there they were in a ditch, all eight of them. CSM 'Barney' Ross had arrived in advance with Major Parry and a couple of men from each company. Private Love was in tears.

'Oh, sir,' he wailed, 'I've lost my rifle and my helmet. What am I going to do?' To lose a rifle, especially at such a critical stage in the proceedings, was a court-martial offence, according to Colonel Otway's stern warning.

'Never mind, Love,' I told him – faintly amused – 'we'll find you another rifle, probably a German one. And keep your head down in the attack!'

Sergeant Bedford, the dependable one, was there, the only NCO from my platoon. My other stalwarts were Sid Capon, Frank Delsignore, 'Johnny' Walker, Les Cartwright, luckless Love and Tom Stroud. I reported to the Colonel every fifteen minutes as other men came in, but they arrived only by ones and twos. What on earth was happening?

On my second or third quarterly-hour visit to Battalion HQ, I realised that something unexpected was happening. Three French civilians had been discovered, loitering in the vicinity of our RV. They said they were on their way to Varaville because of the bombing. Because they were refugees, they had to travel by night to avoid the Germans. But this was not good enough for the Colonel.

'Take them away and shoot them!' he told the Adjutant.

Hal Hudson hesitated, and then asked the CO to reconsider.

'Don't argue with me. They would not be in this area if they were not pro-German. Go on, take them away. I can't afford the risk.'[10]

Hudson was perplexed, and disappeared with them into the woods. I listened but heard no sound of shots. On my next visit to report, Hudson was back again, but without any trace of murder in his features.

At about 02.30 the Battalion total had risen to 110 men at the RV and the Colonel decided that he would wait until 03.00 before moving off. At 02.50, when I went to him to receive orders with the other two company commanders, Parry and Bestley, the alarming fact was brought home to us that we were no more than 150 strong besides those already probing from outside the Battery position.

Except for one Vickers machine-gun (in the capable hands of Sergeant McGeever and Corporal McGuinness); a miserable few lengths of 'Bangalore' torpedo for shattering the main wire; and a very little plastic HE. We had no specialists nor their equipment. Without the 3-in. mortars we would be unable to illuminate the Battery position for the gliders; without the Royal Engineers we had no experts nor heavy explosive with which to destroy the guns; without six-pounder anti-tank guns we were defenceless against armoured opposition; without the parachuting Naval Officers we had no link with *Arethusa*, who might feel inclined to blow us to bits with the Battery.

I don't suppose, though, that anybody fortunate enough to be there had any doubt at all as to what we were going to do. I went back to my troops and told them that we were going ahead with the operation as planned, but because of a very dispersed drop, there were not going to be many of us to polish off those guns. There were no questions. It had been so dinned into us all that we had a job to do that we could not suddenly turn ourselves into spare files and wait there until daylight.

At that moment, 'Dizzie' Parfitt strolled in.

' "Dizzie"!' I exclaimed, 'I'm so glad to see you! And because you're senior to me I hereby relinquish command in your favour. Here is your Company: "C" Company!' I indicated the handful of men with a majestic sweep of my good arm.

'What? Oh,' said 'Dizzie' and loped off to report to the CO.

The diminutive Battalion was led by Allen Parry. There were no other 'A' Company officers. Mike Dowling from 'B' Company was there (though I was able to give him no more than a passing wave) and his Company Commander, Harold Bestley. There was also Tom Halliburton from HQ Company, and, at the very end of the thin red line, Harold Watts led his small medical team of six men. Harold was looking as cheerful and optimistic as ever. That man never looked depressed.

We had 2400 yards to travel undetected, and I suppose we must have taken up some 200 yards with our strung-out crocodile, making slow progress, often lying flat on the ground. Such moments of calm and silence allowed one to absorb the scents and the ambience of the Norman countryside, for this was no tourist package of Gauloise and garlic such as I'd experienced as a boy (on a day trip to Dieppe in 1927). Instead, it was more a case of the delicate 'Sons et parfums tournent dans l'air . . .'[11] It was scarcely possible to gauge any colours in the semi-darkness, but they could be imagined, and I longed to see the richness of Normandy, once the sun was up.

I was forcibly brought back to reality.

This was no holiday.

'Up again – on your feet,' I indicated, as we went on again.

To ground once more. Crash. A German patrol passed close by and went on, unsuspecting. A swishing noise came from a field to our left.

'What is it, sir?' asked Private Capon, close to me on the ground.

'Ssh!'

'What is it, sir?'

I shushed him again with my finger to my lips. He laughed to himself.

It was only cattle in the field, some of them injured by the bombing and rushing about in pain and bewilderment.

I looked up and saw a Lancaster, one of the hundreds of our aircraft in the sky that night, caught in searchlights and hit several times by AA fire. The bomber literally broke in half and two tiny dots of men on parachutes fell out – but only two.

9th Battalion The Parachute Regiment, at that moment comprising eight officers and about 130 men, had reached the road junction where Major Smith and CSMI Harrold were due to meet us. Yes, there they were, talking to the Colonel. They had done sterling work in listening to German sentries talking (although they couldn't be understood) and sizing up the local defence posts and sentries' beats. Now 'Dusty' Miller had been left on the edge of the Battery: the worst time of all for him, completely alone and in danger of being pounced on by a German patrol.

Close behind the 'Trowbridge Party' came Paul Greenway and six men of 'B' Company. They had been engaged in the highly dangerous task of locating and 'delousing' the buried or half-buried mines and then marking the cleared paths by heel-scratches in the earth. They had no mine-detectors, no tape. It was a vital job done with great courage and vigour, and it seemed to me at the time to have been an extraordinary achievement.

George Smith was sure that the way ahead to the Battery was clear of enemy patrols, so we increased our pace along the

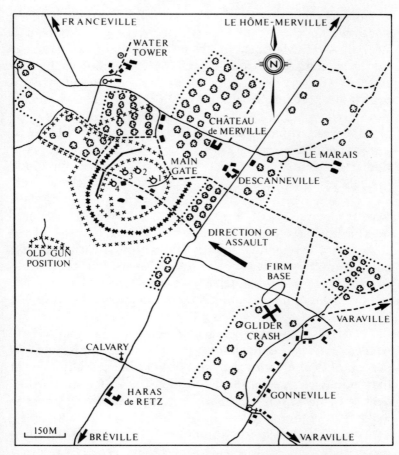

Fig 5  Merville Battery: attack by 9th Battalion The Parachute Regiment

track, fanning out beside the front edge of the orchard that we knew so well from the air photographs. Paul Greenway always carried a flask on the hip, and as the CO approached him, he called out in his normal voice – that sounded like a bellow: 'Have a nip!' There was general amazement at such coolness. If anybody needed a nip after that mine-lifting, it was he. The Colonel rejected the offer with an angry gesture that added to the growing hilarity at this scene.

Colonel Otway established his Firm Base, not far from the south-west corner of the wall which enclosed the Château de Merville while Major Parry advanced with his striking force of all the available men from 'C' and 'B' Companies, to the start line. Allen Parry was in his element as commander of the attack, his previous disappointment over the glider command not only forgotten, but unimportant now.

Time was getting short. The CO had waited at the RV for as long as possible, to try and grasp more men from the drop. But now it was almost time for the GB Force gliders to arrive, and once they landed we had to be on the way in ourselves. There was no time for proper orders, though I knew that my task was, as always, No 1 Casemate, No 1 Gun. We were going to be able to make only two gaps in the wire because of the shortage of 'Bangalores', two parties through each gap, one party to each gun. It was marvellous to see that rugged old soldier, Mike Dowling, preparing to blow our gap in the wire, right in front of me, grinning hugely and thoroughly enjoying himself.

There was some enemy machine-gun fire on the right flank near the main gate of the Battery position. Sergeant Knight had the job of dealing with that, so I didn't take much notice. At that moment I unconsciously recalled Davie Balfour's words from R.L. Stevenson's *Kidnapped*: 'This is the officer's part to make men continue to do things, they know not wherefore, and when, if the choice was offered, they would lie down where they were and be killed . . . for in these last hours it never occurred to me that I had any choice, but just to obey as long as I was able, and die obeying.'

My attention – and probably the attention of us all – was riveted on a glider that suddenly appeared, silently and majestically out of the night, flying low over the guns. We knew the Germans had an AA gun that could be used against us but so far it had not opened up. The glider seemed to hover for a moment as if lost. If only we had a flare – any flare.

No sooner had the glider vanished from sight, heading east, when a second one loomed up, much lower this time. Even

## Silencing the Battery

without artificial light, the navigation of these two gliders was faultless. Then the AA gun did open up, firing bursts of five rounds that appeared like glowing, red balls. The first five loosed off were behind the second glider (the first glider was no longer with us); the second five were closer and then – a flash as two of the third burst hit the glider's tail.

We stared at the huge structure of balsa wood, plywood and wire that represented a container for 22 men, friends of ours, familiar and much liked. Yet we could do nothing to help them. It was like watching a very lifelike display at the old pre-war Aldershot or Tidworth Tattoo, but worse: it was really happening. The glider stood still, close above us, so close that it almost seemed possible to touch it. Then it appeared to give up trying, and with a shrill whistle of air in the wires that were helping to keep it together, it plunged even lower as though trying to find a place to land. Instead it picked up, swooped over No 1 Casemate and straight towards the orchard and . . .

At that moment the 'Bangalores' blew.

It had been 'Go!' in the aircraft, now the word of command was 'Bang!' Without hesitation, because it was a reflex action, I raced forward towards the cloud of smoke ahead, not even wondering whether Mike had done his job thoroughly. Behind me came Morgan, Capon, Sergeant Bedford, 'Johnny' Walker, Stroud, Hawkins, Delsignore, Cartwright and Smith. But Hull and Love remained behind because, without helmets or rifles, there was no sense in going in. The others still came on, and they were all from my 12 Platoon. In the moment before we were mesmerised by the gliders' appearance, I had said to my party: 'This is it. This is what we've all been waiting to do. There aren't many of us but that won't matter. Think of your wives, your sweethearts, your mothers and sisters. Think of what would happen to them if the Germans got to England. Here's your chance to see they don't.' It seemed to have had some effect, because nobody was hanging back. I got that impression from one, swift backward glance. That's all there was time for.

As I passed Mike Dowling on my way through where all that wire had been, I caught sight of him, bending down and making the 'start-up' signal by winding an imaginary engine.

'Double-up, you silly old bugger,' he yelled at me in the din, 'go and find that "S"-mine and tread on it for me.' He roared with laughter.

In action for the first time, I found my angle of vision to be severely limited. I knew that we were on the right flank though whether Sergeant Knight's diversionary party was round by the gate to give us a modicum of cover and support, I neither knew nor considered. And I assumed that 'Dizzie' was leading the group on my left, making for No 2 Gun.

Without realising it, I was blowing away at my silly 'horn', the other arm tucked inside my webbing, because it was useless, though I was holding a grenade in that hand. My pistol was handy to grasp instead of the 'horn'. We seemed to be running into cross-fire and I hoped that Sergeant Knight was going to silence that machine-gun on the right – and quickly. It was becoming a nuisance.

We ran on, shouting blue murder. One man was out on the right flank. 'Hey! Over here! he called. I looked across and saw him standing over an exposed Teller mine, pointing his Sten at it. Smith was near. My throat dried up and the words wouldn't come out. It was too late to stop him. He fired and the mine changed into a fierce ball of fire. He was all right but Smith lost an eye.

'Forward!'

The hard, squat shape of No 1 Casemate was now visible, and I could see that it was encrusted with moulded concrete lozenges like the scales on a huge beast. Its sheer mass was formidable, and the dark entrance, large enough to drive a tank through – had they closed the steel doors we'd been told about?

I seemed to feel something nick me between the shoulder-blades and was aware of Morgan falling down, just behind me. On, on! No looking back. Our number was dwindling. Then I felt a lash across my left thigh. I stumbled and fell. There was

1 Looking into the back of No 1 Casemate as it was at the end of May 1944; one of the steel doors is resting at an angle behind the bench in the centre

2 2/Lt Raimund Steiner, who was appointed acting CO of the Merville Battery on 20 May 1944. He retained command during the Allied landings and until after the German withdrawal in September

3 The 10 cm 14/19 Czech howitzer in action: the long trail, the shield and the large wooden wheels with metal rims are all features of this weapon; the sight, to the left and forward of the side-loading breech, is also visible

4 Maj-Gen. Richard Gale (*l*), General Sir Bernard Montgomery and Brig. the Hon. Hugh Kindersley (*r*) at an inspection of Airborne Troops at Bulford Fields, Wiltshire, 8 March 1944

5 Maj-Gen. Richard Gale, HM King George VI, Brig. James Hill, HRH Princess Elizabeth, Lt-Col. S. Hickie; HM Queen Elizabeth at Bulford Fields, 19 May 1944. The weapon under discussion is a Projector Infantry Anti-Tank (PIAT)

6 Lt-Colonel Terence Otway Commanding 9th Battalion The Parachute Regiment

7 Major Allen Parry Commanding 'A' Company 9th Battalion

8 Captain the Hon. Paul Greenway, second-in-command 'B' Company 9th Battalion

9 The Revd John Gwinnett, Padre of 9th Battalion

10 Mass parachute drop over Wiltshire from Dakotas at the start of Exercise 'Bizz II', 25 March 1944

11 Dakotas of 512 Squadron RAF on the tarmac at Broadwell, Oxfordshire, shortly before D-Day 1944 ('V' for Victory leads). On 5 June, white lines were painted round the fuselage and wings of all Allied aircraft (to prevent enemy infiltration) and remained there throughout the war in Europe

12 Lieutenant Michael Dowling, Platoon Commander in 'B' Company 9th Battalion The Parachute Regiment, killed in the Battery on 6 June 1944.

13 Major John Pooley MC, RA, Commanding 4 & 5 Troops of No 3 Commando, killed in the Battery on 7 June 1944

14 Casemate in course of construction at Colleville, and similar to those at Merville; one of the same type of howitzers as at Merville is outside, pending the completion of its protective concrete covering

15 Vertical aerial photograph of the Merville Battery taken on 20 March 1944 before the bombardments had begun. Nos 3 & 4 Casemates have not yet been built, and the anti-tank ditch has only just been started

16 State of the area of the Merville Battery after the many aerial raids on it up to 6 June 1944 (see Appendix 3)

17 Sgt-Major Hans Buskotte looking through the sight of a howitzer during field exercises

18 Artillerymen of the Merville Battery engaged in an unconventional sing-song. This illustrates the constant importance and companionship to German field-gunners of their horses

19 Sgt-Major Buskotte on his favourite mount in the grounds of the Château de Merville, summer 1943

20 Sgt-Major Hans Buskotte (*l*), Major Karl-Werner Hof and Captain Schimpf (*r*) in May 1944. In the background is the requisitioned Mairie which was destroyed on 20/21 May 1944

21 FM Erwin Rommel (*l*), Captain Lang and Captain Karl-Heinz Wolter (*r*), commanding the Merville Battery, on 6 May 1944; the sloping roof of the small building (*l*) can also be seen in Pl. 20

22 The 2 cm Flak 38 dual-purpose AA gun, nicknamed 'Erika', in a training simulator; this is identical to the weapon, over the old cookhouse in the Battery, which hit Lt Hugh Pond's glider

23 The front of a 10 cm 14/19 Czech howitzer, showing its characteristic shield coming down as a partial mud-guard. This howitzer was captured at Colleville and came from No 2 Battery of the 716 Artillery Regiment, sister Battery to No 1 at Merville

24 Lt-Gen. Erich Marcks's inspection of Merville on 23 May 1944; 2/Lt Steiner (*in helmet, back to camera*) is talking to Marcks, whose stick can just be seen, while other members of the General's staff inspect the damage caused by aerial bombardment

25 *Withdrawing from the Battery after the Battery's guns had been destroyed. The MO sets up his RAP in a bomb crater*: a watercolour by Captain Albert Richards, War Artist, who often saw craters as the reverse of parachutes. He jumped with 9th Battalion The Parachute Regiment on 6 June 1944

26 Col-Gen. Friedrich Dollmann's visit to Merville on 25 May 1944. Steiner (*in steel helmet*) is on the General's right. Behind them is the 'little house with green shutters', a distinguishing feature in the approach to the Battery, reported by the French Résistance

27 The arrival of FM Rommel with admirals, and generals of both the other services, on 27 May 1944. The photograph captures the urgency of the inspection and Rommel's familiarity with Merville is evident from his posture. The mechanical digger in front of No 1 Casemate is removing rubble

28 The top of Buskotte's Command Bunker as it is today, with the remains of the ventilator shaft among the front clump of grass, and the periscope shaft beyond. The building behind was used as a guard room, and also became the Battery kitchen

29 No 1 Casemate at Merville in 1984, viewed from almost the same angle as that forty years earlier (see Pl. 1). This shows how the level of the ground is higher than before, so that one has to walk *down* into the Casemate from outside. No 1 Casemate now contains the Merville Battery Museum

no pain, but I couldn't get up again. 'If you can't feel a wound, it's probably serious,' the MO had told us. How encouraging.

I dragged myself towards a stack of wooden poles and propped myself up beside it so that I had some cover and could also see what was going on. Exasperated by my misfortune – so far and yet no further – I saw my soldiers charging straight for the Casemate. Good for them! They were the brave ones.

Now, instead of sharp cracks of firearms in the open air, I heard muffled detonations coming from inside the Casemates, from both 1 and 2. There were yells, agonised cries and clouds of smoke coming out from the doorways which obviously had not got their steel doors shut.

But those soldiers of mine. How proud of them I felt. They had gone on regardless, not waiting to be led any more. I had never expected them to do otherwise, yet – I had seen them continuing the assault as though I had never been part of it. I laughed out loud. Capon, Cartwright, Delsignore, Stroud, Hawkins, Walker – and Sergeant Bedford now in command – all the best of soldiers.

Meanwhile Allen Parry, not realising that No 1 Casemate and Gun had always been my task from the earliest days of rehearsal, had decided to take it on himself:

> When it became evident that OC 'C' Company was adrift, the CO placed me in command of an ad hoc assault force. I was to select (or detail) any officers immediately available, plus the soldiers, for the assault. I distinctly remember my saying that I would take on No 1 (right hand) Casemate, Mike Dowling No 2, Tom Halliburton No 4. I do not remember who was to command the assault on No 3 Casemate. It may well have been you. . . . If Jefferson and his platoon were destined for No 1 Casemate, I must, inadvertently, have duplicated the effort. I had to go somewhere and do something, so detailed myself for No 1 Casemate.[12]

Men began to fall around Parry as the machine gun fire became more accurate. Suddenly he himself felt as if someone had kicked him hard on the leg. There was a sharp pain and his leg collapsed, toppling him into a large bomb crater. . . . Parry lay for some minutes, dazed and winded by the fall. . . . Eventually he clambered painfully out of the crater and hobbled on towards No 1 Casemate. A scene of carnage met him at the entrance. The ground seemed to be covered with dead and wounded soldiers . . . He told the sergeant with him to . . . make up a charge and stuff it in the breech of the gun. This was quickly done, a fuse was laid and everyone evacuated the casemate for the charge to be set off. There was a satisfactory explosion . . . it was clear that enough damage had been done to the gun to ensure it would not be able to fire even if enough Germans should emerge to man it after the paratroopers withdrew.[13]

Gradually the firing subsided. Only the machine-gun on the right flank continued to fire. Seeing some prisoners being driven from one of the casemates, Sergeant Knight shouted: 'Give them to me!'

They were marched across in rough formation, whereupon Sergeant Knight took over and headed them straight for the machine-gun in the 'Tobruk Stand' on top of No 1 Casemate. The baffled German gunner ceased firing rather than shoot his comrades, and showed a white rag. At this, the firing stopped.

Hal Hudson, the Adjutant, had been hit in the stomach and lay on the ground. While he felt no actual pain, he was entirely unable to move from the waist downwards. Reflecting upon all the work he had put in, training the Battalion and seeing it through the enormous amount of paperwork involved in mobilisation, movement and finally getting them over to Normandy, this did seem a rotten way to end up, so close to the objective. Then he lapsed into unconsciousness. The CO decided to look round, thinking that Hudson was dead.

A concrete building with the AA gun on top of it (crew dead) stood not far from where I was lying. Now that it was getting lighter, I was astonished to see beside the gun, in full view and motionless, a smooth-haired fox terrier dog. As I stared at it, fascinated, and began to laugh, a pensive figure approached, stopped when he saw the stuffed dog and made as though to stroke or touch it. We had been warned to keep well away from any unusual objects in the Battery for fear of booby traps.

'Get away from that, you bloody fool,' I yelled, 'it might be mined!'

'Don't you call your Commanding Officer a bloody fool,' came the reply, and he walked on slowly, alone.

Allen Parry then continues[14]:

> I understood that Nos 3 and 4 guns had been dealt with to a greater or lesser extent. . . . Time was progressing and as we could not communicate with HM Ships . . . it was probable that *Arethusa* would start shelling at the scheduled hour which was now fast approaching. It was at this stage that I ordered the withdrawal to begin. I was therefore unable to visit Nos 3 and 4 Casemates to check what, if any, damage had been inflicted on the guns there.

Bill Harrold ran up to me very fast and stopped.

'I want all your weapons, sir,' he said, and not waiting for me to hand them over, he grabbed everything I had and then took binoculars, compass even and my 'horn' – with a laugh.

'Leave me my watch and fighting knife, won't you?' I asked him, beginning to feel naked. He left only my Army issue watch, then dashed away, satisfied with his loot.

My next visitor was Albert Richards, the War Artist. He and I had shared a room in the mess for several weeks at one stage, and I had grown to like him well.

'Ha! What are you doing down there?' he asked. 'Hang on.'

'What do you mean, Albert, *hang on?*' He was standing a few feet away, drawing very quickly, with a pad of paper in his hand, making a whole lot of angles, his shorthand for the picture that would eventually emerge from them.

'Good!' said Albert. 'I tell you what, I'll put you in the picture, Alan. Poor wounded officer. Ta, ta.' And off he ran to draw some more angles for the picture which was to be called '*Withdrawing from the Battery after the Battery's guns had been destroyed*'. (See Plate 25.)

A medical orderly came towards me, saw me and helped me to the Doctor. Harold Watts was happily ensconced at the bottom of the biggest bomb crater I had ever seen, over in the area between Nos 2 and 3 Casemates, and to the south of them. Any mines that had been there must surely have all been detonated by the RAF long ago, while they were changing the face of the Battery out of recognition. I saw for the first time how earth from the aerial explosions had been lifted and dropped again in huge piles, right outside No 3 Casemate.

The Doctor greeted me warmly: 'Alan, my dear chap, how splendid to see you. Do you know that you're my very first battle casualty! I've got everything ready at last,' and to his orderlies, 'Come along now, get that tea ready for Mr Jefferson.'

Harold had me put down against the sloping side of the crater. I felt defenceless and wondered what sort of a mess my uniform was in, from lying on the ground. That was small consideration for what was to follow. Harold looked at my leg with his head on one side and produced a knife. He carefully slit up the whole length of my best battledress trousers (so carefully pressed by Morgan at Broadwell) to reveal a bloody limb. I was aware of several figures looking down from the top of the crater. Very soon the word got round: 'Jefferson's lost a leg' and with the soldier's gift for embroidery: 'Jefferson's lost one leg and the other one's – well, you know – a bit dicey . . . "S"-mine it was . . .'

Then Albert came back. 'Hallo, Harold,' he called from the rim of the crater, 'how's it going? Oh Alan, you again? You don't half get about.' And off he dashed again, drawing angles, always angles.

Albert's picture has the subtitle: *The MO sets up his RAP in a bomb crater.*[15]

My leg was only superficially injured with a sprinkling of shrapnel that had caused a loss of blood. But Harold said I had to beware of infection and he must send me back to the Field Ambulance at Brigade HQ in case there was further injury. As these days were before general issue of antibiotics, a white powder called M&B was used instead, dusted over wounds. Harold bound me up, chatting away busily, and apparently impervious to what had been going on outside. It all seemed to be a cosy 'inside' at the bottom of that deep crater.

Two orderlies helped me up the long, steep slope to the top,

## Silencing the Battery

and told me to make my way as 'walking wounded' to the RV at the Calvary, all of half a mile away.

Allen Parry

> gave orders for the smoke candles[16] to be lit. The signals officer, Lieutenant James Loring reached into the front of his battledress blouse and pulled out a somewhat bedraggled pigeon with a 'success' message strapped to its leg. Loring flung the bird in the air. It circled twice and flew off – due east, in the direction of Germany. . . . Those who were still on their feet started to move out of the Battery area, herding their prisoners with them and helping the more mobile wounded as best they could. Parry . . . knew there were more who could not be moved in time and who would have to be left where they were. It was an agonizing decision to have to take, but Parry had to weigh the possible loss of their lives against those of the many more who might be killed if there were no withdrawal and the balance came down in favour of saving as many as possible of the assault party.[17]

Shells were now falling round and inside the Battery from German counter-battery fire. I was getting along as fast as I could when I saw Private George Bosher, of 'Jock's' Platoon, coming towards me. He was a burly fellow who wanted to pick me up and carry me away to safety. I'm sure it was far more his kind heart than any First World War flashback: '. . . decorated for getting his officer in from no man's land', but I had to use stern words to Bosher to make him put me down and join the rest of our few fit men who were going on.

Left alone again, I was able to look round and take in the sight of Merville in the morning. It was now light enough to see the tops of the casemates, two of them partly hidden by the mounds of earth that were complementary to the craters beside them. The whole place was an eerie mess of mounds and holes, the earth sticky from recent rain and not a trace of green anywhere. It was a desert of brown and grey filth organised by some giant maker of mud-pies in the craziest of ups and downs.

I was about half-way down the track to the Calvary when an extraordinary sight met my eyes. It was Allen Parry riding in what looked like a child's home-made cart and propelling himself along with a rifle butt. One leg was sticking up in the air and he used the other to prod at the ground. He was waving and shouting in a manner far removed from his normal, quiet behaviour and I thought he must have gone barmy.[18]

'Sorry I can't give you a lift!' he called, proceeding quite fast and laughing all the time. A bit further down the track I saw a sergeant take him in tow with a toggle-rope.

Arriving at the RV at last, worn out and breathless from my exertions, I was surprised to see the remnant of the Battalion still there. I had expected them to be on their way to Le Plein (the next objective) by now. To one side of our soldiers was a huddle of German prisoners, frightened, cold-looking and in some cases only partly clad. Two of our men were guarding them, one was Sergeant Knight. He was being particularly alert, and seemed to regard them as his personal responsibility, walking round them, sometimes jabbing his Sten in the air towards any who moved out of line.

It seemed that there was some sort of conference at which the question of shooting the prisoners was raised. Owing to the temporary distortion of reactions under the stress of battle, I found myself offering to join the firing party. Up to that moment I felt as though I had done nothing for my King and Country, and that my soldiers who had gone in to the Casemate had accepted and shouldered all my responsibilities. This irked me considerably, so if there was now an opportunity for me to fire a shot in real anger, I was all for it.

There was some laughter at my suggestion, because I had no weapon, and could scarcely stand up unaided. The CO looked pityingly at me, half smiled and said something that I didn't hear. It appeared that my offer had been turned down. Oh well, it's the oldest rule in the Army: never volunteer for anything.

Another suggestion about the prisoners followed: to march them in front of the Battalion so that if a minefield was in the way, they would get blown up first. Given the conditions facing us, neither my offer nor the suggestion which followed seemed out of place. Some high-principled individual in this strange debate demurred, saying that such an act would be contrary to the Geneva Convention: it was wrong to use prisoners as an insurance policy against mines. He was told to shut up, and the decision was taken.

The twenty-two prisoners were marshalled in front of the Battalion, now getting ready to move off. 'Battalion'! It was less than the strength of a rifle company. Hugh Pond had joined us from his glider party that had beaten off an enemy attack from the direction of Gonneville, in which CSMI 'Dusty' Miller had joined. There were also a few Canadian soldiers who had been dropped adrift, bringing our total to about 80 fit men, of all ranks.[19]

As they began to move, one of our private soldiers called Lawrence, suddenly appeared, looking very pleased with himself. He was renowned in the Battalion for his ability to reproduce a variety of bird whistles with great fidelity. CSMI Miller caught sight of Lawrence and stopped.

'Where've *you* been then?' he asked, in his sergeant-major's voice.

'I've got here, sir, I've made it,' beamed Lawrence.

'You're late, it's all over,' replied 'Dusty' accusingly. 'So get fell in, you idle, useless man. Get on, shift yourself!'

The fighting men vanished slowly into the morning mist that had risen gently over the fields, like in a film.

I felt fed up and far from home. Now I was like those people standing at the gate of Broadwell Camp when? – it was only last night – when they watched the 9th Battalion marching away.

The wounded were straggling into our haven, a house called on the map Haras de Retz (Haras being a stud farm) down the road beyond the Calvary. We felt reasonably far from the Battery, though nobody had said anything about coming to rescue us, nor do I believe we thought about it either. We merely accepted the immediate resolution to stay calm, take cover indoors, help one another – and wait. We also were 22. Major Parry had settled down; Major Bestley was quiet – well he always was, but now he had a bad leg-wound too. Hal Hudson looked grim. My former batman, Smith, who had lost an eye from that Teller mine, always appeared to have a mournful countenance. Now it was the same, though his face looked a terrible mess. I went over to him and held his shoulder for a moment, saying nothing but hoping to register sympathy. What could I say? 'Never mind, Smith, they'll fix you up with a glass one when we get home.' No. Nothing.[20] Then to Morgan, the good lad who dropped with me as my batman and followed me loyally until he got it through both his knees.

'I think it was that MG, sir. It got us in enfilade as we ran in. I thought it got you in the back, sir. Then it must have fired lower which is when it got me. I'm all right, sir, really I am.' He wasn't. Plucky little chap.[21]

Major Parry asked whether the yellow triangles which we all carried had been taken on to the roof of our château as a signal to friendly aircraft. Somebody said there was one of the orderlies doing it at that moment.

We were thinking about the next event in our lives, and it was going to happen to us all. There were to be three RAF 'stonks' (heavy bombardments) on the coast immediately before the beach-landings at 07.00, 07.05 and 07.10 to keep the enemy's heads down. We had the feeling that these bombs might possibly overshoot the coastline – like most of our Battalion had overshot the DZ – and it was more likely that we would be in the firing line for these 'overs'.

As 07.00 approached, the orderlies and those men who could walk, shuttered the windows in the room where we all lay, and closed the front door as well as the door into the hall. We waited, lying uncomfortably on the bare boards. Hudson was moaning a bit as he drifted in and out of consciousness and the rest of us 'switched off' as we had done in the aircraft coming over to Normandy such a long time ago.

In this vacuum I heard one of the soldiers talking.

'Mr Dowling copped it. I saw him lying out there with his batman. Both dead but peaceful-like.'

'Are you sure?' I called out, horrified. 'Are you sure?'

'Quite sure, sir, it was Mr Dowling all right, I . . .' He suddenly stopped.

Then we heard it. The rapidly increasing roar of many aircraft engines and the *boum-boum-boum* of AA fire. Then came the thunder of exploding bombs. They came nearer and nearer until they were all round us. I pressed myself into the floor not in the conventional position of face down, bottom up, because of my leg. The other way up was far worse. One arm was across my face, small pack protecting my genitals, the rest of me doing its best to squeeze through the nearest join in the floorboards. And I was weeping over Mike.

Then it stopped.

The silence was momentarily as heavy as the air-rending explosions had been. It was glorious. We sat up and looked round. Some of us were white from fallen plaster, but unharmed. I shoved myself round so as to get in a better position for the next onslaught in a little under five minutes from now. That was the worst of it, we knew it was coming, and there were two more — if we were still there for the third one.

Sure enough, at precisely 07.05 it happened again. This time, especially after the blissful silence, the noise seemed more deafening, more of an affront to the system and the mind. I wished I had remained in my first position because now my backside seemed so vulnerable. The house shook and jumped about; my eyes were tightly shut but I knew there was dust dancing round me on the floor because I could taste it. Was it never going to end? How long? A minute? More — less?

These random questions came and went from my mind, criss-crossing my agonising obsession over Mike's death. Could he really be dead? Not Mike, surely, not Mike . . .

Then sudden, wonderful silence once more.

Another check to see what had happened to us all.

Nothing new, except for some signs of shattered nerves. And there was still the third time to be fought through, to be endured. Was it better to know this, or not to know? Well at least one could be prepared mentally for the next possibility of death. And Mike? What of him? Dead already and unprepared for it. He had not got the expression of one who knew death was coming for him, waiting for him inside the casemate. Sergeant Rose certainly knew – I realised that now; and perhaps 'Dizzie' – is that why he was so agonised in sleep?[22] And I? Was I going to die? No, I thought not, but everything going on round us was tempting me to wonder.

The third blast was the worst. I was on my back again, experiencing a sharp, jabbing sensation between the shoulderblades, which at least offered some rebate to the overall blanket of fury. Did the third-wave pilots and bomb-aimers not care about where they were dropping their cargoes? Was there anything to bomb on the coast anyway? If not, why trespass further inland? We may be *hors de combat*, but there's no bloody need to put paid to us for that, thanks. I was feeling angry. Why had we to suffer this indignation? What do they think they're doing up there? *Idiots*! Careless fools!

Then it stopped. Almost. A single explosion rather close, some falling of stones or part of a building perhaps. That was it.

The massive relief we all felt took no account of the danger from German troops in the area. The main and immediate source of fear was over: we had been spared by the RAF.

Gradually we all came back to life and to reality. I felt positively exhilarated, 'Gentlemen,' I said, looking round, 'I think we have all got what they call a "Blighty one"!'

The orderlies busied themselves, settling the more uncomfortable of their patients as well as making tea from the 24-hour packs which each wounded man still had with him.

I had not previously noticed two German medical orderlies who had been through the bombardment with us. But after the bashing that Merville had received over the last few months they were probably more used to it than we were – if the human mind and frame can ever become *used* to such punishment. These two Germans were quietly going about their business in a professional manner as part of our own two medical orderlies' team.

We were all lying about on the floor of what had probably

been the salon of that house in better times. Perhaps it wasn't quite a château but certainly a *manoir*. There were wooden shutters on all the windows (now open again), an old wooden floor, very old to judge from the width of the planks, but no furniture. The place had recently been occupied, it appeared, but all the furniture had been removed except for a heavy piece built into the wall. Hudson began to moan. He looked very pale indeed and was shrugged up in what looked like an uncomfortable position. One of our own orderlies was observing him carefully.

I began to feel that scratch on my back again. It was stinging, but did not seem very important, though I remembered what Morgan had said. My left arm was the worst, but in my shame I still kept quiet about that. My leg felt numb and partly disassociated from the rest, but all the same I was determined to try and find out more about Mike and what had happened. I must go and look.

Nobody tried to stop me – if indeed I told anybody where I was going – but I felt that a companion might be a good idea and ordered the German medical corporal to accompany me. He was a tall man and had a kind of 'fish-eye'. He was older than I, very calm, and obeyed me without demur.

It was becoming quite warm. The road outside the Haras de Retz was still, and the sound of gunfire seemed far away. In spite of the mess from our recent bombing – branches ripped from trees and flung in the road, damaged corners to the house and more craters, the birds were singing and I felt glad to be in the open air again. We made slow progress up the road, the German suiting his pace to my limp, and after several hundred yards in silence, he began to unburden himself.

The only officer inside the Battery position when we attacked it had been the Doctor, a captain and a very good man. When the shooting stopped and this doctor saw some of our wounded, he asked for permission to fetch dressings and other medical equipment for *us*. Permission was given, but on the way back the doctor was killed. The tall man who told me this tale had tears in his eyes. 'It was such a waste of a fine man,' he kept on saying.

All this was in fairly good broken English, for at that time I spoke no German. I was moved by the man's compassion.

'What's your name?'

'Heinz,' I thought he replied.

He asked me the purpose of our foray into the killing-ground and I told him. I told him about Mike Dowling, my best friend for most of my time with 9th Para. Mike and I were going to farm oranges in Spain after the war. I also told 'Heinz' that, believing Mike to be dead, I wanted to find his body and to make certain that it was intact. The German did not reply. He was equally unhappy about the doctor's death.

So there we were, plodding along the road together, a tall German corporal, protected by the Geneva Convention; and a short, unarmed British parachute lieutenant, each grieving over a lost friend and walking straight back into a potentially dangerous place. *Walking?* It was a great effort.

We reached the outer cattle fence, through the cleared paths in the minefield and towards No 1 Casemate when I stopped. I did not like the feel of the place: Death seemed everywhere though I saw no bodies – and that was curious. Looked at from a different angle now, and in daylight, the Battery was unrecognisable from the one which had been implanted on my mind by the aerial photographs and the model. They had all seemed so clean, almost inoffensive. But now, here, what was it?

This thing I saw, the glistening, filthy heaps of earth sheltering those loathsome casemates, might have been a model too, for all the stillness about it. That is what I found so ominous: no sound at all, no bodies, no movement of any kind. I shuddered. And there was something else: no birds were singing at Merville[23].

'I think we've gone far enough.'

'Yes, sir, so do I,' replied 'Heinz' quickly.

He was looking at me in a strange way, almost as if he was planning to overpower me and call for his comrades. But no. How could there be a single German left alive in this place?

'Come on, Heinz, let's go back to the others now.'

He stood there, looking round and shaking his head.

## Silencing the Battery

We began the return journey. He walked and I staggered in silence. The Battery was not only oppressive, but extremely depressing too. 'Heinz' was lost in his own thoughts; mine concerned Mike first of all, and then surprise at the disappearance of all those expected contours in the Battery.

When we got back to the Paras it was long past ten o'clock and our own medics had brewed up. One of them told me that he had been to a nearby house where there were still some French people. They were not at all friendly.

'I only asked for some strawberries,' he said, 'but all she did was glare at me and shut the door in my face. Aren't we meant to be liberating them?'

He gave me some tea and a few strawberries that he had taken all the same. They tasted far better than the tea.

'How does she know whether we're here to stay?' I observed. Corporal 'Heinz' had vanished inside the house and was no longer under my command.

All the rest of the day we hung on, waiting. For what?

Some Spitfires came over, rolling about playfully in the bright sky, and there was a lot more rumbling of gunfire or bombardment west of the Orne. But thank goodness the sun stayed out. I sat there, in the garden, gratefully snoozing in its warmth and nursing my sore arm and 'frozen' leg.

Once or twice I hopped inside to see how Hudson and the others were getting on. Most of the time Hudson was asleep, but his face had gone a dreadful yellow colour and he looked very old. The medical orderly who had taken it upon himself to tend the Adjutant said nothing. He looked me straight in the eyes. I knew what he meant.

At about six in the evening of that very long day – we'd been up and about since the morning of the day before – a vehicle came busily up the road towards us. God bless him! It was John Gwinnett, our Padre. He was in a little pick-up truck driven by Private Allt, and there was room for four men. The two majors were to go first, also Private Smith and one other soldier. John said he'd try to be back for another four as soon as he could, but the roads were rather bad. As we watched them going away, I reflected on their chances of getting through to Le Mesnil where Brigade HQ and the main Parachute Field Ambulance was situated. John told us that Brigadier Hill had been wounded, but was still in command. That was good news. But at least John had got to us once, and he never lacked God's help.

It seemed like hours, and the sun was beginning to go down when – oh joy! – the little truck reappeared.

'We'll take Hal and you, Alan,' John said briskly.

'If Hal's fit to move,' I replied.

'He must be moved, it's his only chance.' John looked unusually stern. 'I've got to get you both out of this – and two more soldiers too, of course.'

Between them the four medical orderlies, two British and two German, carefully carried Hal to the truck and propped him up in the back. There was no cover and the four of us were sitting there like dummies, without any kind of protection. Hal looked more ghastly than ever. I took his hand and pressed it, but when I tried to withdraw my fingers, he hung on. I continued to sit there, letting him hold on to me.

We left. It was getting darker but Allt did not switch on his headlights, so it became increasingly difficult for him to see and to dodge the many obstacles in the road: craters, stones, branches and all kinds of unexpected lumps or pits. At each bump we made, Hal winced and I could almost feel his agony as he grasped my hand as though to crush it. I told John that this journey was doing Hal no good, but we had to rely on Allt to do his best and, everything considered, he was a fine driver.

As we came round a corner, I don't know where it was, some French people ran down the partly concealed drive to a house, shouting and waving. They seemed to be trying to tell us something. Then I heard it:

'*Guet-apens! Guet-apens!*'

It flashed back from my Prep School French[24] –

'Oh, good heavens, a trap!' I whacked John on the shoulder.

'Stop! Stop! They're saying it's an ambush!'

Allt turned very sharply into the drive, nearly decanting us all, and almost taking one of the French women with him. He shot along for a few yards and parked under some trees between bushes. The French people melted away.

Only a few moments later, after Allt had switched off the engine and it sighed into silence, we all heard the clatter of a vehicle, and a half-track came down the road and past the entrance to the drive. We would have met it, head on.

After it had gone past – and it can only have been German – Allt nipped out to make sure that there were no more following. I shouted thanks to the French who were coming out of the bushes. They were very pleased, gathered round us and shook hands. There were lots of 'Vive les Anglais!' and all the patriotic clichés. A middle-aged man had just dug up a bottle and we were all given a swig. It was brandy, very good brandy indeed. Hal had drifted off once more . . .[25]

John Gwinnett was anxious to be on the move again, so with 'Vive les Français! À bas les Boches! Vive la Libération!' and so on, we made our grateful withdrawal and set off again for Le Mesnil.

John Gwinnett turned round to me and smiled.[26]

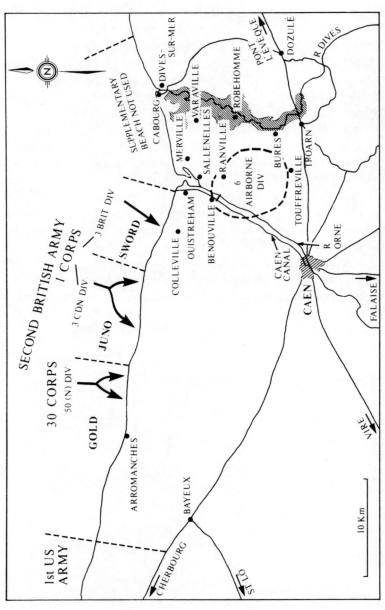

Fig. 6  Second British Army's approach and 6 Airborne Division's position on left flank of the Invasion

# 6
# Pooley

## Another Attack on the Battery

The British 51st Highland Division had landed on 'Sword' Beach on the morning of 7 June[1], well aware of danger from the Merville Battery, and relieved that it was not firing on them. The Commander of this Division, Major-General D.C. Bullen-Smith, was relying on 6 Airborne Division's early commitment to silence the guns of Merville, just as they had preserved the two vital bridges at Bénouville. The larger of these, over the Orne Canal, had since that morning been known as 'Pegasus' Bridge (after the Airborne sign). It was boldly taken shortly after midnight by Major John Howard and his 'D' Company of the 52nd Light Infantry (Oxf. & Bucks.) of 6 Airlanding Brigade. They came down in three gliders beside the bridge, and at 00.26 hrs it was safely in Major Howard's hands, though he and men of 7th Battalion The Parachute Regiment, who soon joined him, had to fight to hold it. This secured a lifeline between 6 Airborne Division's purposely isolated position between the Dives and Orne Rivers, and the bridgehead which they were protecting.

1st Special Service Brigade, commanded by Brigadier the Lord Lovat DSO, MC, had crossed 'Pegasus' Bridge on 6 June to come under command 6 Airborne Division. The units were 3, 4 & 5 Army Commandos with signallers and engineers, and 45 RM (Royal Marine) Commando the only one in the Brigade facing its first action.

When artillery fire suddenly came down on 'Sword' Beach towards midday on 7 June, Major-General Bullen-Smith thought the enemy Battery at Merville to be responsible (though no evidence has survived to support this assumption).[2] He immediately got back to Corps and asked for help. General Gale was requested to silence the Battery once more, but as he had no units of his sorely stretched 6 Airborne Division to spare, he looked to the Brigade under his command.

Both No 3 Commando and 45 (RM) Commando had already been given orders to clear and hold Sallenelles and then move along the coast to Franceville-Plage towards Cabourg. The final push was to be the responsibility of No 3, and by achieving it they would effectively seal off the whole area from the coast to Troarn, with the River Dives as its eastern boundary and the Orne Canal to the west.

The Marine Commando had been expected to be in close contact with 9th Battalion The Parachute Regiment, and for that reason, one of their officers, Lieutenant Peter Winston, jumped with the Battalion.[3]

When Lovat was ordered by General Gale to deal with the Merville Battery on 7 June, he saw that No 3 Commando was the only unit available. Its commander was Lt-Colonel Peter Young DSO, MC, warrior of Dunkirk, Vaagso, Dieppe, Sicily and Italy and many of his troops were, like himself, seasoned fighters. They had come ashore on 'Juno' Beach at 09.05 on 6 June with 45 (RM) Commando and had begun to fight their way inland. Now, though, three troops of No 3 Commando were already committed, and a fourth had suffered many casualties in the landing-craft. That left only two troops available, 4 and 5, so far relatively unscathed. As Lord Lovat was about to brief 45 (RM) Commando for its assault on Franceville, he decided to attach two troops of No 3 Commando to them, these troops to be responsible for the silencing of the Merville Battery.

Lord Lovat consequently briefed the acting CO of 45 (RM) Commando, Major Nicol Gray. Lieutenant-Colonel Charles Reis, who had come ashore in command of them, had been wounded while crossing 'Pegasus' Bridge, and was evacuated on 6 June[4]. Major Gray went to Écarde to receive his orders

## Another Attack on the Battery

and returned to his headquarters afterwards to give his own 'O' (Orders) Group.

A large number of officers awaited him at a point in a field near the quarries west of Amfréville, where 12th Battalion The Parachute Regiment had RV'd after their landing early on 6 June. Major Pooley, second-in-command of No 3 Commando, who was going to lead the two troops, went there with Captain Brian Butler MC, OC 4 Troop. Lieutenant-Colonel Young also went to hear the orders in case there was anything he could do to help. The size of this 'O' Group soon attracted the enemy's attention and they began to be mortared. Hastily repairing to a ditch, they all listened to the rest of the briefing. It was given verbally and was short.

Afterwards, Colonel Young had a few words with Pooley. If there were guns to be destroyed he was going to need explosives, but nothing about that had been said so far. So Colonel Young immediately returned to Brigade HQ where an engineer detachment might provide them. Meanwhile, Pooley was to proceed as ordered.

Major John Pooley had already excelled as a tireless and fearless leader in many previous actions, notably at Agnone where he had earned a Military Cross. He was greatly liked by all ranks: a very tall, slim man with clean-cut features who looked as though he might have come from the Brigade of Guards. In fact he had joined the Commandos in order to avoid remaining an AA gunner. He had been married to a Worthing girl two weeks earlier. Pooley was admirably suited to the task he had been given because he had formerly commanded No 5 Troop and knew them all personally; he was also the explosives expert in No 3 Commando.

Trooper 'Taffy la Barbe' Jones and Corporal Vic Whibley, both Army Commandos, were operating a radio link to Lord Lovat's HQ but had been assigned for this operation to 45 (RM) Commando. They regretted not remaining with their own kind.

Meanwhile 4 and 5 Troops were moving up the road towards Sallenelles, preparatory to striking off eastwards, across country, towards the Battery. Captain Butler explained the plan: 5 Troop under Captain Michael Woyevodsky MC were to put in the attack on the Battery, with fire support from Captain Butler's 4 Troop. Afterwards, No 4 Troop would lead the force to the outskirts of Franceville and then develop east on the edge of the town.

Colonel Young was making all speed to Commando Brigade HQ at Écarde, on the road from Ranville to Sallenelles. When he arrived, no explosives were forthcoming, and it struck him very forcibly that 'they had been invited to perform a very difficult task. How were they to blow up guns without explosives?'[5] So feeling considerably let down, he decided to follow Pooley and to find out how he was getting on at Merville. He was able to do this as his adjutant, Major D.C. Hopson, a very capable officer, was perfectly well able to command the other four troops in the CO's absence.

'Taffy' Jones and Corporal Whibley proceeded towards Franceville with the Marine Commando, but soon became detached from them. Without knowing what was going on, or what they were meant to be doing, they kept moving until, as 'Taffy' Jones remembers[6]:

Advancing along the road to Sallenelles we came under intensive enemy mortar fire and dived into the ditch on the side of the road. This continued for some time and Corporal Whibley, on looking up, discovered that we were on our own, at least on our side of the road. Where the hell was the rest of them? Not knowing what the plans were we had to make a decision. On the other side of the road were Green Berets advancing, our own comrades as we thought, and immediately joined them. On reaching the rise above Sallenelles we halted for a few minutes when suddenly Lieutenant-Colonel Peter Young came out of the shrub and trees to our left with a small party of about four. Heavily camouflaged, he wanted to know how the troop were faring. He wasn't very happy about the situation and was naturally keeping his eye on his own 'boys', as temporarily they came under command of 45, and I don't think he was too happy about that.

Where was 45? We knew they were out on their own without radio contact and their position would be very serious. What to do? Try and find them? . . . There was only one thing for it, go in with Nos 4 and 5 Troops and see how things work out, and so we advanced across country.

Suddenly we came upon these huge craters, the result of RAF bombing raids. Just further on we saw our Commandos in an attacking position behind a hedgerow and small bank.

Colonel Young remembers meeting several parties on his way to Merville that afternoon, including Captain Hodgson, a FOB (Forward Officer Bombardment) who could bring down naval gunfire, but he went away in the direction 45 had taken. Colonel Young's party consisted of his batman, Corporal Christopher (who was very good at spotting mines in time to prevent either of them from being blown up); the MO, Captain E.L. ('Ned') Moore RAMC (Royal Army Medical Corps) and his Sergeant Spears; and Trooper Griffiths, a signaller.

The two Commando troops had reached the area of the Calvary where 5 Troop went right-flanking and into the Battery position from the north. No 4 Troop gave them covering fire from the area of the wood near the Calvary. Colonel Young and his party, approaching the Battery from the west, came upon 4 Troop commanded by Captain Brian Butler MC. Butler explained that 5 Troop under Captain Woyevodsky were making the assault, but he was not certain, at that moment, of their position, especially as 2-in. mortar smoke was covering their attack.

'Taffy' Jones continues[7]:

> Our Commandos seemed to be engaging the enemy, but before we could reach them we had to negotiate these huge craters which were made more difficult by the attention of enemy snipers. Eventually, with more luck than judgement, we arrived at the Commando position. Taking up our attacking position behind the low bank I observed the top of the concrete casemates of the Merville Battery, steel doors closed. Surrounding the Battery was a ring of barbed wire, minefields and an anti-tank ditch. It all looked so formidable, but what amazed me was the number of shell and bomb craters surrounding the complex. Not one crater on the side of the Battery.

It was broad daylight and three o'clock in the afternoon. Although the main attack did not go in from the same direction as that made by 9th Battalion The Parachute Regiment 16½ hours before, it still involved an approach through the minefield. Major Pooley had managed to silence the fire of two MGs (machine-guns) with his own Brens.[8] His order was to go straight through the mines, stepping in the footprints of the man in front. This extremely brave action resulted in the loss of only three men.

Trooper Patterson recalls his own experiences[9]:

> We were immediately met by small-arms fire from our right flank which, combined with the mines and many large bomb craters, made movement difficult. Some of the mines had been brought to the surface by the bombing, and I worked my way round until I was nearly opposite No 3 Casemate. I was firing my Bren gun, one of the few that seemed to be still in working order. Then we got the order to attack . . .

The enemy fire became heavier. Patterson reached the casemate safely and saw some of his comrades, who had managed to open the steel doors, lifting a metal hatch in the centre of the entrance and throwing grenades down below, assuming that this was where the enemy were hiding.

Captain Butler had received no information from Major Pooley about how the attack was going, for some twenty minutes, so taking one section he reached the wood and orchard beside the corner of the wall surrounding the Château de Merville when heavy shell- or mortar-fire came down on him. So he made his way round in the opposite direction and there he met the CO.

'Taffy' Jones resumes his story:

> We still fired on the Battery, but no sign of Jerry. Then a voice called 'Cease Fire!' Figures appeared from the left, NW of the Battery, recognised by their green berets, moving into the complex. It was No 5 Troop clambering over the casemates and dropping hand grenades down the air vents. A great sight to witness. Then orders came for us to advance into the Battery – 'Attack!' first to negotiate the barbed wire, then the minefield.

## Another Attack on the Battery

Word passed back from man to man, 'Step in the footsteps of the man in front', having still to contend with small-arms fire. It was certainly nerve-racking, but fortunately we got through with very few casualties, into and out of the anti-tank ditch. 'Carry on through the Battery and consolidate in area of some houses on the NE side.'

Lieutenant-Colonel Young had moved round to the left and reached the anti-tank ditch when Major Pooley ran past with a German stick grenade in his hand. The CO stopped him to ask how it was going. Very briefly Pooley described the assault so far. There did not seem to be many Germans in the Battery, but those who were managing to hold out did so for some time with fanatical courage, fighting until they died.

As soon as the Germans discovered that they had lost the Battery, it was expected that they would bring down heavy fire on it; so it seemed better to consolidate beyond the objective (which was common tactical doctrine of the period).

Pooley ran on to take charge of the mopping-up operation and the consolidation. Colonel Young signalled to 4 Troop to move across and join them, and he told Captain Butler to clear the houses that could be seen in the consolidation area.

At that moment, Lieutenant Pollock of 5 Troop came up to Colonel Young and said, 'Johnny Pooley's been killed.' Although there had been one or two shots, it seemed that all enemy resistance was over. In the 'Tobruk Stand' of No 1 Casemate a single machine-gunner had gone on firing from his well-defended position. He waited until Pooley had got to within a few yards of the casemate and then opened fire, shooting him through the head. Pooley was killed instantly and lay on his back on the ground. Alan Pollock, a small dark subaltern, was appalled. He reacted in the same way as any other member of 5 Troop would have done at the death of their beloved leader. Pollock, exposing himself fearlessly, hurled a gammon-bomb at the machine-gun position.

Another subaltern from 5 Troop, an ex-regular soldier and Commando since 1940, called 'Bill' Williams was horrified when he reached the vicinity of No 1 Casemate[10]:

I was about forty feet from it when someone shouted: 'Major Pooley's been shot!' Sure enough, I could see him lying there and a few of 5 Troop chaps near him.

Pooley's body had been moved by the time Colonel Young arrived at No 1 Casemate. Young and several others climbed on top of it and dropped grenades down the air vents. They then entered the Casemate from ground level and lifted another metal hatchway in the right-hand compartment and threw more grenades down below.

Colonel Young now realised that his two troops, or what was left of them, were out on a limb, and he decided that they should be withdrawn. They were too far from any main position of the Commandos or of 6 Airborne Division to be supplied with food or ammunition, and could not possibly stay there. As the Brigadier had passed down the order for the attack, only he was able to confirm Colonel Young's view of the situation so he returned as quickly as possible to Lord Lovat 'whom I found at his Headquarters at Écarde. He listened to what I had to say and at once agreed that the detachment must be withdrawn.'[11]

Captain Brian Butler, now in command, was organising the withdrawal and sent Lieutenant Williams on a fighting patrol to the north-east. He thought it now to be more sensible to consolidate all available men in the woods to the west of the Battery pending Colonel Young's return with confirmation of the withdrawal.

'Taffy' Jones was relieved that the battle seemed to be over[12]:

> All serious fighting seemed to have finished and gathering ourselves together including the wounded for a few minutes' respite and patching up as best we could, the MO and the orderlies doing a wonderful job, giving what assistance we could to them. Some were beyond help so we could only let them down quietly on the roadside and make their last moments as comfortable as possible. A cigarette here, a cigarette there and maybe a piece or bar of chocolate, part of our 'iron rations'.

'Bill' Williams was getting his patrol together[13]:

On the order to withdraw, it meant that my patrol was alone. The rest moved on to another area. Whilst treading carefully to avoid anti-personnel mines and engaging the enemy who appeared to arrive in large numbers from different directions, a noise similar to a London tube train rattled my ears and I was pushed against a cottage wall.

Trooper Patterson was on an errand of mercy[14]:

After 4 and 5 Troops had left the Battery, four of us remained behind to try and get as many wounded as possible to safety in a ditch nearby. By this time the Battery was under heavy fire as the Germans had counter-attacked. Another hazard was getting through the mines to reach the casemates where some wounded had taken refuge. We were fired at by heavy machine-guns but I am sure they missed us on purpose as we had a wounded soldier on an old door and we all raised the hand we had free. Now this chap was a member of 9th Parachute Battalion, found in No 4 Casemate. He had his whole leg in plaster or heavy bandages and I think a stomach wound. He kept repeating 'Please don't leave me!' We said we wouldn't. The man was Private Hawkins.[15] We did get quite a few wounded to a ditch nearby when we were suddenly surrounded by German troops, one of whom shot a chap in the stomach who was being assisted, as he couldn't walk owing to a leg wound. There was no escape as we were unarmed and only three of us not wounded. The fourth helper had taken flight whilst we were pinned down in a crater. The Battery was being rained on by self-propelled guns, mortar fire and small-arms and it was impossible to make further attempts, even if we had not been surrounded. The infantry who took us prisoner appeared from a ditch on the opposite side of the road where the wounded lay. They could have come from Cabourg because it was there where they took us after overnighting in the yard of a ruined house or farm. There were about ten Commandos and Hawkins in the ditch.

When Lieutenant Williams came to, he found his captors 'smoking my cigarettes. When I asked for one I received a kick in the ribs. I was taken in handcuffs, alone, to a stable. An old German who had served in World War One gave me some stew (different from a kick in the ribs).'[16]

Cheerful 'Taffy' Jones wasn't at all pleased to be ordered to withdraw, because this cut right across the Commandos' creed[17]:

> Withdrawal! A gateway into a field. *Achtung Minen!* Only way out. Again treading warily we started to cross the minefield – another one! – but also having to contend with the self-propelled gun again catching us in the field. Casualties mounted tremendously. What a mess, men dropping right and left, this was slaughter. In front someone stepped on an S-mine but it failed to explode. What luck! One of our party I picked up, his face split down the middle, and with his arm round my shoulder we made with all haste to the other side of the field. Reassembling on a narrow roadway could not be more than a dozen of us including the walking wounded. The officer ordered us to take up a defensive circle – 'Commandos never retreat.' Certainly no one was happy about the situation and it was decided to withdraw and find our lines, much to the relief of everyone. After all, had we stayed, what would we be defending? At least if we got back we would live to fight another day.

Captain Woyevodsky, commanding 5 Troop, had been the lucky one with the S-mine. The man in front of him trod on it and the canister containing the steel balls shot past the captain's head and failed to explode. Nobody was hurt by it.

The Germans were shelling the retiring party all the time, with the range on the guns now following the Commandos. When they reached safety there were less than 75 men altogether. One section of 4 Troop returned with only eight, having lost 15 men.

The Commandos continued on their way in orderly fashion with 5 Troop leading as before. Near Sallenelles they met a party of 45 (RM) Commando and all of them moved back together although the occasional shell still came down. Throughout the action the wounded behaved magnificently. According to Lieutenant Pollard they were

> extremely patient, uncomplaining, and in the face of their peril of being completely abandoned, extremely cheerful. In particular I

## Another Attack on the Battery

would mention the attitude of L/Cpl Creswick and Tpr Smith, who set an example I shall be a long time in forgetting.[18]

'Taffy' Jones has summed up the action[19]:

> Unfortunately for our part, information re the Battery was not forthcoming; we had no idea what was involved. I believe that this operation was rushed through. The only news at the time we received was the Paras had failed to silence the guns because somehow or someone had lost the demolition charges. We also had no explosive equipment to put the guns out of action.

Lieutenant-Colonel Peter Young is more bitter, for although only one-third of his Commando was involved at Merville[20],

> it was difficult, if not impossible, to dispel the idea that the whole operation had been useless and doomed to failure from the start. Hurried into the fight with only the sketchiest of briefing, 5 Troop had done remarkably well in storming through the minefield, only to lose a loved and trusted leader in the moment of victory . . . Not since Dieppe had the Commando met with such misfortune.

# 7
# Steiner

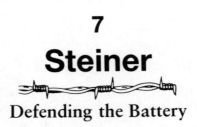

### Defending the Battery

Second Lieutenant Raimund Steiner, in his bunker-OP on the beach at Franceville, shook himself out of sound sleep with difficulty and answered the telephone. It was Buskotte.

'*Herr Leutnant!* A glider has landed in the position and we are engaged in combat. The howitzers are outside the casemates.'

'Bring the guns back inside the casemates and shut the steel doors,' replied Steiner. 'And report back to me as soon as you can.'

It was 00.26 in the morning of 6 June 1944. Steiner stood there shivering slightly in his pyjamas (strictly forbidden, he was meant to sleep fully dressed) for outside it was raining, with a strong wind. Then he went over to Rix's bunker, woke them up with the news and put through a call to Major-General Wilhelm Richter.

Richter was asleep at his well-defended and bunkered HQ in a quarry on the northern side of Caen, a little way beyond the University. With his division spread thinly along a 34km front, two regiments up and one in reserve, his task was to deny Caen to the enemy. He was dissatisfied with the existing conditions, so far as his division was concerned, but at least grateful to Rommel for having reduced the front from a former 50km in von Runstedt's time of direct authority.

When on 6 June at about 00.30 the telephone rang and woke him up, he was not in the best of moods for a start; that it was one of those confounded mountaineers at the other end made matters worse.

## Defending the Battery

'Herr General,' began Steiner, 'an enemy glider has landed inside the perimeter of the Merville Battery and my troops are under attack. I believe that the Invasion has begun.'

'There is complete silence all over Normandy', snapped Richter, 'and one crashed aircraft doesn't make an invasion. Don't get so excited and don't bother me with trivialities.' He slammed down the receiver.

Distaste for Steiner's arm of the service remained in General Richter's attitude and, filled with annoyance and further dislike for the young officer, he went back to sleep on that momentous early morning, satisfied – for once – of his own appreciation of the situation.

Other German general officers in Normandy were still celebrating General Erich Marcks's birthday in Rennes, HQ of 84 Corps. The party had been a surprise for Marcks and was laid on to follow 'war games' that evening to which many senior officers had been called. The subject: Repelling an Allied Invasion. Nobody was disposed, however, to put aside his glass of champagne and go over it all again. It had been well covered for one evening.

Consequently, when Steiner's message to General Richter – and other telephone messages in the Orne area – had been monitored and transmitted to all command headquarters in Normandy, they were treated with scepticism: alarmist and, like all those in the past, grossly exaggerated.

Several staff officers at 716 and 711 Divisional HQs being on the Channel coast, comparatively speaking, were far more concerned than this to try and discover the truth. The regimental adjutant of 716 Division, Lieutenant Karl Heyde, took the reports far more seriously and put the division on full alert. So did his opposite number in 711 Division. Company HQs of 736 Infantry in 716 Division on the east side of the Orne had reported parachute landings and also straw puppets which had been dropped. Furthermore there had been fighting in Bénouville round the Bridge across the Canal, but nothing had been heard from there recently.

Steiner was anxious to hear from Buskotte what was happening, so, returning to his bunker and getting properly dressed, he waited for a report. When it came, the news was grave. An enemy glider had crashed inside the perimeter wire not far from No 4 Casemate, and when a few sentries ran towards it, the occupants emerged and mowed them down. These intruders were not in recognisable British uniform, wore a different type of helmet, had black faces and fought in a 'dirty' manner with long knives as well as with small-arms. German reinforcements arrived and engaged in hand-to-hand fighting with these desperate men and there were heavy casualties. Eventually all the intruders were killed.[1]

The glider, which had caught fire, contained a jeep, some pneumatic drills and flame-throwing equipment; these were taken to be the means for a shock-troop team to force its way inside a casemate, cause destruction, and then make off in the jeep. All this equipment, as well as all evidence of the soldiers' identity, was lost in the glider fire, made fiercer when the liquid-fuel tanks exploded.

This became known to Steiner and Buskotte as the 'first attack'.

Steiner and Rix went outside the bunkers on to the beach at Franceville when they heard the sound of aircraft engines. The time was then shortly before 00.50 and the so-called '1000 Lancaster Raid'[2] on Merville had missed the target and sent bombs down mainly to the south-west of the Battery. Some fell elsewhere, even on Franceville. Nevertheless Steiner reports[3]:

> Bomber formations were flying overhead in unending numbers. They flew so low that one could see the exhausts flaming and glowing. They bombed mainly to the west of the Orne and only once to the east. Parachutists then landed to the south of Franceville and gliders came. They were vast. I did not understand how such things could fly! The bombers and other aircraft came in tight formations and made a great impression on me. The vibration in the air caused the sand in the dunes to crumble. Lieutenant Rix came over to my bunker with two soldiers. We all had rifles and fired at the gliders as they came over. We hit one of them. It swung away, dived to the south and crashed to the east of the Battery.
>
> By now, with such a large number of aircraft overhead,

## Defending the Battery

Buskotte was very apprehensive about the general situation. He went outside to gather as many wounded men as he could find, helping them along the communication trenches to the Command Bunker and then shutting the door. All crews in the casemates were standing by, but when there seemed to be no further cause for alarm, they opened the steel doors again – for better ventilation. The howitzers remained inside.

Steiner asked Buskotte for a Medical Officer to attend the wounded, and Buskotte found one at the infantry HQ at Descanneville. He arrived in the Battery position soon afterwards. The recent bombing, although fierce and heavy, had not touched the Battery, whose inmates began to wonder what next would happen on this early morning, when the enemy were resorting to so many new and unaccustomed tactics.

Steiner decided to visit the Battery and find out for himself what had happened in the 'first attack'. So with a small escort provided by Rix, he made his way up the Avenue de Paris in Franceville toward Merville village. He reached the crossroads at the edge of Franceville, it was still dark, and fighting was going on all round[4]:

> The situation was chaotic: nobody knew who was friend or foe. Houses and trees were on fire and the sky was red. Among this infernal din rang out the sound of small-arms, especially at the crossroads. I followed my instinct and went towards the east, intending to approach my Battery from this direction. When I had got quite close, I saw near the entrance, a little way behind Merville Church, a large German AA gun mounted on a half-tracked vehicle. The SP [self-propelled] gun was firing into the Battery. Evidently its crew were anxious to seek refuge inside the perimeter. I found I could get no further, although I was in sight of my Battery, because of the firing that was going on there.

This was 9th Battalion The Parachute Regiment's assault at 04.30, referred to by Steiner and Buskotte as the 'second attack'.

'Erika', the 20mm AA gun in the Battery position (equally deadly in a horizontal role against attacking troops on the ground) had not fired at Gordon Brown's glider – the first of the two to swoop low over the casemates, looking in vain for light from the British mortars. Either she had jammed again, or else the crew were unprepared. But they fired at the second glider (Lieutenant Hugh Pond) and hit it in the tail with their third burst. Then the crew of the gun were overwhelmed when the attack went in.

Steiner's first thought was, if possible, to bring down fire on the Battery position. He had lost his only wireless operator already, one of the casualties on the approach to the Battery through Franceville. Now the only course was to return as quickly as possible to the OP, running the gauntlet of Franceville again.

There was another, closer witness to the attack: Sergeant-Major Peter Timpf, the FOO with 736 Regiment, No 3 Company, accompanied a platoon on a patrol. Soon after 04.00 hrs, he got the men together and, led by an infantry lieutenant called Valdorf, prepared to move towards Varaville. He remembers[5]:

> On June 6 1944, before your attack, HQ ordered me (as an advanced ground observer) and two radio operators, to join up with our infantry at Merville. While assembling in the village of Merville, still in sight of our casemates, we had to duck because two gliders (waiting for your signal to land) were flying so low.
>
> The infantry's orders (we were a party of 36) were to clear the area behind our guns SE of them of parachutists in order to enable the gunners to fire the cannons and not have to defend themselves against Commandos at their rear. (No one knew then that it would take a force much larger than ours.) When we left the Battery there was one MG on the 'Tobruk Stand' and one 20mm AA cannon in the centre of the position. . . .
>
> Crossing the first hayfield east of the road behind our gun positions, under machine-gun fire, I lost one of my radio men and his equipment which prevented me from requesting artillery support by radio. (I later found out that support would not have been forthcoming anyway.) Under heavy losses, we made our way to Varaville[6]. Our total strength by now was about eight or nine men with three prisoners to guard. Our first one we cut down from an apple tree and had to assign one soldier to walk with him as he had

damaged his leg in the tree. The second was a sniper and we also took another soldier who was with him. Then we ran into two stretcher-bearers but told them to go on and not tell anyone they had seen us, because we did not have the manpower to look after any more. At Varaville, one parachutist was wounded by a British hand-grenade. We found we were surrounded, our lieutenant was wounded and we decided to surrender. We helped carry the wounded parachutist on a stretcher, under guard, to what seemed to be a field hospital. We shook hands and he gave me the badge from his beret which I got rid of, I'm sorry to say, after being questioned about its being in my possession.

Some of the German pioneer bomb-disposal unit, spending their third night in the Battery, were sleeping in No 1 Casemate. It was they who ran out calling 'Russki!' and surrendered immediately (unaware – as we all were at the time – that all Russians in British and American hands were to be handed over to the Red Army and returned to the USSR – if they lived that long.) 'Russki' most of them were, and of an entirely different calibre from the members of 716 and 736 who fought extremely bravely.

Many of the gunners took shelter in the underground chambers of No 1 and No 3 Casemates, or in the many emplacements and weapon pits outside – those which had not been smothered by the bombardments. After the first wave of attackers inside No 1 Casemate, and the attempted blowing-up of the howitzer there by Major Parry's party, a second group of about 15 men from 9th Battalion went in, on the supposition that there was no further opposition. Who sent them in, and why, is not known[7]. Even though it must have been evident to the Germans that the British had not yet withdrawn from the position, they pounced on the 15 men, killed three and captured the others.

The crew of No 4 Gun fared the worst. Their casemate was not entirely finished and had suffered from the bombardments far more than the others because of its hasty, 'utility' construction. All the German gunners inside it were killed partly because they had no side compartments nor any form of protection from a determined assault, in this case a party led by Colour Sergeant Harold Long[8].

A British private soldier called Hawkins from 12 Platoon of 'C' Company was left behind when the Battalion withdrew. He spent the remainder of 6 June inside No 4 Casemate, seriously wounded but undisturbed[9].

Otherwise, the defenders still exercised control of the first three casemates; the Command Bunker and Quartermaster's Bunker had been ignored by 9th Battalion.

During this mêlée, Steiner had reached his OP on the beach in spite of intensified fighting going on round the crossroads at Franceville. He tried to telephone 716 Divisional HQ but unsuccessfully, as the underground cable had not been strong enough to resist the bombardments. The other line eastwards to 711 Division was still open, and the artillery on that side, so far uninvolved, were only too glad to be of assistance. Steiner gave them the co-ordinates of the Battery and asked them to prepare to shoot on his next order. He then got through to Buskotte – that line was still open too – and asked whether it was safe to bring down fire yet. Buskotte told him briefly about the 'second attack', but was not yet in a position to report on the condition of the guns, presumably the reason for the parachutists' attack.

'We've suffered many losses in men,' Buskotte told him, 'but have taken some prisoners. There are many dead of both sides and their bodies are lying about outside. The enemy are no longer engaging us, but have not yet left the position. Now's the time to bring down defensive fire on them.'[10]

Steiner gave his order and immediately shells fell from many artillery batteries to the east of Merville. It was an indirect shoot, without the benefit of visual observation, done off the map.

Then the firing stopped, and once more there was silence at Merville.

Over to the West, the din continued.

It was now light, and shortly before 05.05 hrs.

Buskotte took another look round through his periscope

and saw the different landscape. He resumed contact with Nos 1, 2 and 3 Casemates, telling the crews to remain inside with doors shut because he did not want any more casualties and was still not certain whether the British had really gone away.

Even so, he went outside himself, found several wounded men including the Pioneer Sergeant who had a large piece of shrapnel in his stomach. A communication trench to the Command Bunker was still practicable, and it was along this that Buskotte went to and fro.

He now had six or eight wounded men inside the Command Bunker as well as six fit men. He asked the casemates for reports.

'What is the condition of your howitzer? No 1?'

'All correct. Attempts have been made to damage it, but they've failed.'

'No 2?'

'No 3?'

All three were in full firing order.

'Why did they come here then?' asked Buskotte in amazement. 'The howitzers are undamaged, so are the sights. If they had broken the sights or taken them away, the guns would have been useless! What did they come for?'[11]

Steiner was greatly relieved at the news, and was of the opinion that the mysterious SP gun by the church had hastened the parachutists' departure[12]. But where it came from and where it went was never discovered. Steiner did not see it again.

He regarded the 'first attack' as particularly deadly for he had lost men by those glider-borne attackers who had achieved complete surprise and caught the defenders on the hop. While the next (or 'second') attack by 9th Battalion was put in by a much larger force, and no less determined, Steiner's men were not to be caught napping a second time. Then the counter-battery fire, according to Steiner[13], 'was devastating and decimated the Paras who had already subdued and occupied the Battery'.[14]

Buskotte was anxious to get rid of his prisoners (by passing them back to Cabourg and 711 Division) as soon as possible in case of further attacks. Before he could do so, however, the British Naval barrage began from capital ships with their 15-in. and 16-in. guns 'softening up' the shore-line from Arromanches to Riva Bella. The noise was immense, even at Franceville and Merville, five miles to the East and not in line with the firing. Then came the three waves of bombers to pound the coastal defences (and inland as the wounded of 9th Battalion experienced)[15].

Steiner and Rix were relatively safe inside their bunkers especially as targets were on the western side of the Orne. Nevertheless they received some recognition from the RAF, as the 'overs' landed in and around the Battery.

There was now no doubt about it. This was the long-awaited Invasion by the Allies, and the ferocity of the attacks by land, sea and air, together with the sheer weight of the triple assault was far greater than the Germans had anticipated.

When the sun came up on 6 June, Steiner's eyes met an astonishing sight. He looked across towards Ouistreham and beyond to Riva Bella, surrounding which was a veritable armada. Ships of all kinds and sizes stretched far into the mists of mid-Channel. The sheer magnitude of their presence, with superstructures glistening and glinting in the sunlight, made the huge assembly seem solid, not floating, and earned it the name of *die goldene Stadt* – 'Golden City'. From the distance away of Steiner's viewpoint it all looked beautiful, even enchanted!

Steiner was unable to reach his divisional commander by telephone or by runner – in some ways a relief – but the fact that the Battery was now cut off from Regiment and Division caused a certain unease among all ranks of 1/1716. The German boundary between Divisions (also between Corps and Armies) had run along the Dives River. Merville was to the west of the Dives but now this was no longer a boundary. The Allies and Nature had chosen to make the Orne Canal and River a new dividing-line with the Bridgehead to the west, and 6 Airborne (with 1 Commando Brigade) stood alone on

Merville's side of the Caen Canal. Steiner realised that he needed support – and quickly. A telephone line was open from Rix's Strongpoint to 711 Infantry Division and, probably during the afternoon of D-Day, Steiner was able to speak to the commander, Major-General Josef Reichert. He was far more amenable and sympathetic than Richter had been and agreed at once to 'adopt' Steiner's Battery and the attached troops from 736 Infantry Regiment. This meant that General Reichert would arrange for reinforcements and supplies of all kinds to be sent to Merville on demand. He did make the proviso that, in the event of the Allied attack being repulsed, or its being a feint landing, they would then revert to the *status quo ante*. General Reichert knew Steiner's artillery tasks along the Orne, and expected him to put down fire there in conjunction with any 711 Divisional shoot.

Steiner was comforted by this administrative arrangement and it no longer mattered that he was unable to communicate with his true Division. He decided to order Buskotte to engage targets as on the Range Table (see p. 150) but the canny Warrant Officer seemed to have some sixth sense. In his post-war book *We Defended Normandy*, General Speidel records[16]:

> The German 716th and 352nd Divisions held out bravely in their lineal defences and battle stations under a hail of fire from sea and air and then from land. The intensity of it was such that German troops had never known the like. An umbrella of heavy artillery fire from the Allied armada cut off the battle area from the rest of France. The Allied air force flew some 25,000 sorties during D-Day. Without having actually been in it, it was impossible to estimate the destructive effect on morale of this terrific combined bombardment.

Buskotte's slow reaction to Steiner's order was eventually carried out with Nos 1 & 2 guns. The result was instantaneous. A backlash of fire was returned in overwhelming force by Allied ships and aircraft on the Battery position.

When he had recovered, momentarily, from this, Buskotte remarked: 'It's all very well for the Herr Leutnant to give

| GZ. 3033 | LG | TLRG | ERHG | LIB | BWE. | |
|---|---|---|---|---|---|---|
| BREMEN | 3. | 2878 | 218⁻ | 300 | 0 | 0 |
| CAUB | 3. | 3256 | 246⁻ | 300 | 1¼ | 0 |
| DÜSSELDF. | 5. | 3241 | 190⁻ | 298 | 0 | +7 |
| EMS | 5. | 3243 | 292⁻ | 296 | 0 | +6 |
| ENGERS | 5. | 3343 | 362⁻ | 296 | 0 | +7 |

GZ = GRUNDZIEL: Ground Target applying to this gun 3033
BREMEN – CAUB – DÜSSELDORF – EMS – ENGERS:
        Codenames for targets already ranged
        accurately. Exact targets given at
        Appendix 5, p. 216–17
LG    = LADUNG       : Charge
TLRG  = TEILRING     : Reading on the sight
ERHG  = ERHÖHUNG     : Elevation
LIB   = LIBELLE      : Relative altitude of target
BWE   = BESONDERE
        WITTERUNGSEINFLÜSSE: Changes in direction and
                strength of wind (in pencil)

Fig. 7 Translation and amplification of information on the Range Card taken from No 1 Casemate, Merville Battery. There was one of these boards in each casemate, and it applied only, in detail, to the gun it accompanied

orders from down there, because it's *here* where we shall always catch it!'[17]

A British ship came along, fairly close to the shore off Franceville, loosing off its rocket projectiles known as 'Stalin's Organ' after the Russians' use of them on the Eastern Front. The defenders in the Battery continued to be pinned down

## Defending the Battery

again for several minutes. Buskotte shook his head sadly and wondered whether it was going to be worth while firing again.

Steiner, on the other hand, was fascinated. After all, he had been given *carte blanche* to fire on 'opportunity targets' along with his main fire orders, and there were plenty of opportunities likely if ships came as close to shore again. The 'Golden City', on the other hand, was really too obscure a target to engage with any certainty of success. Whatever was going on round the corner at Riva Bella – presumably beach landings – were completely out of sight from his OP at sea-level, and he lacked the communication to be given observed corrections, were he to fire there. What the Allies called 'Sword' Beach was within the range of Steiner's howitzers, but he fired only on Ouistreham, on the Orne estuary and along the Canal. Nor did he engage 'Pegasus' Bridge either on D-Day, or on D+1. Conservation of ammunition was to be an important consideration.

'*Der Himmel war schwarz von Flugzeugen!*' ('The sky was black with aircraft!') was the constant memory of those who fought for the Wehrmacht in Normandy. Buskotte said 'For every round we fired, we got anything between twenty and a hundred back.'

Steiner had been so impressed by Buskotte's 'personal heroic actions' after both attacks, in bringing back wounded to safety single-handed, that he suggested an award, and General Reichert agreed. Steiner also put in a long list of requirements: men, weapons, ammunition to replace those lost, as well as rations. After a few days they came across the beach from Cabourg, because the whole north coast of France and Belgium, as far as Germany, was open to the Wehrmacht, though Allied bombing had seriously disrupted railways and main roads.

711 Division Supplies sent a Czech 75mm howitzer and ammunition. Like any present which arrives unexpectedly and which is not wanted, this howitzer immediately came into the category of 'surplus to requirement' and suffered mistrust from the start. (It was tried out once, later on, ranged in a

preliminary shoot to support a German attack, but all the rounds fell short and killed some of the German troops. Nobody could tell whether it was the gun, its sights or its ammunition which was at fault, but Steiner and Buskotte agreed never to use it again.)

On the morning of 7 June, round about midday, Steiner received orders for his Battery to take part in a combined shoot by 711 Divisional Artillery and other guns further east. The larger calibre weapons behind Merville were able to shell much further than the 10cm howitzers, which again engaged their normal tasks while others fired 'on Riva Bella and west along the coast'.[18]

That afternoon, Buskotte was in his Command Bunker with several wounded men and his usual staff. The Doctor had been killed[19], and the Pioneer Sergeant had died from his stomach wound. From time to time, Buskotte spoke to Steiner at the OP, by telephone, and heard about the continual firing going on round Franceville. Buskotte also kept watch through his periscope, surveying the Battery position as best he could, with an arc of vision even more reduced by earth turbulence since the last counter-battery fire.

During one of these inspections, Buskotte suddenly gave a cry and stepped back with one arm across his face as though he was about to be struck. Quite close to him he had seen a startling new image in the periscope: many British soldiers, some of them smoking and all appearing to be well equipped and armed. Then, as he moved the periscope slowly round, he seemed to find himself 'face to face' with a British Commando officer, advancing towards him with a .45 pistol. He *fired* the pistol. The image in the periscope vanished.[20]

Buskotte was shaken, and telephoned Steiner:

'*Herr Leutnant!* We are under attack again! I am putting our drill into force, then please bring down fire on the position when you hear from me again.'

Buskotte warned the sergeants in No 1 and No 3 Casemates to bring their howitzers outside as soon as the Commandos began to retire. This was a well-rehearsed drill, and the NCOs knew exactly what to do.

## Defending the Battery

Buskotte's men in the slit trenches and in the casemates fought hard against this new and very determined enemy, but the Germans had the advantage of daylight and of warning. Even so, they lost a lot of men. Those in No 1 and No 3 Casemates who had again gone into the underground chambers were unhurt, despite the grenades which had been thrown down on them. There was plenty of cover, but the noise was deafening.

When the Commandos, suffering severe losses, began to withdraw, the crews of Nos 1 and 3 emerged, climbed the ladders, manhandled the howitzers into position and prepared to fire. The NCO in charge of each ordered the fuse on the nose-caps of shells to be set at 50m detonation, and then began to fire rapid, double ignition with both howitzers. The result was as if a pair of SP guns was firing at the retiring Commandos.

Steiner had meanwhile alerted Rix, who sent a patrol to Buskotte's help. They captured a patrol commanded by a lieutenant. Having achieved a *coup de grâce* with his two howitzers, Buskotte got them back safely into the casemates and then asked for the counter-battery fire. It came down promptly, speeding the Commandos on their way.[21]

This was the last land-based attack on the Merville Battery, though the Royal Navy and the RAF continued to prevent Steiner from feeling altogether deprived of interest.

By 8 June, 716 Infantry Division was no longer a fighting force. General Richter admitted infantry losses of 80 per cent from his four German and two Russo-Polish battalions; from his artillery only two batteries with three guns each were left on the west side of the Orne, but the Merville Battery on the eastern side was still operative though out of Richter's control. The total strength of the combined batteries in the division was only eight officers and 80 other ranks[22]. West of the Orne they were facing 'a superior opponent and his tanks. Air superiority had a devastating effect.'[23]

Nevertheless, and true to his reputation, stubborn Wilhelm Richter developed what became known as his *Schnappsidee* having convinced himself that he was still able to defend Caen with what remained of his division. He should have known that the only possible defence against the Invasion army were the Panzers, and he had none. 21 Panzer Division, the only one near Caen, was not under his command. Adjutant Karl Heyde fully realised the position when he referred to 'the débris of 716'.[24]

All this began to have a serious effect on the morale of the less experienced German troops, and the Allies sometimes sought to take advantage of those who were having second thoughts about continuing the struggle. German soldiers saw pieces of cloth or boards held up by their opponents, on which were written such slogans as 'Hallo, surrender!' in German. Or else 'We have landed with twenty division', or 'Fritz, Karl, Heinrich – come here!'[25]

The detachment of 736 Infantry at Gonneville (a platoon of which had been severely mauled by Lieutenant Hugh Pond and the occupants of his glider) was approached by the French mayor with inducements to surrender to the British. After some deliberation and forceful argument, they did so and were handed over. They were then marched through 6 Airborne Division's lines to the coast, and into the water up to their necks before being unceremoniously hauled on board landing ships. They were taken to England, thence – usually – Scotland and Canada.[26]

The absence of these troops left a hole in Steiner's perimeter defences, the responsibility of Lieutenant Rix, who was furious about his defectors.

Prisoners were being sent in the opposite direction too. All those captured in the Battery, parachutists and Commandos, were thoroughly searched before being sent away. The silk maps, escape kits and general quality of British equipment were all greatly admired by the Germans. In one parachutist's pocket, Buskotte found a plan of the Battery, accurately drawn. But what horrified Steiner, more than this, was a list of the senior personnel of the Battery, their names and the *new dispositions* that Steiner had made on the previous Saturday.[27]

711 Divisional Provost had sent a vehicle to Merville for the

## Defending the Battery

prisoners in the Battery. It was in the charge of a loud-mouthed German NCO.

'There are twenty-two men[28],' Buskotte told him, 'and I herewith transfer them to your safe conduct.'

"Safe conduct?"' sneered the sergeant. 'You don't suppose there'll be as many as that when I get to the other end.'

Buskotte brought him up sharply, demanded his name and number and said: 'And if I do not hear that all your prisoners are completely unharmed on arrival in Cabourg, you will take the consequences – personally. Do you understand me?'

An hour later, a call came through from Cabourg to Rix's bunker to say that twenty-two British prisoners had been safely delivered.

There was anxiety about the bodies – German and British alike – that had disappeared. After bombardments and shelling, the earth inside the Battery had been churned up so many times, burying what had been on top, that relatively few of all those who had died can have been recovered. There were limbs ... and other things.

After 9th Battalion's attack, Buskotte was horrified to see a severed head outside No 2 Casemate. Steiner also saw it and shuddered at the sight. It seemed to have belonged to a negro. The right side of the face was missing from ear to half the chin. The dark, curly hair, black complexion, wide nose and thick lips left them in no doubt as to the man's race.[29] Hitler's Aryan plans did not admit of any contact with the coloured races, and now to find part of one in their own Battery position gave a feeling of fantastic horror, even of nausea. They buried it quickly with the other remains they had found, as well as fifteen almost whole bodies, in a communal grave behind the place where the officers' mess had stood. One of the German soldiers carved a single, simple wooden cross to go over the grave.[30]

When identity discs were found on the bodies of British soldiers, they were removed and sent back to Cabourg for onward transmission, in the accepted international manner, to the Red Cross.

By now Steiner had almost had enough of risking his life twice daily in crossing the road at Franceville and being consistently shot at. But until he received orders to the contrary, he was obliged to keep going up and down the roads that he had grown to know and to fear so much. Commandos had occupied the sector Amfréville – Hauger – Sallenelles, and were facing him across a couple of kilometres of orchards and fields.

On one of his forays, Steiner was held up by what appeared to be a set-piece attack, and retired into strongpoint No 3, a blockhouse, in order to avoid a six-pounder gun that was firing in his direction. There were a number of rather shaken German soldiers there – and a piano. So Steiner sat down and played 'a Schubert song, not very well, and several other short pieces which calmed us all'.[31]

346 German Infantry Division were stationed in the Le Havre area, and up to now had not been involved in any fighting. Now they were ordered to send a battle group to clear 6 Airborne Division from the Bavent Ridge, then sweep round north-west and make contact with Merville. This group, named after its commander, Colonel Hartmann, had collected themselves together on the evening of 6 June. They were composed of two 'Bicycle Mobile Battalions', a light artillery section and some engineers. They were part of 15th Army whose commander, General Hans von Salmuth, believed that 6 Airborne Division was about to attack his western flank. General Gale's aggressive defensive measures were proving their worth, for his role was that of a shield to the Allied eastern flank.

Battle-Group Hartmann was launched in a counter-attack role on 7 June[32]; it arrived in the Varaville area during that afternoon; it was beaten back decisively by elements of 3 Parachute Brigade; it totally failed to accomplish even part of its mission.

From this date, 7 June, it was extremely unwise for any German to attempt to reach Merville from Caen by the direct route (see Fig. 6 p. 128). Otherwise it would entail travelling

## Defending the Battery

from Caen and eastwards, bypassing Troarn (because the bridge across the River Dives was blown) to Dozulé, and then up to Cabourg and 'round the top'.

One man, however, decided that he was going to risk it. Lieutenant-Colonel Helmuth Knupe, CO of 716 Artillery Regiment (who had now not got very much to command) left Caen on 7 June in a *Kübelwagen* (Volkswagen's amphibious jeep). He intended to make a reconnaissance of the Merville area. Knupe, it will be remembered, was a dashing, thrusting personality, who had succeeded Colonel Andersen in command of the Regiment.

Knupe and his driver did not return.

Several days later, his corpse, and that of the driver, were found in a hedge near Troarn with all identification papers and badges of rank and insignia removed from the uniforms. There was a good deal of indignation expressed over this by the German patrol which found them.

Others were either more careful or more fortunate.

Adjutant Karl Heyde, now promoted to Captain, visited Merville on 16 June with a staff officer, Lieutenant Hans Malsch, who had been the Battery Officer there between December 1943 and March 1944. Malsch recalls[33]:

> The Merville Battery, the destiny of which I followed right from the first minute of the Invasion, was occupied by airborne forces (gliders) during the first night. But the garrison was withdrawn into the bunkers and overcame the opponent with artillery support from . . . other batteries . . . when he had penetrated the positions. Enemy losses were high. . . . The Merville Battery remained in German hands until the remnant of 716 Division was transferred from the Caen sector. . . . Because of the valour on D-Day, several members of the Battery were awarded Iron Crosses according to my notes of 16 June. The Battery was fully operational, fully equipped and fully manned. It also participated in the defensive firing in the Quistreham[34] sector during the first days of the Invasion.

Heyde was acting Divisional Commander pending the return of Lt-Colonel Andersen at the end of June and now recovered.

Heyde remembers the atmosphere at Merville on that day[35]:

> I decorated a Warrant Officer of the 1/1716. All hell was let loose in the air while I drove from Caen to Merville. Inside the Battery perimeter everything was quiet as in a fairy tale. I was able to line up the men and make a short speech. During the whole ceremony it was almost unrealistically quiet. Only in the distance could the noise of shooting and of bombardment be heard. The man I decorated was the acting Battery Officer[36]. I was wearing my steel helmet for a change. Normally I didn't do so because it was heavy and uncomfortable.

Heyde was under the impression that Schimpf was in command at Merville, and expected to find him there – after all that is what it said on the establishment sheets. When Heyde and Malsch were greeted by Steiner, and he told them that Schimpf had gone on compassionate leave to Halle on about 20 May, Heyde exploded with rage: '*Schlamlose Lump!*' (Shameless Lout) he declared. 'He would do a thing like that, the irresponsible, selfish, rotten bastard!'[37]

Heyde made more awards at Steiner's OP, this time the WO concerned was Hans Kath.

There was a comic Pole at the OP called Sarochinsky. He and Artur Stange, a Berliner, used their regional accents and turns of phrase to advantage when making jibes at those in authority. They were able to do this and get away with it more often than not, when the average soldier would not dare to try. Sarochinsky ran into Rix's bunker shouting out: 'Quick, give me a bucket, I want to puke. Kath is getting an Iron Cross!'[38] He was not reprimanded.

Malsch's diary has further points of interest[39]:

> Heyde and I were at Merville today to award decorations to men of the 1st Battery. We also went to the strongpoint on the Orne Estuary where the nearest ship of the landing fleet was only 2km away. It was a living, floating island, ships large and small rocked gently at anchor in the Quistreham surf; masts, rigging and funnels shone in the sun. From there as far as the steep cliffs at Luc-sur-Mer was an unending glittering and shining. Small, flat-

bottomed boats went busily to and fro between shore and fleet. Destroyers and cruisers were all round, sending their massive broadsides over us from time to time. It was truly majestic! In the Battery position it was like being on the Moon: crater after crater. Not a speck of earth remained which had not been rooted up by the bombs or shells.

Tired, stretched, dirty – but proud, the soldiers stood by the embrasures and received their well-deserved decorations from Heyde in their button-holes or pinned on their breasts.

On the way back to Caen we called in at Troarn to look in the cemetery for Knupe's grave.[40]

Even before the Invasion had begun, communication between units of 716 was minimal on account of the lack of fuel for transport. In the case of Merville this was accentuated. So any visitor who had the time to gossip, brought welcome news of what was going on elsewhere in the Regiment. Now, with the arrival of Heyde and Malsch, Steiner heard fuller accounts of a strange story which had only been hinted at on the telephone.

Shortly before 6 June, a Lieutenant Steen had arrived on the shore at Franceville and had asked Rix to give him accommodation. Steiner had met him once or twice and found him pleasant, though had not taken a great deal of notice of the man. On 6 June, Steen disappeared in a hurry, leaving behind him a number of personal possessions that were never reclaimed. Mysteriously, too, Steen had been 'promoted'. Steiner continues[41]:

Captain Steen was really crippled. His left hand was partly paralysed and he could not stretch the fingers of that hand. He had been telling fantastic stories about the first hours of the Invasion. Captain Steen telephoned me from Cabourg a few days later, told me that the 1/1716 had been handed over to him to command and that I was to take his orders. He began to issue instructions but I refused to accept them, demanding properly signed orders, not telephone messages. . . . Perhaps this call was just an alibi to make his behaviour in his refuge worthier of credit. . . . He had been telling unbelievable stories about his part in the Invasion and that he had been awarded a medal. Buskotte encouraged me to stand firm, especially as Steen was not the only officer to report great heroic deeds east of the Orne in peaceful territory. Medals were awarded for 'fights' that consisted in firing on our Battery from a great distance and having no direct contact with the enemy!

An enemy freighter was being unloaded in the improvised naval base outside Quistreham. I ordered my howitzers to fire a salvo at 50 metres intervals, i.e. No 1 gun range 7600; No 2 gun 7650; and so on. The second shot at 7640 metres scored a direct hit ... the ship immediately caught fire and went on burning for several days. It was such a spectacular event because it must have been loaded with tracer ammunition. Cascades of tracer exploded into the air, and this firework display could be seen far inland, and out along the coast to Houlgate and even Deauville. I received telephone calls from commanders and units in those areas.

I considered my OP to be the Wehrmacht's closest one to the enemy. Neither the Luftwaffe nor the German Navy had the chance to approach as close. Consequently I was given some very important tasks. I ... sent back many reports on the enemy's activities for the Wehrmacht, the Luftwaffe and the Navy, also weather reports. I got the job of counting Allied shipping and reporting their size and shapes. I had always to report on weather conditions, like % cloud and so on. Being a mountain soldier, this was all new to me.

News of Steiner's 'firework display' had reached Berlin, and on about 20 June two war correspondents visited the Battery. One of them was from the magazine *Das Reich*, a translation of whose subsequent article is in Appendix 6.[42] The reporters did not wish to get too close to the coast nor put themselves in any danger; but when they realised the position of Merville *vis-à-vis* the Commandos' and 6 Airborne Division's commanding positions, they said: 'We cannot report this – nobody would believe it!'[43]

The main reason for the reporters' visit was to get an account for newspapers and radio by way of a demonstration from Steiner of how he had sunk the ammunition freighter. Steiner was not too happy about this[44]:

They didn't dare venture to my OP from where they could have watched the target area, the impressive British warships and supply vessels and all the British front lines from very close, with a telescope. After talking to Buskotte we finally agreed, though reluctantly, to play this charade. I repeated my orders and observations, and Buskotte conveyed them to the gun crews. We actually fired a few shots out to sea. I 'reported' the hits and the gunners shouted 'Hurrah!' Then they had to take cover very quickly because the British promptly answered our 'attack'. But we did not play our parts with confidence and were ashamed of what we had done.

Later we were able to hear it in a 'Western Front Report' on German radio, though with considerable embarrassment at such a fraudulent event. Later I was often asked by war reporters – and so was Buskotte – for all kinds of information. We did not like doing this, and greatly exaggerated reports of what we said were broadcast all the same.

Even though we were being sent supplies of all kinds from across the beach it was very difficult and we were only just able to survive. One day a four-engined Allied supply aircraft was shot down and landed on the beach in front of my bunker about 1½ km away. The soldiers or airmen in it ran off in the direction of the Orne and we did nothing about it at first. Shortly afterwards the British fired on the aircraft and it burst into flames. But the tide came in and put out the fire. This proved a godsend. We had a marvellous feast! We hadn't eaten so well for years – not since the war began. There were preserved foods, ham and cake – a bit singed by the fire, but wonderful to us.

One day a naval car arrived at my bunker with a *Kaleu* (a Captain-Lieutenant), a big, dark and very friendly Viennese naval officer. He told me to help him by giving shelter to some German frogmen. They had 500-kg bombs or torpedoes, armed them, and then swam out towards the 'Golden City', aimed them, and swam away. We had to give them light signals from a certain direction; but when the British saw the frogmen they fired shots and explosive charges in the sea round them. I think two or three frogmen got back safely to the beach, and we heard louder explosions as if they had succeeded in hitting enemy ships.

One day a General Pelz came to my bunker. At twenty-seven he was the youngest Luftwaffe general. I didn't know who he was at first and was, as usual, taken by surprise. I made my report and carried on talking to him. (Either Kath or Rauch afterwards upbraided me for being so forthcoming without checking properly on his identity – he might have been a spy!) He stayed with us until the evening, because one could move safely from my bunker only after dark.

Whenever the British saw or heard anything, they fired at us. It was not so dangerous at night, although they had a searchlight at Quistreham coupled to a quick-firing gun with high velocity that I had not seen used in that way before. They swept our coastline with the searchlight, and when it found a target: *boum*! They hit my 'Tobruk Stand' at least two dozen times, but provided one kept one's head down inside, there was virtually no danger. I warned General Pelz about the gun and searchlight combination, and told him that he would have to duck for cover immediately the light came on.

A bit later, we were outside the bunker and the light did come on. We jumped for cover as the gun fired, and the general thanked me profusely, saying that I had practically saved his life. He said he had not taken my story at all seriously. General Pelz told me that the British ships' intelligence and warning systems were so good that he dared not take his aircraft to within 100km of them. So I asked what the Luftwaffe could do. He replied that in the next day or two he would be flying low over my bunker. Sure enough, a couple of days after he had gone, a twin-engined Heinkel 111 flew so low that I felt I could touch it with my hand. It then made out to sea, so low that it was below the superstructure of shipping.

In mid-July Steiner and the remnants of 736 all withdrew into the Battery position. Steiner still visited his OP but as July saw the Allied weight inside their bridgehead becoming vaster, and its power almost intolerable to those so close at Merville, it was not worth firing any more because of the devastating return. Also Steiner felt that his supply of shells needed to be husbanded against a real emergency.

On 20 July, Captain The Count von Stauffenburg led an abortive assassination plot against Hitler. Very soon the news was all round the Wehrmacht, partly because the plot had been initiated by a clique of generals who now had to pay with their lives for its failure. About 90 per cent of the troops in Normandy were disappointed. 'Oh what a shame,' the soldiers declared ironically, 'our *poor* Führer!'[45] These were the men

## Defending the Battery 163

who were more certain than their families in Germany about the outcome of the war. They had seen the opposing might of the Allies, which had been played down in propaganda, and which they were forbidden to comment on in their letters home.

Hope was beginning to fade altogether among the Merville garrison – a garrison indeed, now that they felt beleaguered. Steiner and Buskotte did their best to keep up morale by parades, weapon cleaning, maintenance and drills, although undue movement was likely to cause attention from rocket-firing aircraft.

In mid-August Steiner was on one of his less frequent visits to the OP, as a matter of form, when he heard his name being called across the water from Ouistreham, by megaphone, and recognised his former batman's voice. This man was a Pole and had deserted to the Allies a short time before[46]:

> *Herr Leutnant* Steiner! You must surrender your position. It is no good. You are surrounded. If you do not surrender, you will be hanged and your troops will all be annihilated. You have no longer any choice, *Herr Leutnant*. Please think carefully.

Apart from the Merville Battery, still 1/1716, there was no representative unit of the old 716 Division in Normandy any longer. The débris, to quote Captain Heyde again, had been sent by train on 21 June to Le Mans, and then on to Perpignan to reform. Steiner had heard that their old and well-liked CO, Hans-Joachim Andersen, completely recovered from his operation, had rejoined them to build up a new artillery regiment with renewed vigour. Perpignan – in that cosy and safe corner of the eastern Pyrenees, close to the Mediterranean! Could not the whole of his unit be extracted from Merville and make their way to Perpignan? What a surprise for old Hans-Joachim.

Then on 16 August came orders to Steiner from 711 Division: *Withdraw*. It was urgent.

# 8
# Paddle

## Expulsion of the Wehrmacht from Normandy

711 German Infantry Division and its neighbours were fully stretched on the ground, suffering aggressive patrols and constant determined attacks from 6 Airborne Division and the Commando Brigade. Allied aircraft continued to be a menace to anyone who moved. Successive attempts to dislodge 6 Airborne Division from along the Bavent Ridge had failed, and now the Germans were obliged to resort to static warfare, a mentally and physically exhausting process for troops who had lost the initiative. These troops were sorely tried (reinforcements were nearly all youngsters aged eighteen or nineteen) and resupply was becoming a grave problem for Rommel's Army Group, static warfare being 'the most materially expensive form of war'[1], especially when the front line is stretched to the utmost.

The Merville Battery was in a very isolated position and Steiner might well be justified in claiming that he held the most advanced position of the Wehrmacht in north-west Europe. This is clear from the map on page 103.

The two opposing armies, logistically, were in diametrically opposed situations. The Allied build-up inside the bridgehead was continuing throughout the eleven weeks since 6 June, and was ready to burst forth in an easterly direction. The Americans had conquered the Contentin Peninsula and were on their way eastwards to join the British-Canadian armies so as to present a consolidated front line.

Beside this threat, which was all too evident to the stock-still

## Expulsion of the Wehrmacht from Normandy

German divisions along the north coast, there had been a number of events during the end of July and the beginning of August which were calculated to disconcert all Germans and to weaken their morale even further. Following the unsuccessful attempt on Hitler's life in July, 200 officers immediately suspected of complicity, and 5000 other people thought to have been connected, had died – many of them after torture of a particularly ferocious kind. Then on 15 August, two armies, one French and the other American, landed in the French Riviera, poised to strike north up the Rhône Valley. On this same day the American 1st and 3rd Armies duly arrived and had hardly taken up a position along the line Mayenne – Alençon, when General Patton was off, due east, towards Orléans. This was a far wider, outflanking movement than the one which was presently going on round Falaise.

The breakout operation was first planned on 7 August, not so much as a determined extension of OVERLORD, but 'in the event of a general withdrawal of the enemy'. Yet there was an inescapable feeling, on both sides, that there must be a sudden – if not desperate – move to break what had developed for the Germans into a stalemate.

The kind of desperation that was seeping through the Wehrmacht is best expressed in a report recounted by Rommel's son, Manfred. The Field Marshal explains his difficulties[2]:

> My functions in Normandy were so restricted by Hitler that any sergeant-major could have carried them out. He interfered in everything and turned down every proposal we made. The British and Americans had only two bridgeheads to begin with, a weak one on the Cotentin Peninsula and a somewhat stronger one near Bayeux. Naturally, we wanted to attack the weak one first. But no; Hitler thought otherwise. The half-hearted dispersed attack which resulted was simply nipped in the bud. If we pulled a division out, Hitler ordered us to send it straight back. Where we ordered 'Resistance to the last round' it was changed from above to 'Resistance to the last drop of blood'. When Cherbourg finally surrendered [27 June] they sent us a court-martial adviser. That was the sort of help we got.

> The troops behaved splendidly.... But all the courage didn't help. It was one terrible blood-letting. Sometimes we had as many casualties in one day as during the whole of the summer fighting in Africa in 1942. My nerves are pretty good, but sometimes I was near collapse.... And the worst of it is that it was all without sense or purpose. There is no longer anything we can do. Every shot we fire is now harming ourselves, for it will be returned a hundred-fold. The sooner it finishes the better for all of us.

It will be recalled that Steiner's ex-batman had deserted and then warned him by megaphone to move out of Merville or to face annihilation. Steiner's orders to withdraw – for he could not move without them – came urgently from 711 Division with only a few hours for them to be implemented. At midday on 16 August the Merville Battery garrison were still in position; at midnight they had gone.

Steiner's way was along the north coast and eastwards as far as he could go, taking the howitzers with him. The evacuation of the Battery and OP-strongpoint occurred simultaneously. The horses at the Haras de Retz were too well off through eating grass, and neglected by not being ridden or exercised to be of any use, so fresh animals were provided by 711 from across the beach. With six to tow each howitzer, two to each limber and several mounts for Steiner and the warrant officers, they needed about three dozen.

Steiner recalls what happened[3]:

> On that dark and rainy night of 16 August we gathered up everything and pulled out. There was only one thing we purposely left behind, that damned 75 howitzer, so perhaps it was this which gave people the idea that our Battery was equipped with such a calibre of weapon.
>
> We went along the beach to Cabourg. There we saw the last German troops for a while. We then travelled east through northern France. I had with me Sergeant-Major Rauch from my Battery and we were virtually going through a no man's land between Allied and German troops.
>
> As we had learned at Battle Schools and in training, we did as the Russians did in the Napoleonic Wars and as the British did at

## Expulsion of the Wehrmacht from Normandy

Dunkirk. I stayed with one gun at the rear as rearguard, with Rauch and one complete gun-crew. The rest of the Battery withdrew while I fired six rounds from my gun.

Fortunately this was always enough to hold up the British advance while they sent their recce troops or spotter aircraft, and it gave us the time we needed to move on again. We had a survey engineer with us called Beck and he always managed to find an escape route when it came to withdrawing again. We also took the precaution of dividing the Battery into groups according to our home areas, as we thought the war was nearly over.

At shortly after midnight on 16 August the Allied breakout, codenamed Operation PADDLE, began, our intelligence having observed that the Germans were withdrawing along the whole front. The brigade designated to capture the Merville Battery was the 6th Airlanding, with the Belgian 'Piron' and the Dutch 'Princess Irene' Brigades under command.[4]

Franceville and the accursed Grande Buisson Farm and Mill had been mined, and German troops held out there against Belgian armour and infantry until they were overwhelmed. Two battalions of the Airlanding Brigade took up positions in the area: 12 Devons in Gonneville, with the Luxembourger Battery of 25-pounders of the Belgian Brigade; and 2nd Oxfordshire & Buckinghamshire Light Infantry whose battalion headquarters were established inside No 1 Casemate of the Merville Battery.

Reconnaissance had shown the place to be deserted, and as he made his way towards his temporary headquarters, Captain John Tillett, the Adjutant of the 'Ox and Bucks', recalls his opinion of what 9th Battalion The Parachute Regiment had achieved, and also what he found there[5]:

> The enormity of the task struck us most forcibly. Not the size of the guns, as we might have expected, quite the reverse of that . . . but much more the still evident extent of the defences.
> 
> Despite the whole area being churned up and deeply pockmarked by the 'rim to rim' bomb and shell craters covering the whole area, the mass of wire, the size of the casemates and the defensive machine-gun emplacements were still very evident. . . .

> We were able to get into the area only along a narrow winding track ... just compounded mud, and either side were these huge craters with the odd unexploded 500-lb bomb still visible here and there. Of course the whole area was almost bare of vegetation. There was the 'usual' smell of death – human and animal – and in No 1 Casemate that distinctive smell of Germans. The Germans appeared to have only just departed and there was plenty of abandoned equipment, blankets, half-eaten foods etc. ... the normal signs of a hurried and recent (war-time) departure.... They even left us some cigarettes.
>
> We noted the fact that some of the casemates had had direct hits from very large bombs but there was no sign of penetration. But the overall impression I recall was one of awe at the fact that 9 Para had managed to penetrate such defences and also that even after such a terrible bombardment on them, the Germans had been brave enough to put up some resistance. My 'office' was set up in a room on the right in No 1 Casemate.... We certainly came across *no* booby-traps.

Thanks to the defenders of Franceville and the Grande Buisson Farm, Steiner had a clear start from his immediate pursuers at the outset of his journey, although he was always in fear of enemy aircraft once the weather cleared. The River Risle was his first major obstacle, if the bridges were not intact; after that the Seine. This was to be crossed somewhere north of Rouen and preferably not too far towards its mouth near Le Havre. He hoped that it would all become easier as they travelled further from the Normandy bridgehead, and towards the First World War plains of Picardy and Flanders.

After crossing the River Risle at Pont Audemer on the third day's march (19 August) they approached the Seine. There a grotesque sight met Steiner's eyes. The withdrawing German divisions were obliged to cross the river on rafts, and there were many troops using this crossing. Those who had gone across already found they could not take with them more than bare necessities, and the whole western riverbank was littered with all manner of objects. Some were (or had been) precious, some trivial and worthless: German officers' and soldiers' loot, souvenirs of their comfortable sojourn in Normany. It was disgraceful. And as more and more soldiers arrived on the bank of the Seine, so the pile of bric-à-brac and antiques grew, only to be smashed, kicked and trampled underfoot, in the general haste to get across the river as quickly as possible.

Steiner found a box of cash, and took the contents for future use. His men quickly cobbled together some rafts strong enough to carry the howitzers, and the whole Battery was conveyed safely to the other side, without mishap — horses included. The cash would now buy horses for the continuation of the journey, a far better proposition than requisitioning them. Steiner remembers how they[6]

came to a beautiful château, in the flamboyant Gothic style, at St Maurice d'Étalan, south of Villequier, and from there we reached Belgium. On 6 September we arrived in Ypres where we met German troops for the first time since Cabourg. They had been in the Paris Guard Battalion, were all officers who had never heard a shot fired, all in the most elegant uniforms and for the first time in danger of facing the enemy! They were hopeless. Their colonel ordered me to take my Battery to the front at Ypres and fire at the first enemy tanks we saw. I refused. He threatened me with his pistol and said he would shoot me if I did not obey him. So I put my howitzer into a garage with a roll-up door, at the same time getting a message to Buskotte to take his three howitzers and make himself scarce as quickly as he could.

My gunners then fired a salvo of six rounds and, at my order, abandoned the gun and ran off.[7] Some enemy tanks arrived a few minutes later, Sergeant-Major Rauch and I fired another six rounds at them and then we fled.

Rauch and I found ourselves on the streets amidst approaching enemy forces. I jumped over a wall with him, only to find myself in full view of a tank. The driver was exposed, Rauch shot him and the tank crashed into a building. We escaped, but felt we had no option but to give ourselves up.

Our captors turned out to be Poles, and they confined us to a cellar. From there we could see through a grille into the street above, where Belgians were dragging collaborators about, with their hair shaved off, and so on. It was an ugly sight.

Eventually I was called before a Polish Colonel and feared for my life. I expected to be executed. He said he knew of me and added: 'You have done your rough work without gloves – but with clean hands.' This chivalrous gesture took my breath away and was one of the most important moments of my life. The Colonel could not guarantee the safety of me or of my men, because he was soon having to relinquish control of us.

This was Lieutenant-Colonel Zdzislaw Szydlowski who commanded the 9th Rifles Battalion in the Polish Armoured Division.[8]

> We were then put in charge of Canadian soldiers who threatened us because some SS troops had recently murdered their Canadian prisoners. They made us bare our arms to see whether we had the SS tattoo marks there. We had no members of the SS in my Battery, but those from other German units, who had been captured and who were SS, tried to hide their tell-tale emblems. In the end, no harm came to them there.
> Buskotte, with the three other howitzers and the main party, got safely to Holland.[9]

But 'safely to Holland' was not as comfortable as it might sound. Completely divorced from his parent division – from any division – Buskotte and his three howitzers were at the command of any unit or any officer who might find them useful, and Buskotte was in no position to refuse an order. Thus he found himself being diverted to Walcheren Island in Holland.

Walcheren is not an island at all, but a bulge at the end of an irregularly shaped promontory approached by an isthmus from the mainland at the mouth of the River Scheldt. A short way up the river lies the important North Sea port of Antwerp, in Belgian territory.

This was General Montgomery's immediate objective, once he had broken out of Normandy and had the Germans on the run. The Allies had left the effective area of supply from Mulberry Harbour, and Cherbourg was even more remote. A large port, forward in Belgium, was now vital to provide for the advance of 21 Army Group, and might even propel them

## Expulsion of the Wehrmacht from Normandy

into Germany itself before the end of 1944.

Montgomery's forward troops reached Brussels on 3 September (the fifth anniversary of the Franco-British state of war against the Nazis) and on the following day Antwerp was in Allied hands with the port intact.

Walcheren now became a vital RAF target. It was a Wehrmacht stronghold with conventional fortifications and a garrison of some 10,000 men which posed a real threat to the Scheldt and prevented Allied river traffic from sailing in or out.

Buskotte and his guns were there, a day or two later, on 9 September when they were caught in the open by a heavy RAF raid. Entirely defenceless without their former concrete protection, the three guns were completely destroyed.

1/1716, the Merville Battery, had ceased to exist.[10]

# 9
# Merville Today

Merville today no longer resembles the Merville we saw at dawn on 6 June 1944. That pockmarked landscape, redolent of a different planet, has gone but the casemates still squat there, glowering at intruders. To many an old soldier it remains a sinister, unwelcoming place. Not all its spirits have been laid to rest.

The land round the casemates is flat now, as it had been before the bombardments began, covered with well-tended grass between the paths; something like the old, outer cattle-wire surrounds the central area of the position, and a circular drive has been created between No 1 Casemate and the open space where the school house used to stand. The row of houses between it and the road junction near the church has been restored and here today is one of the many signs to be seen in the district, pointing to 'les Batteries de Merville'. But we know there is only one.

In their immense clean-up operation in 1945–7, the Normans employed German prisoners-of-war to sort out the mess at Merville. Some were killed when lifting their own mines, but when the whole area was considered safe again, bulldozers pushed the ground flat. Owing to an apparent superfluity of earth, the level of the central area of the Battery is now higher, by more than a metre, than it was in 1944. Consequently one has now to walk down a slope into No 1 Casemate, whereas formerly it was flat. (See Plate 29.)

My first renewed contact with Merville, although not a

physical one, occurred in 1951 when I was asked by Colonel Otway to accompany him to the BBC and give advice on a live broadcast in the radio series *Now it can be Told*. On Sunday 18 March I presented myself in Studio 8 at Broadcasting House, London, at 10.30 in the morning, and found myself among a number of well-known BBC 'voices'. They included Hugh Fawcus (who was playing Colonel Otway), John Slater and Denis McCarthy.

McCarthy had been allotted several different persons' voices including a Lieutenant Jefferson, whose one line near the end of the play was 'Get away from that, you bloody fool, it might be mined!' The cast worked at the script all morning, broke for liquid lunch at whichever local was in favour at that time, and Denis McCarthy beckoned me over to the genial producer, Tommy Waldron. As he had other parts to speak, he suggested that I 'be myself', and this was soon arranged, especially as I was then a member of Equity (the Actors' Union).

The unusual part of it all was the permitted inclusion of the word 'bloody', seldom heard over the air in those days and somewhat at odds with the dinner-jacketed announcer in the studio (we had the Senior Announcer, Stuart Hibberd).

After this aural skirmish at Merville, my real return had to wait for nearly ten years. On 10 June 1960 I began the first of my six visits as a 'guest artist'[1] with the Camberley Staff College annual Battlefield Tour. When I saw Merville again, it frightened me; but slowly, very slowly I began to accept the place in its more comfortable middle age, as I stood on top of No 1 Casemate and related how I remembered 9th Battalion The Parachute Regiment's attack.

In June 1944, a willow post had been set up, close to the triangular building on which stood the AA gun, probably to carry temporary telephone wires. This post survived all the attacks, took root and is now a tree, flourishing after nearly half a century's growth. This is not the only instance when nature has taken over: on top of No 1 Casemate there is a healthy plantation of chives in the spring of every year.

Elsewhere trees, bushes and briars are managing to soften the harsh concrete outlines, other corners are half-concealed among earth and grass.

On 10 April 1969 I went to Merville to take part in a television film for the twenty-fifth anniversary of D-Day, a film I never saw and never shall do now. Owing to a change in independent television franchise, I am told it no longer exists.

As late as the 1970s and well into the nuclear age, there were still military lessons to be learnt by Staff College students from some of 6 Airborne Division's wartime operations. There were also enough former members of the Division who could be called upon to relate their experiences. But it was said to be partly a dearth of armoured and infantry personnel available for the other two presentations ('Goodwood' and 'Epsom') as well as financial stringency in the Armed Forces in 1973 and onwards, which made that year the twenty-seventh and last to see a Battlefield Tour from Camberley to Cabourg.

In 1978 a Trust was set up called 'Airborne Assault Normandy' (AANT) with the purpose of maintaining two museums – at 'Pegasus' Bridge and at Merville – and generally providing information for those who want to retrace and find out more about our battles of 1944. It is also a fund-raising Trust and two British generals have been behind it all along. Lieutenant-General Sir Michael Gray began it in General Sir Richard Gale's lifetime, and then General Sir Nigel Poett joined him. They have put in a tremendous amount of thought, of work, of dedication and have given generously of their own time and resources towards the enterprise. The museums were intended to remain proof positive, for future generations, of what happened in two Norman villages on the early morning of 6 June 1944, and they both attract many visitors from all nations.

In 1981, while preparing for the opening of the Merville Battery Museum in No 1 Casemate, its underground chambers were pumped out by a French engineer called M. Piattier, and a *déminage* (clearance) team from Caen. Major Charles Strafford, once a member of General Gale's HQ Staff in 6

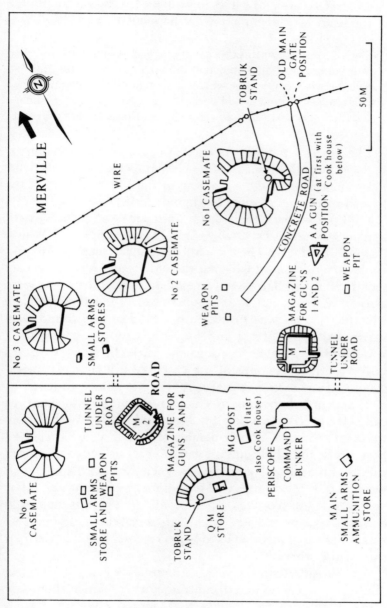

Fig. 8   Buildings in central battery position still identifiable

Airborne Division, now lives in Ranville for the warm months of the year. He remembers what happened[2]:

> When I went down inside the submerged rooms with the then *maire-ajoint*, just after they had pumped out the water that had been there for many years, we saw fins of mortar bombs and bands of cartridges lurking in odd corners. One chap who did *déminage* said there seemed evidence of stocking anti-tank stuff in the place.

The Museum was duly opened in 1982. The ground outside is the responsibility of the French (Municipality of Merville-Franceville-Plage); the equipping of the Museum that of the British (Airborne Assault Normandy Trust)[3].

I did not go back there again until June 1984, the fortieth anniversary of D-Day, when HRH The Prince of Wales, Colonel-in-Chief of The Parachute Regiment, inspected us and spoke to a number of widows, ex-soldiers and regular serving members of 2nd Battalion The Parachute Regiment who were also there, back, not so long since, from the Falklands. The Merville Battery was turned into a kind of fairground with marquees, bands, flags and bunting, hawkers selling their wares and a general feeling of gaiety. Little children ran up and down the grassy slopes of the casemates: a sight so incongruous to the memory, that it moved me almost to tears.

That year I chanced to meet a Luxembourger civil engineer called Jacques Blaat, whose hobby is land-battles. We had been told that a former German member of the Merville Battery had been inside the Museum, but was advised to return at a more suitable time instead of on the day when the British and French were *en fête*. He disappeared without trace, but the news that at least one survivor was still alive, and that he was interested enough to want to come back, was most encouraging. This was the jolt that inspired us to begin research into the German side of the story.

It took more than a year. Sometimes we went up blind alleys, often encountered contradictory evidence, but very nearly all those approached in West Germany were interested, helpful and keen to tell us what they remembered. Some felt that forty years was too long a time to wait to ask questions; others admitted that they would not have been willing to talk much earlier.

Then suddenly on 18 April 1985 I had a telephone call from Blaat in Darmstadt: 'I've found the CO! He lives in Austria. His name is Raimund Steiner.'

Blaat had also found the Battery Sergeant-Major, Hans Buskotte. We visited him at home near Osnabrück in July, where he had invited Fritz Waldmann and Wilhelm Bleckmann. Blaat and I met the three of them on 20 July 1985, the forty-second anniversary of von Stauffenburg's abortive plot on Hitler's life – a fact not lost on any of us and regarded wryly by the Germans.

In the following October I spent two days in Innsbruck with Raimund Steiner; then in March 1986 he, Buskotte and Waldmann all came up to Normandy (driven by Blaat) and I met them there. It was an extraordinary event and by no means an ordinary day. During the night and early in the morning there had been a torrential downpour and when we reached the Battery the water level had risen so much in the remains of No 3 Casemate that it was impossible to enter. On the previous day it had been dry. The wind blew at gale force and made eerie wails round the position. A natural battle seemed to be in progress, but it eventually died down.

This mirrored our individual feelings over the years, for we now felt well-disposed to each other; residual animosity was replaced by a common interest in each other's past, with no little respect for one another, and in our very different memories of the Merville Guns. Of course there were some highly charged moments, how could it be otherwise? But four wives and two small boys helped to prevent lasting wrath or indignation.

Buskotte had lived in Merville from December 1942 until August 1944; it had become his second home and this was his first return. I had been there for less than an hour on a single day in June 1944, but had come back there over and over again, an enthusiastic supporter of the British viewpoint and my own Battalion's achievement.

'I feel haunted whenever I come back,' I told him. 'What must it be like for you – the first time?' The old man burst into tears.

The three defenders explained the purpose of all the buildings – or what was left of them – though not without some difficulty, here and there, and nobody could remember for certain where the latrines had been. Much of this 'tour' is on film.

They looked with interest at the exhibits in the Museum, but would have liked to see more on display to commemorate their own residence; that had not been possible to the founders of the Museum, nor had it suited the spirit of the time.

No 1 Casemate of the Merville Battery was built to last and has now been resurrected as a tribute and memorial to those who fought and died on Norman soil. It represents much more, though, than the triumph of training, determination and courage of a British parachute battalion in its first experience of battle, pitted against determined defenders, battle-trained German soldiers in heavily protected casemates.

The widespread drop of the Battalion, with consequently grave reduction in numbers for the assault – as well as the loss of almost all the explosives – was in spite of the skill and determination of the Royal Air Force who strove to overcome the failure of the pathfinder force.

If one accepts the German evidence: that none of the guns was destroyed, the assault by Parachutists and bombardments by the Royal Navy and Royal Air Force combined to neutralise the strategic importance and *effect* of the Merville Guns in the early hours of the seaborne landings. The gallant, but ill-fated, Commando attack on the following day continued to drive home this British determination to neutralise the guns and subdue the garrison. Thereafter, retaliatory bombardments continued to inhibit any strategic significance Merville might otherwise have retained.

The defeat of an evil was achieved at great sacrifice by Norman civilians and foreign soldiers alike, but I hope that Merville may, in the future, stand as a symbol of an important step towards the far more significant victory of unity and co-operative friendship across national frontiers.

One strange event on 6 June 1944 was my own experience when, metaphorically, that hand of friendship was unexpectedly held out to me. I was unable to recognise it and I did not grasp it. When I took the German medical corporal back into the Battery on that morning, I asked him his name. For forty-one years I had believed that he replied 'Heinz'. In 1985, when I questioned Buskotte about him, he told me that the corporal's surname was Kehlenbach, and only then did I appreciate that he had given me his forename: *Hans*.

Such gestures and incidents, large and small, have recurred throughout the history of warfare and can seldom be acknowledged. (Hans Kehlenbach died at his home in Cologne on 18 January 1966 at the age of fifty-four years), but they should surely be recognised as true tokens of our all too fragile civilisation, which came near, several times, to being shattered during the Second World War.

The Merville Battery Museum is a monument to War – a war against the evils of Nazism. How long should such defeated ends be associated with the succeeding generations of a nation which has become so important in the creation of a united Western Europe? Failings are not isolated to single nations, nor need similar failings be recurrent in any one nation. How important it is that the national response to one phase of history should not be perpetuated as the prejudices of later periods. But this cannot be immediate. One should always be prepared, though, for the time when Norman sons, who never experienced the horrors of war themselves, will at last be able to greet with ease the descendants of those who once occupied their families' homes.

# NOTES

## Chapter 1

1. Bulford Camp is two miles NE of Amesbury, one mile East of the A303. Kiwi Barracks in Bulford was the home of 9th Battalion The Parachute Regiment during the war.
2. At Hardwick Hill, near Chesterfield, Derbyshire. All troops lived in Nissen huts in the grounds of the House (built in 1590 and belonging to the Duke of Devonshire), which was empty. Hardwick was also the Parachute Training School for intensive PT before jumps began.
3. On 2 May 1943, Brigadier Richard Nelson Gale OBE, MC, Director of Air at the War Office, was promoted to Major General and appointed to command the newly formed 6 Airborne Division. After serving in the First World War, and then following a somewhat humdrum peacetime career of soldiering, mainly in India, he had been near to retiring when 1939 came. A real 'soldiers' general', he was well able to converse with and be easily understood by all ranks. His bluff, slightly 'blimpish' appearance concealed a quick mind, a clear brain and an immediate grasp of a military problem or a man's character. He inspired trust and confidence in a moment, and had no difficulty in establishing himself as a tough, though compassionate father-figure of the Division. He could be sharp, very earthy, aggressive and stubborn. His flashes of anger were frightening, but they did not occur very often, thanks to the tactful and accomplished handling which he enjoyed from his ADC, Captain Tommy Haughton.
4. James Hill was an early CO of 9th Battalion. He had left the Regular Army in 1935, after four years' service as a subaltern in the Royal Fusiliers, for the business world in which he was equally successful. This is why the 1944 Army List shows 'Supplementary Reserve. Lieutenants. Hill, S.J.L.' with temporary ranks to War Substantive Lieutenant-Colonel and Temporary Brigadier. He won a MC in 1940 and a DSO in North Africa where he commanded 1st Battalion The Parachute Regiment with distinction. He took command of 3 Parachute Brigade on St George's Day (23 April) 1943, and immediately

impressed his own stoic, determined and God-fearing nature upon all ranks. Tall, spare, muscular and strong in will as in body, James Hill carried a thumb-stick in his right hand as he skimmed over the roughest ground, oblivious of all obstacles. This earned him the nickname of 'Speedy' and woe betide any man who lagged behind. Brigadier Hill was a patient man but required as much from us all as he was able to give himself. At first this seemed far more than we could possibly achieve, but gradually he trained us up to becoming worthy of his smile of approval. He was critical but fair; demanding but grateful; outwardly of granite, but with a warm heart. Even today, at reunions, soldiers stop in their tracks when they see him, give a mental salute, look their best and hope for a friendly greeting from 'Speedy' – which they get.

5 Terence Otway was commissioned from Sandhurst into 2nd Battalion, Royal Ulster Rifles, in 1934. He was posted to 1 RUR in Hong Kong and became Intelligence Officer. This led to an attachment to HQ China Command Ciphers which he left to go to India with 1 RUR. There he saw service on the NW Frontier during 1937–8. From Signals Officer he was promoted to Captain and Adjutant of 1 RUR when they returned to UK shortly before the outbreak of the Second World War. In July 1941 he was promoted to Major and briefly commanded 31st (later 1st Airborne) Reconnaissance Squadron before going to the Staff College, Camberley, in October. Leaving there with his PSC he was appointed Brigade Major of 147 Inf. Bde. in Northern Ireland in April 1942. Three months later he became GSO2 in Military Operations 1 at the War Office until, in May 1943, he was posted to 1 RUR. In April 1944 Major Otway was promoted to command 9th Battalion The Parachute Regiment. His determination to obtain maximum results from his training programme put a fine edge on the weapon which he commanded on D-Day, shortly before his thirtieth birthday. After being concussed in the Normandy Battle, Lt-Colonel Otway was evacuated to the UK in July 1944 and on being regraded A1 in September he was appointed GSO1 in Military Training at the War Office. He now had the DSO. In June 1945 he commanded 15 (British) Parachute Battalion in India but was transferred to HQ 2 Indian Airborne Division as GSO1 in October. In July 1947 he returned to the War Office in London as GSO1 to Director of Land-Air Warfare until February 1949. In the following May he retired from the Army to take up a commercial career.

6 This was the Division that had fought with great courage and distinction in North Africa, earning for us all the epithet of 'Red Devils'. 1st Airborne Division were presently reforming in East Anglia and Lincolnshire in preparation for their next operation which was never in Normandy but at Arnhem in September 1944.

7 Company Sergeant Major Instructor: a physical training WO2 attached to the Battalion. 'Dusty' had been a regular soldier in the Green Howards before the War, and had transferred to the newly formed APTC (Army Physical Training Corps). He was posted to Hardwick and from there to 9th Battalion The Parachute Regiment where he remained. Eventually he became RSM in the field in Nor-

mandy. He was one of the best-known characters in Airborne Forces, having jumped until he was fifty – latterly with the TA – and altogether making more than 500 descents.

8    Charles Paul Greenway, elder son of the 2nd Baron Greenway (cr.1927), was educated at Winchester where he still holds the hurdling record. He continued at Trinity College, Cambridge, as a great athlete: hurdling, long distance running, and soccer. All set for a soccer blue, he injured his knee a week before the Varsity Match and couldn't play. He was commissioned ino The Buffs in October 1940 and transferred to the Parachute Regiment in 1942. When experimental work was in progress, he volunteered to make secret test-jumps with modified parachutes lacking one or two panels. After being appointed Assistant Adjutant of 9th Battalion The Parachute Regiment in 1943, he was promoted 2i/c 'B' Company and went into action with them. His bravery at Merville was emphasised later when, at the Château de St Côme, he stood on a bank in full view of the enemy, directing fire by remote control from *Arethusa* in the Bay of the Seine. After the War he was a Member of Lloyd's. He was an eccentric, generous, a bon viveur and a good mixer. When he succeeded to the title in 1963 he became a popular member of the House of Lords where he managed to address them before he had been introduced. He died in 1975 and was succeeded by his eldest son, Ambrose.

9    HMS *Arethusa* of 5200 tons, was also the name of a class of three other 'smallest possible useful cruisers'. Laid down in 1933 and launched in 1934 from Chatham, she had a complement of 500; six 6-in., four twin 4-in. QF and two 40mm quadruple Bofors guns; she also had six 21-in. torpedo tubes. She could engage targets at eleven miles and the Gunnery Officer was Lieut. Comd. H.T. Burchell DSO. *Arethusa* was on call to 9th Battalion The Parachute Regiment early on the morning of D-Day and her accurate fire was invoked several times after that date. She was scrapped in 1950.

# Chapter 2

1    I last saw the original model at the Depot of The Parachute Regiment in Aldershot in February 1962, when I was asked to talk to some recruits and used it for illustration of the battle. Nobody now knows where it is.

2    John Gwinnett was born in Gloucester in 1916. His father suffered a serious accident in the timber yard where he worked, and died soon afterwards. The notable Mrs Veronica Hensman, wife of the Vicar of St Catherine's Church, Gloucester, saw great potential in John (a choirboy at the church) and persuaded Mrs Gwinnett to let her 'adopt' the boy. John thus became a brother in all but name to the two Hensman

boys. After the Crypt Grammar School in Gloucester, John went up to Leeds University and read Classics. He captained the University Rugby Team and also that of the Universities Athletic Union. He went straight from Leeds to theological college, was ordained in Gloucester Cathedral in 1939 and became Canon Hensman's curate. One day in April 1942, Michael Hensman came home wearing a red beret. 'This sent John scurrying to the Royal Army Chaplains' Department to join the Parachute Regiment.' He was commissioned in November 1942 and in March 1943 he became padre of 9th Battalion The Parachute Regiment. He was 'a remarkable man with that hint of shyness masking a surprisingly firm and resolute character.' John's shining example and outstanding bravery in Normandy is still spoken of with affection and admiration. He married a Hensman cousin, the Lady Doreen Lowry-Corry after the war and had one son. John Gwinnett MC, MA, CF died in 1977. (The author thanks Michael Hensman for this information.)

3   Landing on one's feet without the need to roll over on the ground in the approved style sometimes due to a freak puff of wind, or none at all. It was not regarded in wartime as ideal parachuting technique.
4   John Stagg, Churchill's weather expert, was responsible for predicting the good weather on 6 June 1944 over Normandy, sandwiched between two patches of bad, that had not been observed by the Germans. Stagg also convinced General Eisenhower that the Invasion could go ahead, after it had been delayed for 24 hours. His own account makes fascinating reading. (See Appendix 8).
5   The Battalion Flag is now in the Airborne Forces Museum, Aldershot.

# Chapter 3

1   Fritz Todt (1891–1942) was an early member of national socialist parties in Germany: NSDAP 1922; SA 1931. A qualified engineer, he was put in charge of constructing the Siegfried Line in 1938; then he took over all military construction work and was General Inspector of autobahns, water and energy. In 1940 he became Reich Minister for Armaments and Munitions.
2   Speidel, op. cit. p.27.
3   D. Young, op. cit. p.200.
4   Speidel, op. cit. p.25.
5   Ruge, op. cit. p.153.
6   ibid. p.157.
7   BBC tv film *Destination D-Day*, 1984.
8   D. Young, op. cit. p.198
9   ibid. p.202.

## Chapter 4

1. Buskotte interview 20 July 1985.
2. idem.
3. The Café Gondrée at 'Pegasus' Brige is a famous meeting-place for Airborne troops of the Second World War as well as being a tourist attraction. The patron, Georges Gondrée, died in 1968 and his wife continued until her own death in 1984. Their daughters carry on the business and there is now an Airborne Museum beside the Café.
4. Timpf letters of 28 May and 17 July 1986.
5. ibid. 17 July 1986.
6. Steiner interviews of 26/27 October 1985 and report from those interviews.
7. When Blaat and I were trying (unsuccessfully) to trace the Rittmann company, I was warned not to be too industrious about it . . .
8. Heyde interview, 18 July 1985.
9. Given in full at Appendix 3, p. 198.
10. Buskotte interview 20 July 1985.
11. So called after their modification and use in North Africa.
12. Piekalkiewicz (*Invasion Frankreich*), p.117 trans A.J.
13. ibid.
14. Some German batteries had nicknames; the Merville Battery had not.
15. This figure includes single aircraft strikes as well as mass-bomber raids.
16. Résistance members usually changed their names.
17. The bomb was not retrieved and is probably still there.
18. Steiner interview and report.
19. Bleckmann letter 4 May 1985.
20. There was looting once the Invasion had begun.
21. Bleckmann letter cit.

## Chapter 5

1. 11,500 aircraft; 200,000 sailors and soldiers in the first wave; 713 warships; 4,216 assault vessels; 805 merchant ships; 59 blockships and 2 artificial harbours.
2. 9th Parachute Battalion were not told this. It was untrue. (Lee interview 26 June 1986.)
3. See Appendix 3 p. 200.
4. PRO AIR271/1974
5. Each Dakota carried containers of 20-lb bombs which were released as they crossed the coastline, not only to keep the enemy's heads down, but also to confuse them over the purpose of the sortie.
6. Lee interview cit.
7. The following technical information was provided by Lee and Rees.

## Notes

8   All returning air crews expected an egg for breakfast; only long-range bomber crews were entitled to bacon as well.
9   A balletic leap during which the feet change places in the air four or six times. Ten times would be considered freakish.
10  Golley op. cit. p.86 & Golley/Florentin op.cit. pp.113–14. It is perhaps worth noting that the sound of shots was the last thing that Colonel Otway wished for at this time when we were all concealing our positions in silence. Despite his words in this moment of great stress, he probably did not really intend the French people to be shot.
11  'Les sons et les parfums tournent dans l'air du soir'. Piano Preludes Book I no 4 by Claude Debussy.
12  Parry letter of 12 August 1985.
13  Johnson & Dunphie op. cit. p.51.
14  Parry letter of 8 August 1984. HMS *Arethusa*'s log, in keeping with all RN logs, contains reports only on the ship herself and her condition, but nothing about the battle. However, in his book *Operation Neptune* (pp. 135–6), Commander Kenneth Edwards RN has this to say: 'During the early part of the "fire plan" there was considerable anxiety in HMS *Arethusa* about the progress of a part of the Sixth Airborne Division. . . . For a considerable time the naval supporting craft could get no reliable information which would enable them to give gunfire support to the airborne troops without risk of firing into our own men.

    'The anxiety caused by this shortage of information was most acute with regard to the . . . Battery of 6-in. howitzers east of the river Orne. . . . One glider crash-landed on the battery itself and the battery was duly captured. The *Arethusa* was told that she was to open fire at a certain time unless she received orders to the contrary. Then she was told not to open fire until she was certain that the battery was still in German hands. She never was certain and so she did not open fire.'
15  Albert Richards, born in Liverpool on 19 December 1919, was killed on the advance through Holland on 5 March 1945 when he backed his jeep over an uncleared verge and blew himself up on a mine.
16  A type of pyrotechnic which, when ignited, emits dense smoke that rises some distance in the air as a signal.
17  Johnson & Dunphie, op. cit., p.54.
18  It was only reaction. Major Parry regained his natural poise soon afterwards.
19  Lieutenant-Colonel Otway ordered Segeant Knight to count heads (in spite of the fact that he was not the senior NCO present) and he remembers that there were 80 fit men able to go on.
20  Smith was evacuated to the UK and got his glass eye. He then went to Arnhem in September and earned an MM – one of the few soldiers to take part in both major actions and the only member of 9th Parachute Battalion to do so.
21  I did not see Morgan again.
22  Parfitt and Rose, together with the Battalion's 2i/c, Major Charlton, were all killed near the Château de St Côme on 9 June.
23  Nor have I heard any singing there since.

24  *Hedgcock's French Primer.*
25  Hal Hudson lived, after many operations. In a letter to the author in September 1985 he wrote:

> I was hit in the middle of the minefield about 15 yds from the Battery perimeter. Presumably by mortar as the fragments remaining in my innards to this day are certainly not a machine-gun bullet. I suppose a mine could have produced a similar effect. It was an academic matter as far as I was concerned at the time!

As Sir Havelock Hudson he retired from Lloyd's, having been their Chairman from 1975 to 1977.

26  John Gwinnett got us safely to Brigade HQ at Le Mesnil where it and 224 Parachute Field Ambulance were both situated in farm buildings, approached by a bumpy drive winding its way through trees, and well concealed. I spent the night sitting upright, and asleep for most of the time, in the back of a small car. The next day was a fine one and I lay on a grass lawn, sleeping in the sun. Major Alastair Young RAMC was the senior Medical Officer present, and he asked me about Hal Hudson who was being operated on by Captain Tom Gray RAMC.

This was done with an Ever Ready razor blade, and was the first of many stomach operations which Hudson had, and which saved his life. When I, in turn, sought information about his patient, Major Young refused to answer. About an hour later, I asked Major Young what Hudson's hopes were. He fixed me with his eyes and gave a barely perceptible shake of his head, turning away with a great sadness about him. Later that morning, my Company Commander Ian Dyer turned up together with some men of 'C' Company whom I recognised and was glad to see. Ian greeted me, but had a surprised look on his face. 'So you made it, Jeff!' he said. (Afterwards he told me that he thought, by my pale complexion, that I was dying.) Later there was a general alarm, and I could see a couple of large German tanks nosing about not more than two fields away. We all kept rather quiet. On 8 June, D+2, some of us, including Major Parry, were driven to Divisional HQ in Ranville where we spent the night being liberally dusted with M&B powder by the medical orderlies and being heavily mortared by the Germans; and on 9 June we left in a DUKW (an amphibious troop-carrying vehicle) for the coast. At 'Sword' Beach – where there were still bodies of Commando soldiers on the wire – we entered the water and were on our way to an empty LST (tank-landing craft) when a single enemy aircraft flew over and dropped a bomb on the beach. It hit an ammunition dump which went up with a great explosion. Minor bangs, flashes and explosions continued for some time afterwards, and the DUKW driver seemed reluctant to board the LST and then have to return to the shore.

After several false efforts at climbing the ramp of the DUKW, the driver was threatened not to repeat his demonstration of bad driving. We embarked and returned that afternoon to Southampton, where we arrived early in the following morning. I remained with Major Parry and after one night at a hospital in Farnborough, Hants., we were sent on a hospital train to just outside Swansea in South Wales. When we were booked in, the staff took it for granted that we had come from the Italian Front, but when they discovered we were the first from Normandy, we were made much of. We were joined shortly afterwards in our ward, by Lieutenant 'Sandy' Smith (later MC) who was one of John Howard's Platoon Commanders at 'Pegasus' Bridge and had been badly injured in his right wrist by a German stick grenade. After only six days, Major Parry and I caused ourselves to be discharged from Morriston Hospital and went our own ways, he back to rejoin the Battalion in Normandy, I to get proper treatment for my arm in Edinburgh. (The ruptured biceps muscles turned out to be far longer in mending than my leg-wound). After excellent treatment at the Royal Infirmary in Edinburgh I returned to Bulford and was appointed OC Home Details, so in a sense I was where I would have been posted – to 'R' Company, the nearest equivalent of Home Details – had Frank Tavener been allowed to retain his Mortar Platoon on 8 January 1944. The Battalion returned home again on 7 September and I met them at Southampton Docks. Many faces were completely unfamiliar although there were still a number of old friends among them. I handed over to the CO, was marked A1 (completely fit) again, and rejoined to take over command of the 3-in. Mortar Platoon.

## Chapter 6

1  None of the histories of the Normandy Landings, official or otherwise, has much to report about the 'second wave' which came over the beaches on D+1.
2  According to Commander St Clair Tisdal, Beachmaster on 'Sword', the weight of enemy shell-fire during the first week of the Invasion was so great that on about D+6 'Sword' was evacuated for a while, and Commander Tisdal established his station at Courseulles on 'Juno' Beach.
3  Killed in Holland in January 1945.
4  He was again wounded on the way back to the UK.
5  P. Young letter of 2 January 1985.
6  Jones report of 27 November 1985.
7  ibid.
8  This was daylight and the Germans were thoroughly alerted.
9  Patterson interview on 21 July 1985 and letters April 1985 – April 1986.
10  Williams letter of 2 October 1985.
11  P. Young, op. cit., p.154.
12  Jones cit.

13  Williams cit.
14  Patterson interview cit.
15  Of 'C' Company 9 Battalion The Parachute Regiment. See p.137.
16  Williams cit.
17  Jones cit.
18  3 Commando War Diary App. 'A' No.3 p.2 (PRO WO218/62).
19  Jones cit.
20  P. Young op. cit. p.155.

# Chapter 7

1  It is unlikely that this glider was British.
2  See Appendix 3, pp. 200–1.
3  Steiner interview and report.
4  ibid.
5  Timpf letters of 30 August 1985 and 10 October 1985.
6  It is possible that the machine-guns of Timpf's patrol were firing on the right flank of 9th Battalion's attack. Reports of three German machine-guns firing on to both flanks from 9th Battalion do not tally with the Germans' declared shortage of weapons. Timpf's patrol would then have crossed the top of DZ 'V' on their way to Varaville, where they ran into elements of 1st Canadian Parachute Battalion and were captured. They were taken to the section of 224 Field Ambulance attached to the Canadians. Some of the Germans interviewed always refer to 6 Airborne Division as 'Canadians', whether because of the one Canadian Battalion in 3 Para. Brigade, or because of the preponderance of Canadians at the Dieppe Raid, is not clear.
7  There is no information about this from 9 Parachute Bn.
8  Major Parry states (p. 113, para. 6) that he detailed Lieutenant Halliburton to take No 4 Casemate. He makes no mention of appointing a C/Sgt and a CSM to command assaults. In the event, C/Sgt Long led the attack on No 4 Casemate, and CSM Ross that on No 3.
9  George Hawkins was taken PoW, recovered and was eventually repatriated. He now lives in Crowborough, Sussex.
10  Buskotte interview, 20 July 1985.
11  ibid.
12  It is doubtful whether any member of 9th Battalion was aware of the presence of a German SP gun, though in *Operation Neptune* it states on pp.136–7: 'By 9.30 on the morning of D-day, however, all the main batteries facing the eastern sector of the Assault Area had been silenced, at least temporarily, although the beaches and anchorage in the SWORD area were being subjected to an increasing volume of shell fire from German mobile guns operating in the woods south of Franceville. These mobile guns were exceedingly difficult to locate and engage as

## Notes

13  they moved as soon as they came under accurate fire.'
13  Steiner report cit.
14  Questionable. AJ remembers the artillery fire as 9th Battalion were withdrawing (and he was one of the last out of the Battery because he could move only slowly). The shelling was initially wild. Had the Battalion not withdrawn when they did (although for an altogether different reason) Steiner might well have been correct.
15  See Chapter 5, pp. 121–2.
16  Hans Speidel, *We Defended Normandy* (1951), p. 96.
17  Buskotte interview, Normandy, March 1986.
18  Steiner, Buskotte, Waldmann interview, Normandy, March 1986.
19  See Chapter 5, p. 123.
20  This was Captain Woyevodsky of No 3 Commando (see Chapter 6, p. 133
21  See Chapter 6, p. 138.
22  1947 report on his 716 Division by Lieutenant-General W. Richter.
23  Rudi Schaff's letter of 30 December 1984.
24  Heyde letter of 18 March 1985.
25  Bleckmann interview, 20 July 1985.
26  Timpf and Steiner.
27  Buskotte interview, Normandy, March 1986.
28  The defenders of Merville took 22 prisoners (Paras and Commandos); 9th Battalion took 22 prisoners; and 9th Battalion had 22 wounded officers and men after the attack.
29  Despite AJ's insistence that there were no Negroes in 9th Battalion The Parachute Regiment, Buskotte and Steiner are firmly convinced that the severed head was negroid. It is possible that a very close explosion can have swollen nose and lips and suffused the features with clotted blood. The face would, if one of the 9th Battalion soldiers, have been covered with black camouflage paint, but that does not necessarily indicate negroid features and black, tight curly hair.
30  These bodies were later removed to the Airborne Forces Cemetery at Ranville, but their tombstones bear no reference to their first burial place. It is not now possible to ascertain who they were. (War Graves Commission, September 1986.)
31  Steiner interview, Normandy, March 1986.
32  Kortenhaus letter of 17 October 1984.
33  Malsch letter of 10 February 1985.
34  The Germans always called the place 'Quistreham'.
34  Heyde interview of 18 July 1985.
36  Johannes Buskotte.
37  Heyde letter and interview cit.
38  Bleckmann letter cit.
39  Malsch letter cit.
40  They were chancing it with 8th Parachute Battalion's numerous and offensive patrols in the area, even though the Troarn cemetery is at the western end of the town. Even so, the French would not have allowed a German officer's body to have been buried in their cemetery.

41 Steiner report cit.
42 Although this report has an immediacy, it is written in propaganda fashion (whimsical and poetical) to appeal to Germans at home. So far as the military events are concerned, they are confused and exaggerated; the bombing and its effects are not.
43 Steiner report and interview; Bleckmann cit.
44 ibid. Steiner.
45 Bleckmann interview of 20 July 1985.
46 Steiner report cit.

## Chapter 8

1 T.E. Lawrence quoted in *Encyclopædia Britannica* ed.cit.
2 Liddell Hart op.cit., pp.495–6.
3 Steiner interview and report cit.
4 Dollar & Kayser op. cit. pp. 58–62.
5 Tillett letters of 8 & 16 July 1986.
6 Steiner cit.
7 The Curator of the 'Ypres Salient Museum 14–18' states: 'This gun, together with many others which were captured in the Ypres area at that time, has been scrapped. In Sept.-Oct. 1944 a very large quantity of captured German artillery pieces, and damaged Allied guns, were brought together in a salvage dump on the old drill-field near the powder-store of the pre-First World War Belgian Infantry Barracks called The Esplanade. To my knowledge *all* these guns and other material from that dump have been sold as old iron and scrapped.'
8 Information from Polish Institute, London.
9 Steiner cit.
10 When Buskotte left Ypres, he had no idea what had happened to Steiner, Rauch and the gun crew who had protected him while he and the main party escaped. Raimund Steiner was handed over to the British and sent to England on a vessel which had a shell-hole in its side. Over it a sailor had written: 'Ouistreham 7 June 1944'. Steiner was convinced that this ship had been hit by a gun of the Merville Battery and when he told the sailors, it led 'to much good-natured joking' between them. Steiner became a PoW in Scotland and was repatriated to Innsbruck in 1945.

Buskotte was not nearly as fortunate. He left Walcheren on about 10 September and travelled eastwards to the South-Eastern Front between Czechoslovakia and Hungary. He was in Czechoslovakia when Germany surrendered on 8 May 1945. Thousands of Czech slave-labourers went on the rampage while German troops – though officially troops no longer – hurried westwards to escape the Russians. On 12 May Buskotte was making for the American lines when he was shot in the back without warning by a young Czech extremist. He was rescued by regular Russian troops who tended him and treated the bullet-wound which had narrowly missed his heart. When he was fit to travel again, Buskotte was sent to Russia as a PoW until 1949. Then finally, 12 years and 20 days after he had been conscripted (in 1937), Buskotte was able to resume his chosen occupation as a butcher in Osnabrück.

Steiner and Buskotte met one another again in Frankfurt on 23 March 1986. There, they and their wives and Fritz Waldmann were collected by Jacques Blaat and driven to Normandy to meet the author.

## Chapter 9

1 The name given to ex-members of Second World War units whose battles were the subject of Staff College presentations and discussions. Guest Artists gave first-hand, personal accounts to the students during a week on the former battle-ground in Normandy.
2 Strafford letter of 2 January 1985.
3 The Merville Battery Museum is open to the public between mid-May and early September every year.

# APPENDIX 1

# British Army

(a) Order of Battle : Commanders
  C-in-C Land Forces:     Gen. Sir Bernard Montgomery KCB, DSO
  2 Army incl u/comd:     Lt.-Gen. Sir Miles Dempsey KCB, DSO, MC
  1 Corps, incl u/comd:     Lt.-Gen. J.T. Crocker DSO, MC

    6 Airborne Division     Maj.-Gen. Richard N. Gale OBE, MC
      6 Airlanding Brigade     Brig. The Hon. H.K.M. Kindersley MBE, MC
      5 Parachute Brigade     Brig. J.H.N. Poett
      3 Parachute Brigade     Brig. S.J.L. Hill DSO, MC
        8 Parachute Bn.     Lt.-Col. A.S. Pearson DSO, MC
        9 Parachute BN.     Lt.-Col. T.B.H. Otway
        1 Canadian Para. Bn.     Lt.-Col. G.F.P. Bradbrook
    224 Para. Field Ambulance     Lt.-Col. Thompson

under command 6 Airborne Division:
  1 Special Service Bde.     Brig. The Lord Lovat DSO, MC
    3 Army Commando     Lt.-Col. P. Young DSO, MC
    4 Army Commando     Lt.-Col. R.W.P. Dawson
    6 Army Commando     Lt.-Col. D. Mills-Roberts DSO
    45 (RM) Commando     Lt.-Col. C. Ries

## Appendix 1

(b) Composition of a Parachute Battalion:
  Battalion Headquarters
    Intelligence Section
  Headquarters Company
    Company HQ
    Signals Platoon
    3-in. Mortar Platoon   six Mortars in three sections
    Machine-gun Platoon    four Vickers .303
    Anti-Tank Platoon      eight PIATs
    Pioneer Platoon
  'A' Company   Company HQ
                3 Rifle Platoons (numbered 6–8)
  'B' Company   as 'A' Company (numbered 9–11)
  'C' Company   as 'A' Company (numbered 12–14)

  'B' Echelon   Administrative Officers, cooks, drivers etc.

  *Total*: 29 Officers and 584 ORs

(c) Composition of an Army Commando:
  Commando HQ
  Heavy Weapons Troop:   two 3-in. Mortars
    (No 2 Troop)         two Vickers .303 MGs
  5 Troops each:    3 officers
    (1, 3, 4, 5 & 6)  62 ORs

  Total: 24 Officers and 440 ORs

## APPENDIX 2

## Instructions issued to Commander 3 Parachute Brigade

1   Your primary task is to ensure that the battery at 155776 is silenced by P-30 minutes. No other commitment must jeopardise success in this enterprise.

If, as appears possible, the battery is being made into a positive fortress, your plan should include a coup de main assault by glider on the position itself.

2   Whilst your attitude of mind must be that you cannot contemplate failure in the direct assault, you must be prepared to have to deal with the battery by naval gunfire. Therefore the first priority of all naval support allotted to 6 Airborne Division is the neutralisation of this battery, if it is not captured by P-30 mins: in the event of casualties to FPBs allotted primarily to this task, the alternative FOB waves at my disposal will be earmarked for this task by me.

The detailed arrangements which have been made regarding
(a) Signals to be displayed on capture of the battery
(b) Wireless messages and codewords to be sent on capture of the bty
(c) The time naval ships will open fire in the event of non receipt of these signals will be issued as soon as they have been confirmed.

3   If neither of the above signals get through the HQ ship or the allotted cruiser, the cruiser will engage the battery with air observation in the absence of definite calls for fire from FOBs.

4   As soon as the battery is silenced you will secure the LE PLEIN feature which you will hold until relieved by 1 SS Bde.

## Appendix 2

5  In addition to the task of silencing the battery at 155776 you will demolish the bridges at TROARN 177680 – BURES 1770 – ROBEHOMME 1972 and VARAVILLE 1875 by H + 2 hrs. You will leave dets to cover these demolitions. 1 SS Bde will relieve your detachment at VARAVILLE.

6  On completion of these tasks the roles of you bde will be to hold the area BOIS DE BAVANT – TROARN with the object of
   (a) denying this high ground to the enemy
   (b) interfering with any attempted army movement WEST from TROARN.

If circumstances permit you will send out patrols as far SOUTH as LA RAMET.

In the event of your being unable to hold TROARN you will withdraw to the high ground to the north. You will not withdraw further NORTH than the road junction at 140702 without orders from me.

(SGD) RN GALE<br>
Major-General<br>
Commander<br>
6 Airborne Division

## Appendix 2

## British Officers in action at Merville

*6 June 1944*

| | |
|---|---|
| Lt.-Col. T.B.H. Otway | CO 9th Parachute Battalion |
| Maj. A.J.M. Parry | OC 'A' Company |
| Maj. H.R. Bestley | OC 'B' Company |
| Maj. G.E. Smith | OC 'HQ' Company |
| Capt. H.H.T. Hudson | Adjutant |
| Capt. the Hon. C.P. Greenway | 2i/c 'B' Company |
| *Lt. M.J. Dowling | Pl. Comd. 'B' Company |
| †Lt. T.C. Halliburton | Pioneer Pl. Comd. |
| Lt. A.R. Jefferson | Pl. Comd. 'C' Company |
| Lt. J. Loring | Signals Officer |
| †Lt. G.D. Parfitt | Pl. Comd. 'C' Company |
| Lt. H.C. Pond | Pl. Comd. 'A' Company (*in glider*) |
| Lt. D.G. Slade | Assistant Adjutant |
| Lt. F.J.J. Worth | Intelligence Officer |
| Capt. H.H. Watts RAMC | Medical Officer |
| †Capt. A. Richards (att.) | War Artist |

*7 June 1944*

| | |
|---|---|
| §Lt.-Col. P. Young DSO, MC | CO No 3 Commando |
| *Maj. J.B.V. Pooley MC | Commanding 4 & 5 Troops |
| †Capt. B.D. Butler | OC 4 Troop |
| Capt. M. Woyevodsky | OC 5 Troop |
| Lt. G. Pollard MC, MM | 4 Troop |
| Lt. A. Pollock | 5 Troop |
| ‡Lt. H. Williams | 4 Troop |
| Capt. E.L. Moore RAMC | Medical Officer |

\* killed in the Battery
† killed later, elsewhere
‡ taken PoW

§Lt.-Col. Young was there as a self-confessed 'umpire' together with Capt. E.L. Moore RAMC and 3 ORs. They had not been ordered to take part in the attack.

## Appendix 2

### Strength of 9th Battalion The Parachute Regiment before and after their action at Merville, 6 June 1944

| | |
|---|---|
| Left RV on DZ for Battery | 150 |
| Trowbridge Party (Smith) | 3 |
| Taping Party (Greenway) | 6 |
| Battery Recce Party (Slade) | 4 |
| Pond's Glider (alive) | 21 |
| Others (not 9 Bn., joined after battle) | 13 |
| | 197* |

*Otway; Bestley, Parry, Smith; Greenway, Hudson; Dowling, Halliburton, Jefferson, Loring, Parfitt, Pond, Slade, Worth + MO, + War Artist + 181 ORs ........ 197

| | | |
|---|---|---|
| Killed in glider | 1 | |
| Known killed, not found† | 2 | |
| Buried by Germans | 15 | |
| Captured by Germans | 22 | |
| Wounded, left in Battery‡ | 3 | |
| Wounded, to Haras de Retz (Bestley, Parry; Hudson; Jefferson + 18 ORs)§ | 22 | |
| Own Medics with them§ | 2 | 67 |
| On these figures, Bn. strength | | 130 |
| Fit men counted afterwards | | 80 |
| ORs unaccounted for | | 50 |

† Lt. Dowling & Batman

‡ Privates Cartwright and Hawkins both of 12 Platoon made PoW on 6 June 1944. Private Mower made PoW on 7 June 1944.

§ 14 ORs at Haras de Retz and 2 Medical Orderlies made PoW

# APPENDIX 3

# Royal Air Force

### Intelligence Reports

(1) An unidentified United States Intelligence Report of November 1943 defined the Merville Battery as being armed with '155mm Howitzers and Guns'.

Intelligence Information up to April 28 1944:

(2) 4 ?150mm (5.9 in.) Howitzers. Range 14,600 yds. Rate of fire about 5 rpm. 96-lb shell. Centre line NE Arc of fire 130°. At present mounted in open circular emplacements, diam. 36 ft, probably with concrete beds; wheels of gun-carriage shackled to pivots of mounting. In front of each existing emplacement a concrete casemate is being constructed. Work started in June 1943. No 1 Casemate complete; No 2 nearly complete; Nos 3 & 4 – work proceeding slowly. No 1 earthed over, earth banked up to cover roof. Gap left in rear for entrance, and one in front for gun port. These casemates contain gun compartments with embrasure in front, room for detachment on duty and one or two magazines. Thickness of concrete probably 6ft 6in. Open emplacements and casemates arranged in an arc facing ORNE estuary. The Battery in casemates will have an arc of fire of 90°–130° but guns in open emplacements have all-round traverse. Slight camouflage of roads and services.

Accommodation at gun positions, men and stores in concrete casemates and a few older concrete shelters

## Appendix 3

undergound. Off-duty personnel billeted in Merville-Franceville village. Battery OP almost certainly within Infantry Strongpoint on R bank of ORNE 138789. Communications: buried cable and probably also wireless. Armament 3 × ?20mm AA guns possibly not all present. Identity: ? Army Static Coastal Troops.

(3) 9/10 May 1944. Merville/Franceville Gun Position.

56 Lancasters from 460, 625, 100, 12 & 626 Squadrons of No 1 Group attacked the target in clear weather with visibility marred by haze that made it difficult for crews to identify the green assembly-point markers. Bombing appears to be very accurate, numerous bomb-bursts being concentrated round the markers and most crews consider the attack to be successful. Some light, and a few bursts of heavy AA were the only defences over the target. No fighter opposition and no aircraft are missing. All crews claimed to have hit the primary. Time over targets 23.41 – 23.58. Bombing heights 2000–10,000 ft. No searchlights. 307.6 tons of bombs were dropped, 20 × 250 Marker Bombs.

(4) 19–20 May 1944. Sallenelles map ref. 155776. Another attack with 41 Halifaxes, 15 Lancasters, 3 Mosquitos (Halifaxes and Lancasters of 6 Group RCAF; Mosquitos of 8 (Pathfinder) Group) attacked the gun emplacements in moderate visibility. A fair concentration round the markers is reported, but haze prevented a fair assessment of results. Flak defences were very slight and fighting activity negligible. No aircraft are missing. Time over target 01.30–01.38. Bombing heights: Mosquitos 22,000 ft; Halifaxes 7500–8500 ft; Lancasters 7000 ft. 217.2 tons of HE were dropped.

4 × 150mm howitzers. 2 direct hits on No 1 Casemate may have caused damage. Roads cut. Considerable sympathetic detonation of mines outside positions. Near misses on Casemate 1: 7; Casemate 2: 5.

Sometimes called Merville-Sallenelles. Concrete on No 1 Casemate laid bare at south side. Casemates are protected by considerable thickness of earth all round and appear in themselves to have great solidity. Wire perimeter of Battery severed in 7 places; crater on proposed extension of A/Tank Ditch at south, and communication trenches severed.

(5) Pre-D Day Batteries Joint Fire Plan Top Secret 23–28 May 1944

4 × 150mm Howitzers: Sortie by 55 Lancasters on 27/28 May
289 tons HE
20 × 250 Marker Bombs
Believed Ex concentration

55 Lancasters from Special Duty Flight and from these Squadrons 460, 625, 100, 576, 166, 550, 101, 12, 626 & 300 of No 1 Group. Crews claimed to have attacked the target. It was free from cloud but there was considerable ground haze which made visual identification of the target impossible. Reports indicate that a good concentration of bombs was achieved in the vicinity of the markers and it is thought that the attack was successful. Ground defences were nil and only four sightings of enemy aircraft, all in the target area, are reported. One aircraft is missing from this operation.

Time over target 0155–0206. Bombing heights 6000, 9000 & 11,000 ft

(6) 5/6 June 1944 Merville/Franceville
This raid was carried out by RCAF Squadrons of 6 Group, together with 3 Mosquitos from 8 (Pathfinder) Group and bombers as follows: 13 Lancasters from 419 Squadron; 15 Halifaxes from 428 Squadron; 18 Halifaxes from 431 Squadron; 17 Halifaxes from 434 Squadron; 17 Halifaxes from 427 Squadron; and 19 Halifaxes from 429 Squadron.

Total: 13 Lancasters and 86 Halifaxes.

80 aircraft attacked the target and 19 returned without having attacked it due to being unable to identify it. Weather was 10/10 cloud with tops 5000–9000 ft but horizontal visibility was good.

PFF markers were seen cascading but they quickly disappeared into cloud so that bombing had to be done on the red glow reflected through the cloud. Assessment of results is impossible but one large explosion was reported. Slight light flak but no searchlights in the target area. Cherbourg Peninsula was active with light and heavy flak. Several enemy fighters seen in target area. No casualties and no aircraft missing.

Time over target 00. 30. Bombing ht 9000–12,000 ft. Total of bomb-load carried was 339.4 tons of which 315 tons of HE were dropped.

(7) According to an observer on the ground afterwards, there were 3800 craters in the area of the Merville Battery (Florentin, *Opération Paddle*, p. 152).

## Appendix 3

### The Drop – as reported by Stanley Lee, ASC, DFM Chief Squadron Wireless Operator of 512 Squadron RAF in Wing Cdr. Coventry's aircraft

As 512 Squadron approached DZ 'V' at 00.50 on 6 June 1944, we found no 'Eureka' beacon, no wind indicators, no markers of any sort. Fortunately the visibility was good and visual map reading was possible. Since all pilots and navigators had studied models of the area and had watched countless showings of a film of the approach to the DZ, there was now little difficulty in identifying it.

As each pilot continued his slow descent to an average height of 550 ft over the DZ, he was either told that the whole stick was away, or else he put on the red light and jumping had to stop. There were two reasons for this. Either the aircraft had reached the end of the DZ, or it had gone down to below the safe height for jumping, reckoned as less than 500 ft (though some jumped from lower than that and got away with it).

Bearing in mind what we had been told about mines round the DZ, pilots and dispatchers exercised caution, and in several cases the red light went on to stop jumping before all sticks had gone out. In other cases the soldiers, very heavily laden and running on a metal floor in boots with smooth, rubber soles, slipped and fell, holding up the rest of the stick. Pilots took some risk in turning. It meant flying round in the correct direction for return to England, but then going west and re-entering the stream of aircraft approaching the coast, rather like driving from a slip-road into a dense stream of traffic on a motorway. Several made as many as three runs-in, including our own leading aircraft in which I was wireless operator, and dispatcher for the jump, piloted by Wing Commander Coventry. We saw no dust or smoke from the Lancaster raid on the Battery, and experienced no flak at all.

Many of the dispatchers commented on the determination shown by the parachutists in their desire to leave the aircraft, and in their extreme frustration when the red light stopped them. In the leading aircraft, on its *third* time round, one of the soldiers warmly shook my hand and thanked me for the chance to get out. As he waited in the door for the green light to go on, panting to be away, I looked down and saw flashes and signs of battle on the ground. This struck me as a poor alternative to getting back to the mess for breakfast. 'My officer'd never forgive me if I wasn't down there with him,' said the soldier and – as the light went on – 'buy you a beer later. . . .' and he was gone.

No pilot refused to go round again if it was necessary, although here and there the red light was ignored by one or two men who jumped after the southernmost limit of the DZ had been passed. Then they were in trouble, blown by a wind which was gusting to 25 mph, from a height of 550 ft, falling in an ESE direction. Any soldier who jumped from an aircraft on the port (eastern) side of the 'vic', especially if they were drifting slightly as they approached the DZ, would then be taken even further SE during the 47½ seconds it took the aircraft to cross the DZ. He may well have landed one and a half miles ESE-SE of the DZ.

The main body of the Battalion were dropped over DZ 'V' between 00.49¾ and 01.17 hours ('V' for Victory being the last aircraft to fly home). The Wind was 310/25 with 10/10 cloud at 3000–6000 ft, lowering to 1000.

# Appendix 3

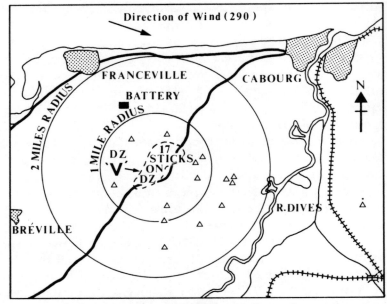

Fig. 9  DZ 'V' and approximate positions of sticks of 9th Battalion The Parachute Regiment. Each triangle represents the middle of each stick.

## The Drop – as described in official report

There was considerable controversy over the accuracy of the 9th Battalion's drop afterwards, which shocked the air crews of 512 Squadron. They were absolutely certain that they had found the DZ, if not on the first run-in, then certainly on the second. Nobody reported seeing enemy fighters and none reported any interference from flak or having to take evasive action to avoid any. There was some light flak a little distance away, and one aircraft was seen to crash in flames, but it was not from 512 Squadron. At times there was considerable turbulence in the air from the large number of aircraft in the area, mostly at the same height. Every one of the thirty-two aircraft of 512 Squadron returned to Broadwell without a scratch, let alone any dents or perforations in fuselage or wings.

Wing Commander Coventry, upset by reports of a scattered

## Appendix 3

drop which had filtered back from Normandy, wrote a strong memorandum to his superior officer, Group Captain Crofton, of which this is an extract:

3  after cross-examining each crew I found that –
   (i)   the 'C' pulse on Gee was poor and therefore accurate fixes could not be obtained.
   (ii)  the ground aids were non-existent from 00.50 hrs and until my last aircraft left the DZ.
   (iii) the DZ was only 1 min. 15 sec. from the coast and was quoted at 38 Group briefing as the most difficult.
   (iv)  other streams were crossing us breaking up vics and making straight runs very difficult.

4  Until concrete evidence is obtained from the 9th Btn. I have come to the conclusion that my squadron carried out a drop which qualifies 90% of them as pathfinders and that they require no different or further training.

5  I would like to suggest that as we are responsible for any troops which we carry that in future we be allowed to send out own pathfinders. Although it has been assumed that some of our troops were dropped inaccurately there has been no question as to whether pathfinders reached the correct DZ. I feel very strongly about the fact that these accusations have been made without any foundation and entirely contrary to all reports I have had re 9th Btn. from the Army.

In submitting Wing Commander Conventry's report to 38 Group Headquarters, Group Captain Crofton added the following:

One important point which is not brought out in Wing Commander Coventry's summary, is the fact that not only did each Vic leader navigate independently throughout the operation, but also, the rest of the formation was navigated independently. Thus on the occasion when formation had to be broken, there was no difficulty experienced in running up to the DZ, as there certainly would have been had navigation not been continuously and carefully done.'

This correspondence was in progress round about 20 June. The 9th Battalion remained in Normandy until early September by which time they had a different commanding officer, and much had happened to them in between. The files yield no follow-up to the argument, though there is some further clarification from a number of different sources.

The official RAF 'Report on the British Airborne Effort in Operation Neptune by 38 & 46 Transport Support Groups RAF' was published in typescript in about October 1944 (it is undated). The relevant paragraphs are these:

*Drop of Main Body of 3 Parachute Brigade on DZ 'V'*

78   71 Dakotas of 46 Group were detailed, to drop from 00.50 hrs.

79   Visibility was good; 7–10/10 cloud at 2000 ft; wind 290/25 at 2000 ft. No ground aids were operating on the DZ.

80   All aircraft reported dropping between 00.49¾–01.17 hrs except for one report which is missing. Of 1294 troops carried, 1287 were dropped, 4 had exit difficulties, 2 were injured and one was sick.

81   Reports from 3 Parachute Brigade indicate that only about 30 of the 71 sticks were dropped on the DZ or within one mile of its centre. Most of the remainder were dropped in the low-lying country to the east and south-east of the river DIVES

It should be noted that of the 71 Dakotas mentioned in para 78 above, only 32 referred to 9th Battalion. The rest, from squadrons other than 512, relate to 3 Parachute Brigade HQ and to 1st Canadian Parachute Battalion who also dropped on DZ 'V'.

A survey of the part played by the Royal Air Force in airborne operations, published by the Air Ministry in 1951 under the title of *The Second World War: 1939–45: Royal Air Force:* AIRBORNE FORCES *Air Publications* 3231 states:

The Events of 5–6 June 1944

Operation 'Tonga'

*First Stage*
Six Albermarle aircraft of 38 Group carried the men of the 22nd

## Appendix 3

Independent Parachute Company to the three main dropping zones 'K', 'N', and 'V'. These were the Pathfinders and it was their duty to set up Eureka beacons and illuminations on the DZs to guide in the main force following behind. Two aircraft were allocated to each zone and all went well until they reached their areas. . . .

The third zone, 'V', proved to be an unhappy choice. Although apparently quite suitable when viewed from the air, the area, being in a valley, had become extremely wet and treacherous owing to the flooding of the river. The ground was like a bog and all the equipment of one stick was lost or damaged while the other stick was dropped wide and did not arrive until the main body was due to drop. There were also many irrigation and other ditches which prevented rapid concentration. Although a later aircraft reported that Eureka beacons were working on 'K' and 'N' and lights were visible on all three zones there is no doubt that those on 'V' were inadequate and it was this zone which had the highest proportion of scattered drops. The work of the Pathfinders can have far-reaching repercussions but the fact that zone 'V' was unsuitable made it impossible for them to carry out their tasks. The mistaken choice of the ground for zone 'V' might have had very serious consequences had enemy resistance been stronger.

. . . 11 gliders scheduled to land on 'V' . . . carrying heavy equipment for the Merville raid, were mostly unsuccessful. The weather was unfavourable with low cloud and bumpy conditions and several pilots reported that the Lancaster bombing raid on the Merville Battery had caused considerable dust and smoke which obscured the landing zone. The outcome was that four gliders landed in a semicircle 1¾ miles from the landing zone while, of the remainder, three were compelled to cast off owing to cloud over the French coast; two landed on zone 'N' and two others nearby, consequently most of the equipment was not available for the attack on the battery. . . .

Close behind the gliders came the main bodies of the two parachute brigade groups. The weather was much the same except that lower cloud (2000 ft) was experienced over zone 'V' where no ground aids were working. The bog-like nature of the ground in this zone made the landings by the main body extremely hazardous; it impeded movement and rendered the task of mustering the troops at their rendezvous points all the harder.

Of the 11 gliders mentioned in the second paragraph of this report, only five were carrying stores and explosives for the Merville Battery raid, but none of it was available in time. 271 Squadron supplied tugs for these gliders, one of whose pilots was the comedian, Jimmy Edwards.

The 'Report on Operations, 6 Airborne Division' part I, issued in typescript, has in para 8:

> *Summary of Glider and Para Landings*
> . . .
> (b) *Parachute*
> The parachute drops were not as concentrated as might have been expected. This may have been due to the fact that only half an hour was allowed to the Independent Parachute Company for its work. It was desirable to keep this time as short as possible, . . . but since the DZs were comparatively easy to find, the risk was accepted.
> It is impossible to give accurate strengths of battalions in the first few hours of darkness, but the 3 Parachute Brigade Battalions certainly had to carry out their tasks at well below 30% strength.
> One unforeseen repercussion of the unintentional scattering of troops was that the German was misled as to the area and extent of the airborne landings.

Finally, the story of the drop is told, slightly differently, but with the same emphases, in *The History of Airborne Forces in World War II* from the War Office (HMSO, 1951):

> **The Airborne Assault of 6 Airborne Division**
> Pathfinders
>
> 17 Two sticks of pathfinders from 22nd Independent Parachute Company should have been dropped on each dropping zone but in each case only one stick was accurately dropped. In three cases two or more runs over the target were needed to get all the troops out, one aircraft completing its drop on the third run, 14 minutes later. All the radar and visual beacons for dropping zone 'V' (1st Canadian and 9th Parachute Battalions) were lost or damaged, and one aircraft carrying a pathfinder team intended for dropping zone 'K' (HQ 3 Parachute Brigade and 8th Parachute Battalion) put its passengers down on dropping zone 'N' (5th Parachute Brigade). Not realising that they were on the wrong dropping zone, the 'K' pathfinders set up their beacons and lights on dropping

zone 'N', before the 'N' pathfinders, who had been dropped some distance away, arrived and erected the correct beacons about 30 minutes later. In addition some of the pathfinder personnel set up their lights in standing crops, and they were not seen from the air.

### 3 Parachute Brigade

22 Most of the pathfinder equipment for dropping zone 'V' was damaged on the drop, so only two green lights were exhibited when the main body arrived there and few crews saw them, in addition to which they were hampered by dust and smoke blowing across the run-in from the bombing of the Merville Battery by the Lancasters. The main body had a very scattered drop, Brigadier Hill and several sticks of 1st Canadian and 9th Parachute Battalions being dropped near the River Dives. Their position of course was not known and unfortunately on their way to join their units later in the day, this party suffered heavy casualties in killed and wounded from our own bombing, Brigadier Hill being slightly wounded.

## The 00.26 Glider landing at Merville

(See Chapter 7, p. 142)

Steiner and Buskotte have reported that all the occupants of this glider were killed by their soldiers. In this event no news of the fate of its occupants can possibly have reached Allied sources at the time. Nor have any bodies since been recovered that clearly relate to the incident.

No member of 9th Battalion reported seeing the glider. Admittedly few, if any of them, were so far out beyond No 4 Casemate where it is reported to have landed; it burnt out quickly; the parachutists were not looking for a glider; it was dark, though the nature of the ground might have concealed it.

Nevertheless, the manner in which the area was afterwards searched, without revealing any vestige of typical metalwork, and the strange nature of this solitary invader from the sky at a totally unaccountable hour, must tend to cast a shadow of doubt upon the whole event.

The reported time of the glider's arrival – 00.26 on 6 June 1944 – disqualifies it from belonging to 6 Airborne Division. The only gliders in the area at that time were the six of Major John Howard's for the Orne *coup de main* parties. They have all been accounted for. Eleven gliders due to land on DZ 'V' for 3 Parachute Brigade (including 9th Battalion) cast off at 00.45 from 1500 ft. The RAF's flight-plan was so tight and has been so well documented since that it is most unlikely to have been a 'regular' mission. Nor can it have been with US forces, since none of their gliders took off from the UK before 00.19 on 7 June. Among its contents, according to Buskotte who speaks as an eye-witness, were those unfamiliar pneumatic drills. If the glider was an 'irregular' SAS taskforce on a special demolition job, there can never be any disclosure of information.

Steiner and Buskotte have always been vehement in their assurance about the glider. General Richter, too, in his postwar report about the 716 Infantry Division, relates that 'at about 00.30 I received a report that the Invasion had begun.' It was at this time that Steiner says he telephone Richter.

It is a chilling thought, nevertheless, that the glider's arrival could have fully alerted the Merville Battery garrison ready for the 'second attack' (as they still call it) by 9th Battalion. All Buskotte did was to 'clear up the mess' and double the sentries. No further evidence is available.

The case rests.

# APPENDIX 4

# German Army

Order of Battle : Commanders

| | |
|---|---|
| C-in-C West | Field Marshal Gerd von Rundstedt |
| Army Group 'B' | Field Marshal Erwin Rommel |
| 15th Army (E of Orne) | Colonel-General Hans von Salmuth |
| incl. 81 Corps | Lt.-Gen. Adolph Kuntzen |
| incl. 711 Inf. Div. | Maj.-Gen. Josef Reichert |
| 7th Army (mainly W of Orne) | Col.-Gen. Friedrich Dollmann |
| incl. 84 Corps | Lt.-Gen. Erich Marcks |
| incl. 716 Inf. Div. | Maj.-Gen. Wilhelm Richter |

Composition of 716 Inf. Div:
Infantry Divisions 736, 642 (Öst) both forward on coast and on both sides of Orne
    125 in reserve
    716 Artillery Regiment

Composition of 716 Artillery Regiment:
III Section (not yet formed)

  II Section     3 Batteries 10cm howitzers all W of Orne

  I Section:     3 Battery 'Graf Waldersee'
              4 × 150mm all self-propelled
              at Plumetot far W of Orne

              2 Battery
              4 × 10cm Czech howitzers
              Ouistreham W of Orne

              1 Battery
              4 × 10cm Czech howitzers
              Merville E of Orne

Infanterie-Division     – 14 –     Stand: 15 Dezember 1943

Offizier-Stellenbesetzungsliste des Artillerie-Regiments 716(656)

| Dienst-stellung | Dienst-grad | Name Vorname | R.D.A. (Ord.Nr.) | Lebens-alter Taugl. | Zivilberuf bei Offz. d.B.u.z.V. | Bemerkungen In solcher Stelle seit |
|---|---|---|---|---|---|---|
| *Stab Artillerie-Regiment 716 (Stab Art. Rgt. 656)* | | | | | | |
| Regts.-Kdr. | Oberst-leutnant | Andersen | 1.2.42 (193) | 48 g.v.H. | | 8.7.43 |
| Regts.-Adj. | Oberlt. | Lancelle | 1.2.43 (1113) | 23 k.v. | | |
| Ord.-Offz. | Lt.d.R. | Schulze Ernst | 1.5.43 | 33 k.v. | Optikermeister | |
| Offz. (W) z.Zt. unbesetzt. | | | | | | |
| *Stabsbatterie Art. Regt. 716 (Neuaufstellung)* | | | | | | |
| Battr.-Fhr. | Lt.d.R. | Weiss Kurt | 1.3.43 | 30 k.v. | Eisenhändler | |
| *Stab I./Art. Regt. 716 (Stab I./656)* | | | | | | |
| Abt.-Kdr. | Major d.R. | Hof Karl-Werner | 1.8.42 | 45 k.v. | Apotheker | 28.5.42 |
| Abt.-Adj. | Lt.d.R. | Hofheinz Günter | 1.1.43 | 33 k.v. | Syndikus | |
| Führer A.V.Ko. | Leutn. | Collin | 1.12.42 | 19 k.v. | | |
| *Stabsbatterie I./Art. Regt. 716 (Stabsbatterie I./656)* | | | | | | |
| Battr.-Führ. | Hptm. d.R. | Bote Hans-Ludwig | 1.3.43 | 49 g.v.H. | Pfarrer | 6.9.41 |
| Nachr. Zugf. z.Zt unbesetzt. | | | | | | |
| *1./Art. Regt. 716, Geschützart: le F.H. 14/19 (t) (1/656)* | | | | | | |
| Battr.-Führ. | Oblt. d.R. | Wolter Karl-Heinr. | 1.7.40 (739) | 30 g.v.H. | Landwirt | 1.3.41 |
| Beob.-Offz. | Ober-fähnr. | Brandenburg | | 28 g.v.H. | | |
| Battr.-Offz. | Leutn. | Malsch | 1.12.42 (1947) | 20 g.v.H. | | |
| *2./Art. Rgt. 716, Geschützart: le F.H. 14/19(t) (2./656)* | | | | | | |
| Battr.-Führ. | Oblt. d.R. | Ebenfeld Siegfried | 1.4.42 | 29 g.v.H. | Lehrer | 4.8.40 |
| Beob.-Offz. durch Wachtmeister besetzt | | | | | | |
| Battr.-Offz. | Lt.d.R. | Trippen Josef | 1.7.43 | 34 k.v. | Fleischer-meister | |

– 15 –

# Appendix 4

### Erinnerungsprotokoll über den Einsatz des Artl. Reg. 1716 in den ersten Tagen der Invasion im Juni 1944

Zusammenstellung: K.Heyde, ehem. Oblt.u.Reg Adj. Artl.Reg. 1716
H.Collin, ehem. Ltn.u.Abtlg.Adj. I/1716
H.Hammen, ehem. Ltn.u.Abtlg.Adj. II/1716
R.Schaaf, ehem. Oblt.u.Battr.Chef lo/1716
Battr.Graf Waldersee

Das Artl. Reg 1716 gehörte zur 716.Inf. Div. und wir mit seinen beiden Abtlg. (insges. 6 Batterieen) in der Normandie eingesetzt. Der Gefechtsabschnitt reichte von Merville (rechts der Orne) bis Port en-Bessin.

Sitz des Reg. Gef.Stabes war Caen.

Reg. Kdr. am Tage der Invasion    Obstltn. Knupe
Reg. Adj.                         Obltn. K. Heyde
Ord. Offz.                        Ltn. Malsch

Zum Artl. Reg. 1716 gehörten :
*I. Abtlg.*  Kdr. Major Hof
        Adj. Ltn. Collin
  Sitz: Höhe 61 bei Colleville (verbunkert)

1. Batterie:   Merville 4 × 100mm verbunkert
          Battr. Chef Hptm. Schimpf
          Battr. Offz Ltn. Tubbesing

2. Batterie:   Quistreham (Wasserturm) 4 × 100 mm verbunkert
          Battr. Chef Hptm. Engels

3. Batterie:   ehem. lo/1716 "Battr. Graf Waldersee"
          auf Selbstfahrlafetten 4 × 150mm
          in Feldstellung bei Plumetot
          Battr. Chef Oblt. Schaaf

*II. Abtlg.*  Kdr. Major G. Grünewald
        Adj. Ltn. H. Hammen
        Ord.Offz. Ltn. Mette
  Sitz: Gefechtsstaand 2 km. nordwestl. Crepon

5. Batterie:   Crepon (Ausweichfeuerstellung) 4 × 100mm
          Feldstellung
          Battr. Chef Oblt. K. Theimer

## Appendix 4

|  |  |
|---|---|
|  | B.-Offz. Ltn. Blank |
|  | Battr.Offz. Ltn. Güther (Günther) |
| 6. Batterie: | Ver s.Mer (La Mare-Fontine) 4× 100mm verbunkert |
|  | Battr. Chef Ltn. Mitschke (?) |
| 7. Batterie: | Vaux sur Aure 4 × 100mm offene Feldstllg. |
|  | Battr. Chef Hptm. Franke |

eine III. Abteilung bestand im Artl. Reg. 1716 nicht.

# APPENDIX 5

## The 10cm Czech Howitzers at Merville (10cm le FH 14/19(t))

Specification:

| | |
|---|---|
| Calibre | 100mm |
| Length of piece | 2400mm |
| Length of barrel | 2175mm |
| Length of rifling | 1899mm |
| Weight travelling | 2025/2855kg |
| Weight in action | 1490/1505kg |
| Traverse | 5° 38' |
| Elevation | −7°30' to 48° |
| Maximum range | 9800/9970m |
| Muzzle velocity | 395/415 m/s |
| Shell weight | 14/16kg |
| Rate of fire | 8 rpm |

(Different weights depended upon equipment used; different range muzzle velocity and shell weights depended upon type of ammunition used.)

Produced in the Skoda Works, Pilsen, Bohemia in 1916 for the Austro-Hungarian Artillery.

### Skoda 100mm Model 14/19

Essentially a revised and updated version of the Model 14, the Model 14/19 was one of the more important equipments in the

Czech Army artillery park in 1938 when it served as the 10 cm houfnice vz.14/19. During the Second World War these guns served with the German Army as the 10 cm leFH 14/19(t) and they were used in some numbers. Other nations that used the M.14/19 were Hungary, Poland, Jugoslavia and Greece. In Poland the gun was known as the 100 mm haubica wz.1914/1919 but became the German 10 cm le FH 14/19(p). Jugoslav guns served as the 100 mm M.14/19 and became the 10 cm le FH 316(j). The few guns in Greek service that fell into German hands became the 10 cm leFH 318(g). Many of these captured weapons were passd to the Italian Army where they were sometimes fitted with rubber wheels and other revisions – as such they were known as the Obice da 100/24 and many were used for coastal defences.

## The Tasks of the Merville Battery
(from the Range Card shown on p. 150)

The range card from No 1 Casemate of the Merville Battery establishes that the howitzers were expected to fire on a variety of targets and not only on 'Sword' Beach – as it came to be called. Steiner and Buskotte could recall only that the targets were 'the Orne Canal locks and key road junctions etc.'.

Gunnery of this kind is very precise. Instead of degrees (360 to a circle) the Germans used a far smaller measurement called a *Strich*, with 6400 to a full circle. The figures in the third column of the range card, under TLRG, represent the bearing: 6400 (or 0) *Strich* = due South and, going clockwise, 3200 *Strich* = North. It was immediately obvious that the guns could not fire in these directions from inside the casemates and even without appropriate range tables it was clear that all the shots on the given bearings would fall in the sea.

For security reasons, however, it was a habit of German gunners to code the bearings on their range card ± a pre-arranged figure in 100-*Strich* from the true bearing. We found that if 1400 *Strich* were deducted from each of the figures in the

## Appendix 5

third column of the range card, it makes the best sense, and we assume the same alteration applies to all five targets.

Making allowance for the charge of shot used (under LG) and the elevation (under ERHG) and combining them, the howitzers were ranged as follows:

1 ENGERS T-junction of the coast road at Colleville Plage and the road going inland to Colleville. By increasing elevation on this bearing, ENGERS also covers about two miles of 'Sword' Beach.

2 EMS In Ouistreham, the first X-roads on the straight minor road off the coast road going SE towards Caen along the west bank of the Caen Canal.

3 DÜSSELDORF The locks on the Orne Canal and the Caen road alongside.

4 CAUB The east end of the Pointe du Siège between the Caen Canal and the tidal mud-flats of the Orne River. Increasing range, this bearing coincides with the northern beach of this peninsula.

5 BREMEN The Moulin du Buisson on the short N-S stretch of the coast road between Sallenelles and Franceville east of the Orne River. Increasing range, this bearing also covers part of the beach in the Baie de Sallenelles.

It will be seen that the howitzers were ranged on four targets west of the Orne Canal and one immediately east of it. Control was from No 1 Howitzer in No 1 Casemate and all four could switch from one target to another when ordered to do so. Together they neutralised all four roads in the area going inland from the coast towards Caen; the Canal locks; and the island site of the Pointe du Siège. This is in sight of the Battery and might be said to menace it. The emphasis upon the roads to Caen probably lies in the (mistaken) German view that the Allies needed a port for supply, and Caen was the only one in the Baie of the Seine apart from the securely defended Le Havre. The Germans did not know about 'Mulberry'.

(I thank Professor Steiner and Major Strong for, between them, providing the necessary information and skill to reconstruct the orders on the range card and decipher them; also to the unknown person who saved the range card and presented it to the Airborne Forces Museum in Aldershot.)

### Blowing the Merville Guns

The guns were to have been destroyed by Royal Engineers carrying special explosives ('beehive charges') used to blow in the steel doors of the casemates if they were shut, and others placed on the guns inside. They were hollow charges, similar in effect to the PIAT bomb where all the explosive force was directed and concentrated in one direction. The main contingent of REs and their explosives were due to be delivered in gliders on DZ/LZ 'V', but they did not arrive. A small, supplementary group of REs with a limited amount of explosives were in the 'GB Force' gliders, but only one of them landed anywhere near the Battery, and too far away to be of assistance in the attack.

All soldiers of 9th Battalion carried some plastic HE which, when crammed into a stockinette holder and fitted with a detonator was known as a Gammon Bomb or No 82 Grenade. It was primarily for use against tanks but was all that the soldiers had to use against the howitzers.

Unfortunately it was thought best to place the bombs against the breech block. That is the strongest part of any gun as it has to withstand the major force of explosion. When

## Appendix 5

ignited, any plastic explosive or normal grenade will burst outwards, finding the line of least resistance and will not penetrate inwards. It is conceivable that such an explosion might unsettle any sensitive breech-mechanism if there was any, but an engineer, had he been present, might have been able to apply more scientific use of the limited resources available.

The historic way of 'spiking' a gun was to put a round reversed in the muzzle, load another round normally in the breech, stand well back and pull the toggle. But the Czech howitzers in the Merville casemates needed primers to activate the round in the breech. The soldiers of 9th Battalion were not gunners and could not be expected to know this, nor to recognise and find the primers and insert them with the round in the breech. Thus 'one down the muzzle and one up the spout' would, in this instance, have produced no result at all.

If, as has been stated, old bits of metal and 36 (Mills) grenades were put down the muzzle and it was not 'tamped' (i.e. stuffed tightly to enclose what was inside it) the explosive force was bound to escape, resulting in the clouds of dust described. As the 36 Grenades were made of softer metal than the tempered steel of the inside rifling of the gun barrel, they would have had little effect on the subsequent firing of the weapon.

(The author is grateful to Brigadier F.H. Lowman CBE, DSO, then CRE of 6 Airborne Division, and to Brigadier R.F. Semple MBE, MC, also a Royal Engineer of 6 Airborne Division, and a specialist in blowing up 'Rommel's Asparagus', for this information.)

# APPENDIX 6

## At the Orne Estuary

An article from the German magazine *Das Reich* (end July 1944), written by Naval War Correspondent Helmut Berndt (translated by Major Mike Strong REME)

This forward bunker on the eastern flank of the Normandy battle area has virtually four fronts. The first two are the Orne and the sea, the third is the sky which is never free from enemy aircraft that dive to attack even solitary soldiers. During the past eventful days the fourth front has moved further to the south but could return this way overnight.

This bunker is our most forward position at the mouth of the Orne. Only sand dunes, undergrowth, mines and wire obstacles lie between here and the river. The strip of land between the bunker and the sea is similarly protected, the barbed wire looking even more conspicuous on the beach. As with most forward positions, this bunker is known to the enemy and often comes under fire.

In the bunker's concrete turret, or 'Tobruk Stand' the Battery Commander sits as usual, on an ammunition box, by his rangefinder. He scans all round with his binoculars. 'Fog again,' he says to himself. A small boat appears and behind it are banks of sea mist which hide the landing places and the ships. Nevertheless the superstructure and turrets of *Nelson* and *Rodney*, and the pylon-masts of *Nevada* are recognisable, also other ships offshore. Most of the bigger ships lie at anchor; through the haze they resemble an imaginary city with winking towers in the mist – 'The Golden City', as the troops call it.

## Appendix 6

Lieutenant Steiner turns his periscope towards the coast. Riva Bella is over there – in former days it was a spa, famed for its cuisine. Now the beach is cratered, many houses have been flattened and, further to the left, Ouistreham is in a similar state.

Once the lower Orne was like a little paradise. On the narrow canal, patrol boats pass through parkland, past distant châteaux and farms. Tall hedgerows, crowded rows of trees border the meadows where contented cattle lie. Alongside the canal, near the road, is the tiny railway with small engines and open wagons like a toy train. It is hard to imagine violence here. Who could believe that war was possible here? . . .

Steiner turns the crosswires of his periscope on to the lighthouse in the estuary where earlier he had been firing in order to smash the beacon. Then he checks the houses that have survived the hail of fire, and the people in the street. Also he takes a quick look at the big square where, a few days earlier, the British were playing football – until he broke it up!

He makes a quick count of the shiny, silver barrage balloons which encircle the landing zone. He verifies that there are still forty-eight of them, then turns the periscope through ninety degrees. Over there lie solitary destroyers, also a cruiser and gunboats. He knows some of them already, others keep changing position. Now they fade slowly from sight as the mist comes in from the sea in grey banks, a few kilometres offshore. There is not much more to be seen.

Lieutenant Steiner calls to the sentry below. Something is happening in the fog. He peers through the periscope. He can see more clearly now and he resumes his seat. Something is happening out at sea. Four boats emerge like shadows from the milky-grey mist. Rocket boats succeed in penetrating to an extent hitherto unknown in war. These boats were developed from combined operations experience, and are the size of gunboats, with the usual camouflage.

They attack us at high speed, throwing white foam from their bows. They come past us with multiple rocket-tubes flashing. We count between twenty-four and thirty-six tubes on each boat and then we see spurts of flame coming from them. The projectiles rush and moan through the air and explode around us. They fall in groups, in a narrow strip, their bladed tips burrowing into the sand dunes and exploding with unusual force. A great blast-wave follows the explosions, then shrapnel. With their great concentration and simultaneous action, they light up the beach and start a fire in the ruins of a nearby village.

We can no longer stay in the 'Tobruk Stand', but Steiner must give his fire orders and he grabs the telephone. Shortly afterwards, shells howl over the bunker towards the sea, passing through the yellow clouds of dust above the beach, towards the still flaming tubes of the enemy boats.

'Cease Fire, Battery; Cease Fire!'

Battery Sergeant-Major Buskotte, passes the order from his commander in the coastal bunker to his gun crews, and the howitzers fall silent. The gunners take off their steel helmets again, and the gun-loaders wipe away the sweat. Gunsmoke drifts through the casemate doorways.

'We gave it to them!' One of the young artillerymen removes the wadding from his ears and begins to pick up the empties.

It is amazing to realise that these young men were school-boys only a short time ago. They have been familiar with their weapons for only a few months, and it is as if they had just finished the campaign in Poland. The past few weeks have been most eventful for them, even before the Invasion started.

Starshells and illuminating flares flicker in the sky, then bombs whistle down on to the Battery. The enemy knows our position from aerial photographs. He wants to weaken our position before a flanking attack. He drops one-tonne bombs which make huge craters. The bunkers shake under the blast, but they survive and the guns remain serviceable.

These various bombardments were, however, just a preliminary. The Battery was a threat to the British strongpoint on the Orne and was continually firing at it. In this, the German gunners were successful. They covered the roads on the other side of the Orne, destroying vehicle concentrations and anti-aircraft guns, shelling gunboats and freighters which came near the coast. They were not involved, however, in sinking the ships whose masts protrude from the sea off Riva Bella. Once they scored fifteen hits on a gunboat, and one evening they hit an ammunition ship which caught fire after a few shots; the ammunition exploded and the night sky was lit with all colours until early next morning.

Their Battery Commander also directed fire on to the troops- and tank-landing craft. The British dived head first into the sea when the Battery opened fire on them. The gunners themselves cannot see the results of their work, they follow orders. They aim the guns, see the flash, hear the thunder and say a grim farewell to each round. Enemy intelligence knows the location of the Battery well, as they have suffered many hits. In the course of time, the Battery's appearance has changed. The barrack buildings which they occupied earlier are completely destroyed, the roadways are battered and the craters are full of water.

They have been fired upon continuously. Once it was land batteries on the other side of the Orne, then they were fired upon by ships' guns, and this combination produced a remarkable curtain of fire. It is hard to recall a day when there was not repeated shelling of their positions. Aircraft fly overhead. Fighter-bombers hunt low over the landscape, four cannons projecting from their wings, soon reaching the Battery. At night they come in even greater numbers.

But that is no great problem: the men can endure a great deal.

They are often bombarded from nearby woods in such regular fashion that they count every shot. When they are off-duty they sleep late in their bunkers, awakened only by machine-gun fire or by mortars or hand-grenades, and listening to find out whether they are required to stand-to. Soon they roll on to their sides and sleep on, as they do not know when they will get another chance.

They are sad that the small wood – which is now the front line – is no longer green: the wood in which they spent many hours in earlier days. The trees are smashed and the greenery has disappeared in recent bombardments.

Now and then they think of their fathers' experiences in the First World War. But today they need no longer just talk of war, because this battle on the invasion front excels all else in brutality, hardship and fire-power of weapons.

They put up with so much and have become accustomed to things that would earlier have frozen the blood in their veins. Have they become battle-hardened, or are they just pretending to be nonchalant?

When the two medical orderlies go out, coughing, to bury a dead man, and have to seek shelter from the enemy gunfire, they leave the corpse on its stretcher beside the open grave while they seek shelter for themselves. They already disassociate themselves from the dead man. They no longer notice the smell of putrid decay which pervades the craters and ruins. They are only seventeen or eighteen years old. But they know that there is more to come.

One night was particularly bad. The countryside was in near darkness; the moon appeared only through gaps in the moving clouds; the bunkers lay in deep shadow.

A cargo-glider flies low over their positions, they fire at it and it goes down in flames behind the wood. Another lands not far away with a special task. As well as a large crew it carries flamethrowers, compressed air drills and explosives in order to clear the bunkers. . . .

This battle in the dark was unnerving. They could not tell friend from foe – control was difficult. However Buskotte knew that the direction of the main attack was from the landward side.

'To the rear, infantry attacking. Range 500 m, fire at will!'

The howitzers, dragged from their bunkers, stand ready to fire. The lanyard is pulled and, in direct fire, the shells explode in the open fields.

The howitzers were not intended for this sort of battle. They were supposed to be used against targets at sea, at long

## Appendix 6

distance, not at a few hundred metres. The men are gunners, not infantry.

But close-quarter battle is unavoidable. The gunfire blazes orange again, the charges explode in the barrels. But the enemy gets closer, in a large semicircle. Here a shadow jumps up and sinks into a crater. Over there crouches a dark shape as the earth swallows it.

They are now 200 metres away. They bring their machine-guns and mortars into the Battery position. We are outnumbered.

What use are rattling machine-gun salvoes, hand grenades and rifles when they are surrounded by attackers five times their number?

The howitzers can fire no more, the hand grenades have been thrown, the machine-guns are silenced. The enemy breaks into the position. But they throw him out again.

They inflicted heavy casualties on the British but also some of the defenders were lost as grey morning dawned in the countryside.

They held their position but the enemy, who sheltered in a nearby village and were reinforced by other troops from the landings, were determined to win this key position. So the day passed, and the night, and by midday on the second day the next crucial test began.

From the ruined houses there is some movement! Small, but its purpose is becoming clearer as the defenders use their binoculars.

The guns are dragged out of the bunkers again. Again their barrels are aimed at the khaki dots in the fields. Again cartridge-belts rattle through the machine-guns and bullets travel flat over the ground. But the attackers come from two directions. When close combat seems imminent, Buskotte has only one option. He orders a neighbouring battery to fire on the position.

As night falls, our men are again in charge of their position. They wait for reinforcements which must soon reach them in order to reduce the enemy's numerical superiority. Before they arrive, the third attack is launched. The British send their fighting-bombers in support. They attack at low level, firing at our guns and soldiers. Meantime, as the enemy have many aircraft, their parachutists move in from crater to crater and from bush to bush.

It is hard for an individual soldier to understand how, in some situations, his weapons are not entirely effective. The same manœuvre as those of previous days seem to be developing once more.

'Everyone into the bunker!' The order comes from across the cratered field. The gunners get their machine-guns and machine pistols, and pull back. The steel doors are closed and the gun-slits are opened. The bunkers have taken on the appearance of grey concrete and iron with protruding gun barrels.

Meanwhile Buskotte has telephoned to Lieutenant Steiner. Although the Tommies had cut some of the cables, this link has survived to permit communication and fire control.

Shells come down nearby, throwing sand high in the air, but it was too far away. Buskotte observed the fall of shot through his periscope: 'Still too far,' he says into the telephone, and his voice has a concise tone which Steiner can discern from the other end.

The British have reached the bunker. Buskotte sees them running. He sees one with a pistol aiming at his periscope and then the glass shatters. They can no longer see what is happening. They are almost blind inside their concrete block and can neither follow the enemy's movements nor spot the fire of neighbouring artillery. Only the firing-slits give them contact with the outside world. Behind them the soldiers hold their weapons in tense fingers. Soon the British might come with explosives and flame-throwers. . . .

There is one of the enemy – there another. . . . Their machine-guns fire, and the sound echoes loudly under the bunker's roof. Three of the attackers fall in front of the steel door. The gunners stand, tight-lipped, at their slits. Nobody will come from their front, but they will certainly find other

## Appendix 6

ways. Perhaps they will bring drilling equipment.

If only their own artillery shots would fall nearer! But time goes on . . .

Time seems wasted in the bunker with so many men together in one room. This is no way to fight a battle, here behind concrete walls in half-darkness. No one has a proper field of fire. No one can see the enemy.

What about our guns? Have the enemy blown them up?

Mighty explosions rock the bunker, but it is not the British, it is our own artillery firing on to our position, right on target. Shell after shell comes howling down. One makes a small crater, throwing up a shower of splinters. With only short pauses, the heavy guns hammer away continually and throw up the earth again and again. Some shells fall close to the bunker, then echoes of more distant shells reverberate, then a shell shatters on the bunker-roof, and the soldiers inside are thrown against one another. In the small space, bunk-beds fall over and dust fills the air.

Nobody could survive this barrage without substantial overhead protection.

When the air in the bunker becomes so thin that the lungs protest and carbide lamps go out; when the smell of blood from the wounded becomes unbearable, then the gunners open the shutters. Dead and wounded lie about the battlefield, otherwise there is silence. Only the ships' guns rumble in the distance and fighter-bombers criss-cross the sky. The gunners make for their still-serviceable howitzers and take aim again at the enemy fleet.

## Appendix 6

## THE TIMES Saturday 24 June 1944 (page 3)

## PARACHUTISTS TAKE A BATTERY

### Feat in Normandy Landings

The parachutists of the 6th British Airborne Division were the men on whom the success of the establishment of the bridgeheads in Normandy depended. One battalion rehearsed the taking of an enemy battery for months. It was their responsibility to ensure that these four guns were put out of action before the sea borne invaders arrived on the beaches.

Captain Albert Richards, a young war artist, who trained with the division and jumped with them has given an account of their exploit in which he says:

> I am sure we lost men in the marshy ground on which most of us landed. After searching round in the dark we found the rendezvous, but we were far from the full complement. Ahead of us was a special party, consisting of a major and two PT sergeants, whose job was to breach the minefield known to surround the gun site. They were to have the task completed by the time we arrived.
>
> We moved carefully, taking cover in country which happened to be well suited to our needs. We met several French men and women. There was also a bomb-crazed cow which threatened to give away our position. It was not until we came close to our objective that we were seen and mortared. There were not many casualties, though they put down a good barrage. All the time we were on the look-out for gliders which had been instructed to crash-land on the gun site, and give us help. One now came into view, wheeling silently above the objective like a gigantic hawk waiting to sweep on its prey. They got this glider down safely, but 50 yards away from the battery.
>
> We now linked up with the special mine-breaching party, who told us the site had beeen bombed so heavily there was little they could do to ensure a safe path by normal anti-mining methods. The whole area was pitted with tremendous craters. The CO of the battalion then decided that the assault company, or what was

left of it, should go forward and guard what gaps could be found, while 'B' Company blew the inner wire defences. The enemy brought all his small arms fire to bear on us. The battery crew were fully alive to their danger and were defending themselves desperately. Our fellows did not seem to take the slightest notice of the hail of bullets. Led by their colonel they went forward as planned. Their courage was wonderful. Every man knew his job and went straight to it. No orders were issued. None was necessary.

Inside the battery terrific hand-to-hand fighting developed. Stens barked, grenades were lobbed into galleries, and within 15 minutes it was all over. Gun crews had been winkled out of their emplacements; 50 prisoners, some startlingly young and others equally old, were shepherded out. They seemed dazed by the speed and surprise of the attack. We destroyed the four battery guns by demolitions. We thanked God we had been able to silence them in time. The first of our invasion forces were not due to land on the beaches for two hours. Our casualties we carried from the site to a paratroop MO who had set up an emergency reception station in a bomb crater. I cannot pay too high a tribute to paratroop RAMC personnel. They did wonderful work in most difficult conditions.

# BIBLIOGRAPHY

## I Books

Belfield, E. & Essame, H., *The Battle for Normandy*, Pan, London, 1967, pp.66–70.
Carrel, Paul, *Sie kommen!* G. Stalling Verlag, Oldenburg & Hamburg, 1960, pp. 45–51.
Carier, Raymond, *Der 2 Weltkrieg 1942–44* Band II, Piper Verlag, Munich, n.d., pp.878–9.
Chamberlain, P. & Gander, T., *World War II Facts and Files: Light and Medium Field Artillery*, Macdonald & Janes, London, 1975, pp.8–12.
Collier, Richard, *Ten Thousand Eyes* Collins, London, 1958, pp. 74–7, 166–71, 310–20.
Crookenden, Lt-Gen. Sir N., *Dropzone Normandy* Ian Allan, London, 1976, pp.174–81, 200–9, 246–7.
   *9th Battalion The Parachute Regiment Normandy 1944 – the first six days*, private printing, n.d., pp. 1–20.
Dollar, J. & Kayser, R., *Histoire de la 'Luxembourg Battery'* Imp. Cent. Soc. An. Luxembourg, 1982, pp. 56–62.
Edwards, Comdr. Kenneth, *Operation Neptune*, Collins, London, 1946, pp.135–7.
Ellis, L.F., *Victory in the West* Vol.I, HMSO, London, 1962, pp. 152–5.
Ferguson, Greg, *The Elite: Against All Odds*, Orbis, London, 1985, pp. 18–19.
Florentin, Eddy, *Opération Paddle – La Poursuite*, Presses de la Cité, Paris, 1983, pp.92–3, 150–3, 158–9.
Gale, Gen. Sir R.N., *Call to Arms*, Hutchinson, London, 1968, pp.140–3.
   *With the Sixth Airborne Division in Normandy*, Sampson Low & Marston, London, 1948, *passim*.
Gleeson, James, & Waldron, Tom, *Now It Can Be Told*, Elek, London, 1951, pp. 11–31.
Golley, John, *The Big Drop*, Janes, London, 1982, *passim*.
   *La Nuit des Canons de Merville* (trans. Florentin, E.), Presses de la Cité, Paris, 1983, *passim*.

# Bibliography

Grall, Jeanne, *1940–1944: Le Mur de l'Atlantique en Images*, Eds. Libre-Sciences, SPRL, 1978, pp. 134–7.

Hamilton, Nigel, *Monty: Master of the Battlefield, 1942–1944*, Coronet, London, 1985, pp.475 *et seq.*

Hastings, Max, *Overlord, D-Day & the Battle for Normandy 1944*, Michael Joseph, London, 1984, p.88.

Hayn, Friedrich, *Die Invasion von Contentin bis Falaise*, (Die Wehrmacht im Kampf band 2) Kurt Vowinckel Verlag, Heidelberg, n.d., p.41.

Hilton, Frank, *The Paras*, BBC Publications, London, 1983, pp.195–200.

Hogs, Ian, *German Artillery of World War II*, Arms and Armour Press, London, 1975, pp.38–41.

Howarth, David, *Dawn of D-Day*, Collins, London, 1959, pp.50–63.

Jackson, Gen. W.G.F. *'Overlord': Normandy 1944*, Davis-Poynter, London, 1978 pp.172–9.

Johnson, G., & Dunphie, C. *Brightly Shone the Dawn*, Warne, London, 1980, pp.41–55.

Liddell Hart, B.H. (ed.), *The Rommel Papers*, Collins, London, 1953, pp.451–87, 495–6.

Lovat, Brig. The Lord, *March Past*, Weidenfeld & Nicolson, London, 1976, pp.314, 322–9.

Paine, Lauran, *D-Day*, Robert Hale, London, 1981, pp.128–37.

Piekalkiewicz, Janusz (trans. Garvie, F. & Fowler, N.), *Secret Agents, Spies and Saboteurs*, David & Charles, Newton Abbot, 1974 pp.38–53.

*Invasion Frankreich*, Sudwest Verlag, Munich, 1979, pp.64–5, 92–3, 88, 117, 137–8, 141, 166.

Ramsey, Winston G. (ed.), *After the Battle* Vol. I, London, New York, 1977, pp.7–10.

Ruge, Admiral Friedrich, *Rommel in Normandy*, Macdonald & Jane's, London, 1979, pp.65–6, 92–3, 120–3, 136–41, 152–9, 161–4, 168–79

Ryan, Cornelius, *The Longest Day*, Gollancz, London, 1960, pp.106–8, 134–8.

Saunders, H. St. G., *The Green Beret*, Michael Joseph, London, 1950, pp.270–2.

*The Red Beret*, Michael Joseph, London, 1950, pp.178–89.

Sawyer, John, *D-Day*, Four Square, London, 1960, pp.29–34.

Speidel, Dr Hans, *Invasion 1944: Rommel and the Normandy Campaign* Greenwood Press, Westport, Conn. 1971, pp.3, 5, 21–55, 78–81, 88–9, 115–19.

*We Defended Normandy* (trans. Colvin, I.) Herbert Jenkins, London, 1951, pp.95–6.

Stagg, J.M., *Forecast for Overlord*, Ian Allan, London, 1971, *passim*.

Stjernfelt, Bertil, *Alerte sur le Mur de l'Atlantique*, Presses de la Cité, Paris, 1961. pp.104, 281.

Trevor-Roper. H.R. (ed.), *Hitler's War Directives 1939–45*, Pan, London, 1966, No.51, pp.218–24.

Wheldon, Sir Huw, *Red Berets into Normandy*, Jarrold, Norwich, 1982, pp.20–5.

## Bibliography

Wilmot, Chester, *Struggle for Europe,* Collins, London, 1952, *passim.*
Young, Brig. Desmond, *Rommel,* Collins, London, 1950, pp.189–214.
Young, Brig. Peter, *Storm from the Sea,* William Kimber, London, 1958, pp.139–56.
*Encyclopaedia Britannica,* 15th (1985) Edition.


## II Official Publications consulted, in chronological order of publication

| | |
|---|---|
| COSSAC: *Overlord* 6 Airborne Div. in outline plan | PRO WO205/2 |
| Pre-D Day Bombing reports on Coastal Batteries | PRO WO205/172 |
| History of 46 Transport Support Group RAF | PRO AIR38/238 |
| 38 Group Operation order No.500 Operation *Neptune* (typed) | Middle Wallop |
| 512 Squadron Operations Diary | PRO AIR271/1974 |
| Photographs of 38 Group Ops Room Boards for DZ/LZ 'V': Operation 'Tonga' 5/6 June 1944 | Middle Wallop |
| 9th Parachute Battalion War Diary | PRO WO171/1242 |
| No 3 Commando War Diary | PRO WO218/65 |
| No 45 Commando War Diary | PRO ADM202/82 |
| Report on British Airborne Effort in Operation *Neptune* by 38 & 46 Groups RAF (typed) | Middle Wallop |
| Analysis & Report of Radar Equipment in British 6 Airborne Div. Operations night 5/6 June for 'Tonga' | PRO AIR25/588 |
| 38 Group correspondence over 'Tonga' | PRO AIR37/286 |
| Current Reports from Overseas No.49 (5 August 1944) | HMSO 1944 |
| 2 Oxf. & Bucks L.I. War Diary | PRO WO171/1357 |
| 6 Airborne Division, Report on Operations in Normandy 6 Jun-27 Aug. 1944 (typed) | Private Source |
| Report on Operations by 6 Airborne Division 5 Jun-3 Sept. 1944 (typed) | Private Source |
| *By Air to Battle* The Official Account of Airborne Forces | HMSO, 1945 |
| Kampf der 716 Division in der Normandie vom 6.6.44–23.6.44 von Lieut. Gen. Wilhelm Richter (Allendorf 31.5.1947 – typed) | Private Source |
| History of Airborne Forces in World War II | War Office, HMSO 1951 |

## Bibliography

Second World War AIRBORNE FORCES
   1939–45 Royal Air Force     Air Ministry (A.H.B.)
Staff & Students' booklet on 'Overlord'. Data &     Staff College,
   plans     Camberley
6 Airborne Division Intelligence Summary by
   Major G. Lacoste MBE July 1977 (typed)     Private Source

PRO    = Public Record Office, Kew, London
WO     = War Office
HMSO = Her Majesty's Stationery Office
Middle Wallop = Archive of the Museum of Army Flying, Middle Wallop, Stockbridge, Hants.

# INDEX

AANT (Airborne Assault Normandy Trust), *174, 176*
Agnone, *131*
aids, air navigational, *100, 101*
Air Force, Canadian (RCAF), *80*
  German *see* Luftwaffe
  Royal (RAF) photography, *44, 77*
    dinghies, *49*
    mess party, *54, 55–6*
    raids on Germany, *70, 72, 98*
    bombardments, 6 June 1944, *120–2, 148*
      intensity of, *151, 153, 178*
    destroys Merville guns, *171*
    38 Group, *55*
    44 Group; 24 Sqn, *54–5*
    46 Group; 512 Sqn, *54–5*
      plan, *94, 97, 98*
      route, *98*
      flight, *98–102*
      drop, *102*
      skill of, *178*
    Women's Auxiliary (WAAF), *23, 50, 51, 58*
aircraft: Albermarle, *94*
  Dakota, *54, 98, 101*
    description of, *95*
  Flamingo, *54*
  Halifax, *80, 89*
  Lancaster, *80, 89, 90, 94, 108, 142*
  Whitley, *55*
Alençon, *165*
Allt, Private, *125, 126, 127*
Amfréville, *131, 156*
Andersen, Lt.-Col. Hans-Joachim, *76, 79, 157, 163*
Antwerp, *170, 171*
*Arethusa*, HMS, *37, 106, 115*
Army
  Belgian:
    Piron Brigade, *167*
    Luxembourg Battery, *167*

British:
  21 Army Group, *170—1*
  1 Airborne Division, *34*
  6 Airborne Division, *29, 53, 55, 129, 130, 148, 156, 164, 174*
  Battle School, *27–8*
  CCS, *47*
  Royal Engineers, *36, 37, 41*
  22 Indep. Para. Coy, *94, 101–2*
  3 Para. Bde., *156*; Bde. HQ, *126*
    224 Para. Fld. Amb., *47, 126*
    9 Para. Bn, *see under*
      Parachute Regiment
  5 Para. Bde
    7 Para. Bn, *129*
    12 Para. Bn, *131*
  6 Airlanding Bde, *167*
    12 Devons, *167*
    52 LI, *129, 167*
    1 RUR, *27, 43, 53, 58*
  1 SS (Commando) Bde, *129, 148, 164*
    HQ, *130, 131, 132, 136*
    No 3 Commando *see under*
      Commando
    No 45 (RM) Cdo, *129, 130, 132, 138*
  Staff College, Camberley, *34, 173, 174*
Canadian, *164, 170*
German *see under* Wehrmacht
Netherlands:
  Princess Irene Bde, *167*
Polish:
  Armoured Div, *169*
  9th Rifle Bn, *170*
Unit, *34*
United States:
  1st & 3rd Armies, *165*

Badoglio, Marshal Pietro, *82*

234

# Index

Bavent (ridge), *156, 164*
Bayeux, *165*
beaches:
   'Juno', *130*
   'Sword', *129*
Beck (German engineer), *167*
Bedford, Sgt Eric, *40, 105, 111, 113*
Bénouville:
   Bridges at, *85, 129*
   'Pegasus' Bridge, *70, 129, 130, 141*
'Bernard', Denise, *80, 81, 84*
   Jacqueline, *80, 83, 84*
Bestley, Maj. Harold, *106, 107, 113, 119–20*
Blaat, Jacques, *176, 177*
Blaskowitz, Field Marshal Johannes, *62*
Bleckmann, Lt. Wilhelm, *93, 177*
Booby-traps, *26, 114*
Bosher, Pte George, *117*
Boulogne, *59*
Brittany, *64*
Broadwell, *42, 51, 55, 56, 116, 119*
Browne, Lt Brian R., *48*
Bulford Camp, *24, 32, 41, 45*
   'Special', *40*
Bullen-Smith, Maj.-Gen. D.C., *129*
Buskotte, Battery Sgt-Maj. Johannes, *68, 75, 77, 80, 81, 84–5, 86, 87, 88, 89, 91, 92, 140, 141, 143, 146, 147, 149, 151, 152, 153, 159, 161, 163, 169, 170, 171, 177, 178*
Butler M C, Capt. Brian, *131, 132, 133, 134, 135, 136*

Cabourg, *70, 72, 86, 130, 137, 148, 151, 154, 155, 157, 159, 166, 169, 174*
Caen, *70, 71, 74, 85, 140, 153, 154, 156–7, 158, 159*
Café: Franceville, *70*
   Gondrée, *70*
   Merville, *70*
Calais, Pas de, *65*
Capon, Pte Sidney, *40, 105, 108, 111, 113*
Carentan, *61*
Cartwright, Pte Leslie, *40, 105, 111, 113*
Charlton, Maj. Edward G., *37*
Cherbourg, *59, 64, 165, 170*
Chilton, Capt. & Q M Albert, *28, 42, 56*
Christopher, Cpl R.W., *133*
Colleville, *76, 79, 80, 83, 84, 85*
**Commando, No 3**: task, general, *130*
   description of, *130*

   officers in, *130, 131*
   briefing of, for Merville, *131*
   approach march, *131–2, 133*
   attack on Battery, *134–5, 152–3*
   in casemates, *134, 136, 153*
   death of Pooley, *135–6*
   medical, *136, 137*
   withdrawal, *136–7, 138, 153*
   patrol from, *136–7, 153*
   German artillery fire on, *138*
   in minefields, *133–5, 137–8*
   conclusions, *139*
Convention, Geneva, *119, 124*
Cotentin, *164, 165*
Coventry, W/Cdr Basil A. ('Champ'), *95*
Creswick, L/Cpl, *139*

*Daily Telegraph*, *53*
Deauville, *160*
Delsignore, Pte Frank, *40, 105, 111, 113*
Detmold, *68*
Dieppe, *64, 65, 107*
   Raid, *59, 67, 130, 139*
Dives River, *129, 130, 148, 157*
   Estuary, *100*
'Dizzie' *see* Parfitt, Lt G.D.
Dollmann, Col.-Gen. Friedrich, *87–8, 89*
Dowling, Lt Michael J., *26, 27, 28, 40, 41, 43, 48, 53, 107, 110, 111, 112, 113, 120, 121, 122, 124, 125*
Dowling, Cpl, *42, 45, 46*
Dozulé, *157*
ducks, bakelite, *35, 39, 104*
Dunk, Pte, *40, 99*
Dunkirk, *61, 130, 167*
Dunes, Les, *74*
Dyer, Maj. Ian C., *22, 26, 39, 43–4, 105, 113*

Ebenfeld, Lt Siegfried, *83, 84*
Écarde, *85, 130, 132, 136*
Eisenhower, Gen. Dwight D., *54*
   message to French, *96–7*
Enterprises Rittmann, *72, 84*
'Erika', *see* Merville Battery A A Gun
Essex Regiment, 10th Bn, *28*
'Eureka', *see* aids, air navigational

Falaise, *165*
Fawcus, Hugh, *173*
Ferme du Boisson, Grande, *78, 91, 168*
Finland, *82*
Flitton, L/Cpl, *58*

# Index

Fontainebleau, 61
'Fortress Europe', 59, 67
Franceville (-Plage), 70, 85, 93, 130, 132, 142, 144, 146, 148, 168
  OP on beach at, 76, 85, 86, 152, 158, 160, 162, 163
  crossroads at, 143, 146, 156
  bakery at, 71
  inhabitants of, 93
  bombers & gliders over, 142
frogmen, German, 161
Front, Eastern, *see* Russia

Gale OBE, MC Maj.-Gen. Richard N., 32, 53, 130, 156
GEE, *see* aids, air navigational
Gestapo, 71, 72
gliders: GB Force, 34, 37, 56
  Pond's, 110–11
  'Mystery', 93, 140, 141, 142
  over Franceville, 142
Goebbels, Dr Joseph, 59, 60, 71
'Golden City', 148, 151, 158–9, 161
Gonneville, 119, 154
  Calvary at, 117, 118, 119, 133
  Mayor of, 154
Gordon-Brown, Capt. R. ('GB'), 34, 37, 43, 52
  Force, 34, 37, 56, 110, 111, 143–4
Göring, Hermann, 62, 64
Gough, F/Lt Anthony, 94, 97
'Graf Waldersee', *see* Wehrmacht 716 Arty. Regt.
Gray KCB, OBE, Lt-Gen. Sir Michael, 174
Gray, Maj. Nicol, 130
Greenway, Capt. The Hon. C. Paul, 35, 40, 108, 109
Griffiths, Tpr, 133
Gwinnett, Revd. John, 48–9, 56, 125, 126, 127

Halliburton, Lt Thomas, 107, 113
*Hamlet*, 51
Haras de Retz, 70, 119, 123, 166
Harper, Sgt 'Tich', 40, 44, 52
Harrold, CSM I 'Bill', 35, 108, 115
Hartmann, Col., 156
  Battle-Group, 156
Hawkins, Pte George, 111, 113, 137, 146
Hauger, 156

'Heinz', Cpl, 123, 124, 125, 179
Henderson, Johnny, 22
Heyde, Lt (Capt.) Karl, 73, 141, 154, 157, 158, 159, 163
Hibberd, Stuart, 173
Hill DSO, MC, Brig. S.J.L., 21, 32, 52, 126
Hitler, Adolf, 59, 60, 61, 62, 64, 65, 67, 88
  attempt on life of, 162, 165, 177
  on Invasion, 64, 65, 79
Hodgson, Capt. (FOB), 133
Hof, Maj. Karl-Werner, 76
Hollinghurst, Air Vice-Marshal, 94
Hopson, Maj. D.C., 132
howitzers, Czech 10cm, 68–9, 74
Houlgate, 72, 160
Howard, Maj. John, 129
Hudson, Capt. & Adj. H.H.T. ('Hal'), 28, 39, 45, 106, 114, 120, 125, 126
Hull, Pte Percy, 111

Inkpen, 22
Innsbruck, 81, 82, 86
Isle of Wight, 64

Jefferson, W/Cdr 'Jeff', 55
'Jock' *see* Lepper, Lt C.E.
Johnston RAMC, Capt. A. ('Johnny'), 47, 48
Jones, Tpr W.E. ('Taffy'), 131, 132, 133, 136, 138
ju-jus, 51
Jüngling, WO, 83

Kath, WO Hans, 76, 158, 161–2
Kehlenbach, Cpl Hans, 179
Knight, Sgt Sidney, 110, 112, 114, 118
Knupe, Maj. (Lt-Col.) Helmuth, 79, 81, 84, 157, 159
Krancke, Admiral, 62
Kriegsmarine (German Navy), 62, 64, 74, 160, 161

Lawrence, Pte, 119
Le Havre, 59, 64, 86, 156, 158
Le Mavais, 78
Le Mesnil, 126, 127
Le Plein, 91, 118
League of Nations, 68
Leave, 31, 32–2
Legrix, Charles, 69
Lepper, Lt C.E. ('Jock'), 22, 43, 105

# Index

Long, C/Sgt Harold, *146*
Loring, Lt James, *104, 105, 117*
Lovat D S O, M C, Brig. The Lord, *130, 136*
Love, Pte, *105, 111*
Luc-sur-Mer, *158*
Luftwaffe (German Air Force), *31, 32, 60, 63, 160, 162*
   Heinkel III, *162*
Lutz, L/Cpl, *71–2*

Malsch, Lt Hans, *76, 157, 158, 159*
Marcks, Gen. Erich, *86–7, 141*
Mayenne, *165*
McCarthy, Denis, *173*
McGeever, Sgt 'Mac', *106*
McGuinness, Cpl 'Marra', *106*
Meise, Engineer-Gen., *77*
**Merville (or Sallenelles) Battery**, *66, 129, 130, 148, 149, 156, 158, 164, 172*
   armament of, supposed, *26, 74*;
      actual, *68–9*
      projected, *87*
   photographed by R A F, *44, 77*
   model of, *44*
   1/1716 arrive at, *69*
   construction of, *74*
   Casemates, *37, 72–3*
      No 1, *73, 75, 85, 86, 89, 91, 112, 113, 114, 124, 136, 145, 147, 152, 168, 172, 173, 176, 178*;
         range-card from, *150*
      No 2, *112, 113, 115, 147*
      No 3, *88, 89, 113, 115, 116, 133, 145, 147, 152, 177*
      No 4, *89, 113, 115, 142, 145–6*
   installation of howitzers in, *72, 74*
   British scrutiny of, *73–4*
   Allied intelligence about, *74*
   Command Bunker for, *73, 76, 77, 85, 143, 146, 152*
   Quartermaster's Bunker for, *73, 78, 146*
   air raids on, *77–8, 78–9, 80, 88, 90, 91, 116, 133*
      deaths from, *80, 81, 90*
   A A Gun 'Erika' in, *78, 90, 91, 110, 111, 114, 143–4, 173*
   Rommel's 1st visit to, *77*
      2nd visit to, *89–90*
      officers' mess at, *80*
         destroyed, *80–1*
      Steiner takes command of, *85*
      Gen. Marcks's visit to, *86–7*

   Gen. Dollmann's visit to, *87–8, 89*
   pioneer general's visit to, *89*
   Making good after raids on, *90, 91, 92*
   Mass said at, *91*
   reorganisation of tasks in, *92, 154*
   pioneers at, *92, 145*
   'mystery' glider lands at, *93, 140, 141, 142*
   9 Para. Bn's attack on, *110–14, 143*
      withdrawal from, *117*
      medical unit at, *122–3, 125, 126*
      bodies in, *114, 138, 146*
   counter-battery fire on, *117, 137, 138, 146, 147, 153*
   3 Cdo directed to attack, *130*
      attack on, *134–6*
      withdrawal from, *136–8*
   pioneer sergeant at, *147, 152*
   war correspondents at, *160–1*
   wounded in, *147*; adoption by 711 Div., *149*
   howitzers of, in action: land, *149*; in defence, *153*; sea, *160, 161*
   withdrawal of 1/1716 from, *163, 164, 166, 167*
   howitzers of, at Walcheren, *170*
      destroyed, *171*
   75mm howitzer at, *151–2, 166*
   appearance of, dawn 6.6.44, *117*
      10.00 6.6.44, *124*
      15.00 7.6.44, *133*; 16.6.44, *159*
      afternoon 17.8.44, *167–8*
      6.6.84, *176*
      24.3.86, *177–8*
   museum at, *174, 176, 178, 179*
Merville: Café, *70*
   Château de, *69, 70, 75, 76, 110, 134*
   Church, *143*
   Mairie, *69*
   Village, *69, 93, 143, 144, 148*
   Water Tower, *85, 86*
Miller, C S M I G.D. ('Dusty'), *34, 35, 108, 119*
mines & minefields, *26, 35, 36, 86, 115, 118, 119, 120, 133, 134, 135, 137, 138*
Montgomery K C B, D S O, Gen. Sir Bernard, *22, 57, 170*
   appreciation of Rommel, *66*
Moore, M C, R A M C, Capt. E.L. ('Ned'), *133, 136*
Morgan, Pte, *40, 48, 100, 111, 112, 116, 120*
'Mulberry', *170*

Murmansk, 82

NAAFI girls, 58
Navy, Royal: barrage, 148, 150, 178
    fire, retaliatory, 149–50, 161
    German, see Kriegsmarine
Newbury, 22
Norway, 82

Orléans, 165
Orne: area, 141
    bridges, 70, 85, 129
    canal, 74, 86, 130, 148, 149
    estuary, 74, 87, 100
    river, 69, 71, 76, 125, 129
    German strongpoint on, 156, 158
Otway, Lt-Col. T.B.H., 21, 32, 34, 39, 42, 43, 44–5, 52, 53, 95, 105, 106, 108, 109, 110, 114, 115, 118, 173
Osnabrück, 68
Ouistreham, 71, 86, 93, 148, 157, 158, 160, 162, 163

pack, ration, 24-hr, 30–1
**Parachute Regiment: 9th Battalion,** 22, 28, 29, 32–3, 55, 94, 104, 119, 143, 167, 173
    formation, 28
    task for Operation, 24–6
    briefing, officers, 24–6, 42, 43
        ORs, 44
        battalion, 52
    mobilisation, 29
    training, 30, 31
    exercises, 30, 31, 33–4, 39–41
    leave, 31, 32–3
    battery, mock, 32, 40
    plan, 34, 52
        parties in, 34–6
    'A' Coy, 34, 36, 52, 56
    'B' Coy, 27, 35, 36, 110
    'C' Coy, 23–4, 36, 39, 105, 110
        12 Pl., 22, 29, 33, 36, 40, 41, 42, 48, 111
    'HQ' Coy, 35
        3-in. Mortar Pl., 36, 37, 40
        MMG Pl. 36
        Anti-tank Pl., 48
    flag, 49, 56
    final preparations, 53–6
    flight, 98, 99, 100, 102
    DZ 'V', 55, 94
    drop, 102, 104, 204

DZ RV, 35, 104, 105
    French at, 106
    missing elements, 106
    approach march, 107–9
    forming up, 110
    gliders, 110–11, 143, 144
    attack, 111–14, 143—6, 155
        War Artist in, 115, 116
        medical, 115–17
    withdrawal, 117, 146
    Calvary RV, 118
    departure of, to Le Plein, 119
    wounded of, 119–20, 122–3, 125, 126, 127
    Post-War, 176
2nd Bn, 176
Parachutes: description of, 49–51
    fitting of, 49, 51
    drawing of, 51
parachutists, foibles of, 51
Parfitt, Lt G.S. ('Dizzie'), 22, 23, 42, 43, 44, 56, 105, 107, 112, 122
Paris, 64
Parry, Maj. Allen J.M., 28, 34, 35, 36, 39, 40, 104, 105, 106, 107, 110, 113, 114, 115, 117, 118, 119, 120, 145
Patterson, Tpr Stephen, 134, 137
Patton, Gen. George S., 165
Pearson DSO, MC, Lt-Col. A.S., 21
Pelz, Luftwaffe Gen., 161, 162
Perpignan, 163
Peters, Lt G.F. ('Pete'), 30
Piattier, M., 174
pigeons, carrier, 91, 117
Poett, KCB, DSO, Gen. Sir Nigel, 174
Pond, Lt Hugh C., 37, 119, 144, 154
Pont-Audemer, 168
Pooley MC, RA, Maj. John, 131, 132, 134, 135, 136
Prince of Wales,, HRH The, 176
prisoners, execution of, 106, 118, 155
    British, 137, 145, 154
    German, 114, 118, 119, 145, 147–8, 154
    Russian, 145

Quakenbruck, 68

radar-station, German, 42, 45
Ranville, 132, 176
ration-pack, 24-hr, 30–1, 122
Rauch, Wo, 76, 161–2, 167, 168, 169
'Rebecca', see aids, air navigational

## Index

*Reich, Das*, 72, 160–1, 219–26
Reichert, Maj-Gen. Joseph, 149, 151
Reis, Lt-Col. Charles, 130
Rennes, 141
Résistance, French, 74, 84
Richards, Capt. Albert, 115, 116
Richter, Maj.-Gen. Wilhelm, 82, 83, 140, 149, 153
Risle, River, 168
Riva Bella, 74, 83, 86, 148, 151, 152
Rix, Lt, 76, 80, 86, 140, 142, 143, 148, 149, 153, 154, 159
Robinson, Capt. T.E.A. ('Robbie'), 36, 43, 105
Rommel, Field Marshal Erwin, 59, 61, 62, 63, 64, 65, 76, 78, 140
  strategy of, 63–4
  qualities of, 65–6
  at Merville, 77, 89–90
  despair of, 165–66
Rose, Sgt, 40, 122
Ross, CSM A.E. ('Barney'), 39, 48, 105
Rouen, 72, 168
Ruge, Vice-Admiral Friedrich, 65, 77, 79
Rundstedt, Field Marshal Gerd von, 60, 62, 63, 140
Russia, conquest of, 67
  Germans attack, 82
  fronts: Crimea, 82
    'Eastern' (generalised), 60, 68, 75, 81
    Southern, 60
    Stalingrad, 67, 82

'S'-Mine, *see* Sprung-Mine
St Maurice d'Ételan, 169
Sallenelles, 85, 130, 132, 138, 156
Salmuth, Gen. Hans von, 156
Sarochinsky, Pte, 158
Schaaf, Lt Rudi, 75–6
Scheldt, River, 170, 171
Schimpf, Capt. 79, 81, 158
Seine, Bay of the, 64
Seine, River, 168–9
*Signal*, 72
Slater, John, 173
Smith, Maj. George E., 34, 36, 40, 108
Smith, Pte Frederick, 40, 111, 112, 120, 125
Smith, Tpr, 139
Smyth M C, Lt Hugh E., 28, 37
Solbad Hall, 82
Spears M M, Sgt, 133

Speidel, Gen. Dr. Hans, 62, 77, 149
Sprung-mine, 24, 26, 112, 116, 138
'Stalin's Organ', 150
Stange, Pte Artur, 158
Stauffenburg, Capt. Count von, 162, 177
Steen, Lt ('Capt.'), 159, 160
Steiner, 2/Lt Raimund, 81–93, 140, 141, 142, 146, 148, 151, 152, 153, 154, 156, 159, 160, 161, 162, 163, 166, 168, 169, 170, 177
Stevenson, R.L., *Kidnapped*, 110
Strafford, Maj. Charles, 174
Stroud, Pte Thomas, 105, 111, 113
Szydlowski, Lt-Col. Zdzislaw, 169, 170

Tarrant Rushton, 56
Tavener, Capt. Frank H., 29, 30, 42, 57
Thorn (German Officers' School at), 82
Tillett, Capt. John M.A., 167–8
Timpf, WO Peter, 70, 75, 86, 144
'Tobruk-Stand', 76, 92, 114, 135, 144, 162
Todt, Fritz, 61–2
  Organisation, 61, 72, 77
Troarn, 130, 157, 159
Trowbridge, Admiral, 35
  Party, 34, 35, 108
Tubbesing, Lt Karl-Heinz, 79, 81

Udine, 82

'V'-Bombs, 59
Valdorf, Lt, 144, 145
valour, German awards for, 151, 157, 158, 159
Varaville, 106, 144, 145, 156
Voluntary Serice, Women's, 49

Walcheren, 170, 171
Waldmann, Sgt (W O) Fritz, 75, 177
Waldron, Tom, 173
Walker, Pte H.T. ('Johnny'), 40, 105, 111, 113
Wall', 'Atlantic, 59, 60, 61, 62, 67, 77
Waterloo (station), 32
Watts, R A M C, Capt. Harold H., 46–7, 107, 113, 115, 116
**Wehrmacht**, Afrika Korps, 59
  Arbeitsdienst, 68, 81
  Army Group 'B', 59, 62, 77, 164
    15 Army, 156
      711 Inf. Div., 149, 164
        HQ, 141, 146, 148

Provost, *154–5*
Artillery, *152*
346 Inf. Div. *156*
84 Corps, *86, 141*
716 Inf. Div, *67–8, 77, 149*
   HQ, *141, 146*
716 Artillery Regt, *67–8*
   No 1 Bty (1/1716), *see* Merville
   2 Bty (2/1716), *83*
   3 Bty (Graf Waldersee 3/1716), *79*
   6 Bty (6/2716), *73*
736 Inf. Regt, *75, 76, 85–6, 93, 141, 144, 145, 154, 162*
   M O from, *123, 143, 152*
Bomb Disposal Unit, *92, 145*
Field Artillery, *63*
Paris Guard Battalion, *169*
7 Panzer Div, *61*
12 SS Panzer Div, *66*
21 Panzer Div, *66, 154*
91 Airlanding Regt, *61*
111 Mountain Arty Regt, *82*
112 Mountain Arty Regt, *82*
West Woodhay, *21–2, 23, 32, 37*
   House, *22*
Wheldon, Capt. Huw, *43*
Whibley, Cpl Victor C., *131, 132*
Williams, Lt H. ('Bill'), *135, 136, 137, 153*
Winston R M, Lt Peter, *130*
Wolter, Capt. Karl-Heinrich, *75, 79, 80, 81, 84*
Worth, Lt F.J.J. ('Joe'), *24, 52*
Woyevodsky M C, Capt. Michael, *132, 133, 138*

Young D S O, M C, Lt-Col. Peter, *130, 131, 132, 133, 134, 135, 136, 139*
Ypres, *169*